Freedom and the Welfare State

By the same author:

Client-Worker Transactions

The Social Worker in Family Situations

Paupers: The Making of the New Claiming Class

Poor Parents: Social Policy and the Cycle of Deprivation

Freedom and the Welfare State

Bill Jordan

Department of Sociology
University of Exeter

Routledge & Kegan Paul

London, Henley and Boston

First published in 1976
by Routledge & Kegan Paul Ltd
39 Store Street,
London WC1E 7DD,
Broadway House,
Newtown Road,
Henley-on-Thames,
Oxon RG9 1EN and
9 Park Street,
Boston, Mass. 02108, USA
Set in 10/11pt Press Roman
and printed in Great Britain by
Unwin Brothers Ltd
© Bill Jordan 1976

ISBN 0 7100 8425 0

Contents

I am very grateful to a number of colleagues, friends and relatives for helpful discussions of various parts of this book during its writing. They include Professor Duncan Mitchell, Professor Robert Leaper, Bob Witkin, Dermont Walsh, Sarah Pelissier, Paul and Lesley Wolfarth. Many of my students and ex-students will also recognise bits of themselves in parts of it, but those from whose dissertations I most directly borrowed were Peter Jeffries, Diane Hart and Julian Kohn. My thanks are also due to Mrs Jill Soughton for her patient and prompt typing of the manuscript, and to Mrs Colleen Hutchings, Mrs Sue Ridler and Mrs Margaret Jerry for additional assistance. But I am most particularly grateful to Jean Packman for encouragement, interest and sharing in the whole of this book at every stage, from preliminary plans to final amendments.

1
Three Traditions

To what extent is freedom compatible with attempts by the state to promote the welfare of its citizens? Does liberty reside in independence from state interference? Are welfare institutions necessarily agencies of social control which impose constraints on individual autonomy? Do some people require the state's protection, and if so, should they enjoy the same rights and liberties as independent citizens? These questions are the starting point of this book.

But it is not meant to be an abstract and philosophical discussion of these issues. My interests are in social policy and social work—not in building theoretical models of society, but in the ways people actually think and feel and live together. As a framework for the development of an analysis of these questions, I have identified three elements which seem to me to be likely to influence the future relationship between freedom and welfare in our own society. These elements are really no more than constellations of attitudes; but they have come to form separate and recognisable traditions which have run through society like underground streams, coming to the surface in politics, in literature, in philosophy or in everyday life. Each of these traditions has a history of its own, sometimes expressed in an extreme crystallisation of values at a certain point in time, sometimes in more subtle, long-term and subterranean influences upon people and events. There are other such traditions; I have selected the three most relevant to welfare issues and institutions.

The present-day expressions of these three traditions in relation to the questions I want to consider are, first, the new Conservative political philosophy; second, the libertarian ideology and lifestyle; and third, the new role of social work as part of a strategy for dealing with social problems. The crucial issues in the current debate about the Welfare State between these three elements are their conflicting views of the relationships between welfare and freedom, and between the state and its citizens.

The Conservative Party's claim to represent the first tradition I wish to identify is quite recent. Only since the 1974 elections has the new leadership of the Conservative Party enunciated principles which call into question the expansion of the social services and increases in welfare expenditure. In September 1975 Mrs Thatcher made a speech in New York in which she questioned the use of state intervention to promote equality between citizens, suggesting that it was destructive of national prosperity, and damaging to individual liberty. The speech confirmed increasing evidence that the new Conservative leadership was reaffirming objections to the provision of services that were first stated by nineteenth-century Liberals.

Broadly, these objections rest on the following presuppositions; that private enterprise in industry is the most efficient method of maximising production and thus prosperity for all; that individual enterprise and responsibilty should be encouraged and rewarded as much as possible; that every man should provide out of his earnings for himself and his family; that very few people need free provision of welfare services or benefits; and that most people prefer to make provision for themselves, to choose how to allocate their resources between their various needs. These presuppositions lead to a number of conclusions about welfare. First that state intervention, in so far as it attempts to impose collective solutions on individual citizens, reduces their autonomy and freedom of choice. Second, that benefits and services provided without charge by the state are neither properly valued nor economically used. Third, that the provision of free services diminishes initiative and independence and destroys people's powers to find their own solutions to problems. And fourth, that the high level of taxation required by the expansion of social services slows economic development and undermines individual energy and ambition.

The notion of society which this tradition postulates is of a system of obligations. The political and economic order are based on definitions of what people in different social roles have a right to expect from each other, and the duties they owe each other, which are seen as functional for this system. Freedom therefore resides in the opportunity to live one's own life and make one's own choices within the limits set by these rights and duties. The state should not infringe this freedom more than is absolutely necessary, and then should avoid doing so in such a way as to upset the balance of mutual obligations between citizens. So much has this nineteenth-century liberal view of society become part of our cultural heritage that, however subterranean its tradition may have been during the post-war period, modern Conservative politicians have only to use certain phrases to evoke the whole constellation of values associated with it.

The second tradition is opposed to the first in almost every respect. What I shall call the libertarian standpoint is, in its present expression, as much a style of life as a counter-argument. It is the tradition of anarchism and syndicalism rather than that of authoritarian and centralist communism, though it springs mainly from Marxist sources. Starting from the proposition that in a capitalist society all other social relationships are derived from the productive process, which rests on exploitation, it does not go on to develop a rival structure of a unified society with an alternative productive organisation. Instead it emphasises that the family and the state, like the factory, are institutions by which the individual is estranged from his true potential, for they demand that he take his place in relationships and processes that perpetuate the unjust distribution of power. The libertarian standpoint distrusts all forms of authority, and all intermediaries between the individual and effective action. It is only by resistance against all authority in every formal institution that the individual can express himself and be free. The libertarian point of view is highly critical of the present Welfare State in several respects: its centralism, its bureaucratic structures, its denial of participation and control to recipients of provisions. But it also draws attention to the extent to which the institutions of the Welfare State attempt to control society's most potentially dissident members, the people who are not sharing in the benefits of prosperity, the deviants and the nonconformists. Resistance against these institutions thus becomes particularly relevant to the struggle for freedom. For libertarians, freedom resides first in breaking down traditional definitions of social obligation and then in substituting a new perception of relationships in which individuality, spontaneity and self-direction will be positively pursued. The concept of welfare as state provision is challenged by a notion of an ideal relationship between individuals, in which needs will be recognised and met. Libertarianism thus opposes the Labour Party's traditional view of welfare.

Libertarian writers like Marcuse, Laing and Cooper, Germaine Greer and the sociologists of the interactionist school conceptualise the disillusionment of one part of the middle class with the post-war Welfare State; the new Conservative leadership expresses the disillusionment of another section. Both suggest that our present institutions are destructive of freedom, but their views of freedom are very different. When Sir Keith Joseph launched the new Conservative philosophy with his speech on the population in October 1974, his attack was principally on left-wing intellectuals and their influence on the morals of the poor, with their ideas about freedom without responsibility. Conservatives tend to see libertarians as products of a Welfare State which has removed the sense of the individual's social obligations. Libertarians see the Welfare State as reinforcing traditional values.

The third tradition is rather more difficult to identify and define. It has tended to express itself in the administration of the social services rather than in political philosophy, and has found few such eloquent spokesmen as the first has had. It is the paternalism of the old Poor Law, and particularly of the first three decades of the nineteenth century; the attempt to use social provision to buttress and buffer a section of the population deemed to be incapable of organising its life without such support. It is based on a notion that the casualties of material progress should be looked after by the state, partly for their own sake, and partly for its own, for it sees them not only as inadequate or irresponsible, but also as often dangerously unruly and lawless. It believes that assistance should be very carefully provided in such a way as to enable a degree of supervision, influence and control to be exercised over those who require it. It is not particularly interested in questions of freedom, for it assumes that those who need provision are only too willing to sacrifice a good deal of their liberty for this relief, and that it is in their interests, and those of the state, that they should do so.

In the past ten years, this tradition is the one which has most clearly emerged in the administration of the Welfare State. In particular, it has emerged in the way in which social work has been used for two functions it did not perform in the 1948 version of the welfare provision. First, whereas it was previously segregated from the business of giving material and financial aid, social work is now entrusted with responsibilities for providing discretionary benefits, usually to the poorest sector, and making sure that they are reflected in 'improvements' in their life styles. Second, whereas before social work was virtually only involved in the investigation and supervision of deviant behaviour on behalf of the courts, either during or after a court hearing, it is now increasingly used as an alternative to a court appearance. Powers given to social workers to supervise both the deprived and the deviant have significantly altered the civil and social rights of a sector of the community. These processes have, in an unspectacular way, slowly changed the relationship between freedom and welfare in the Welfare State.

In becoming involved in these tasks, social work has come to occupy the territory of the third tradition I have identified; yet its origins lie in the first, and it has also had one sortie into the second. Nineteenth-century social work was built upon a respect for clients' freedom within a context of clearly defined social obligations. It reflected the current liberalism in its avoidance of interference except in essentials. Not until the inter-war years did a section of the social work profession become identified with anything approaching a libertarian standpoint; then, in the wake of Freud (in psychology) and leftist politics, it sided with the breaking down of the constraints of traditional morality and formal institutions, and espoused individual self-fulfilment and autonomy. Alternating between these two conflicting traditions, social work was finally swept away by the rising tide of the third, of protective paternalism. While claiming still to uphold 'client self-determination', it opted in practice for a *preventive* principle, justifying interventions in terms of forestalling various kinds of catastrophe—family breakdown, neglect or rejection of children or the elderly, institutionalisation, destitution, homelessness, mental illness, court appearances. By showing itself willing to step in to prevent all these disasters from occurring, it made itself the natural tool for a policy which required a professional skill both to translate selective assistance into behavioural modifications, and to supervise the day-to-day lives of people defined as potential burdens or threats to society. The social work services are thus in the process of becoming, like a system of poachers' nets, the means whereby the poorest and most deprived members of the community are denied escapes from their situations. Classified as potential threats to themselves and their children, social work's clients pay the price for assistance in loss of freedom and of full citizenship.

If (speeded on by the economic crisis) we are approaching a crossroads · in social policy, there seems to be some point in reviewing the interrelations between these three elements over the question of welfare and freedom. To do justice to this task, I feel that it is first necessary to analyse the concepts of freedom contained in each tradition, and then to consider the problem of state intervention in the light of the issues raised by this analysis. But the analysis of freedom which follows as Part One of this book is intended to apply to all citizens, and not simply to recipients of welfare provision. If we believe in a state which attempts to promote the welfare of all its citizens, then we need to analyse how we understand and value our freedom before we can discuss state intervention in others' lives. To treat the issue of welfare as separate from the other rights and obligations of citizenship is to presuppose that state intervention only takes place in the event of social inadequacy or moral inferiority. I deliberately start with an analysis of freedom and social obligations in the most general terms, to avoid any such assumption.

Furthermore, the study will be as concerned with personal liberty and with interpersonal obligations—between individuals, between family members—as with civil and social rights. Libertarian writers have drawn attention to the very close connections between the conventional expectations of personal and family responsibilities and the formal obligations of institutional role relationships. They have also suggested that the overthrow of traditional values in personal and family relationships is both a necessary and a sufficient condition for the breaking down of formal institutional roles, and that any true welfare state requires a prior revolution in the personal sphere. The relationship between personal and political liberty will therefore be examined.

In Part One of this book, I shall be mainly concerned with the first two traditions I have identified. The third has not developed its own characteristic notion of freedom, but asserts that, for the needy, assistance is more important than citizenship. It therefore serves mainly as a counterpoise. What I shall do in this part is consider possible justifications for intervention in others' lives with assistance or advice, and how these can be reconciled with notions of freedom. This will lead to an analysis of the justifications for professional interventions by social workers. I Part Two, I introduce the paternalistic concept of welfare, and go on to show how social work has come to serve its ends. In Part Three, I discuss whether freedom and state intervention for welfare purposes are compatible. The whole subject of freedom and welfare is so complex that it is difficult to divide it up in a logical way, so as to present a single thread of argument throughout the book. Thus the contents of a number of chapters could have been introduced at several different points, and the order in which ideas are discussed is bound to be somewhat arbitrary. What I hope will emerge by the end is that an important struggle between three very different notions of freedom and welfare is at this moment taking place in our society. The dilemmas raised by this struggle are fundamental to the definition of the sort of society ours is to be—issues that have been debated and discussed in philosophy and literature for several centuries. It is a struggle which is too deep and complex to be confined within the banal context of party political bickering about social policy, or to be fragmented between the competitive claims of the social sciences.

Part 1
Freedom

2
Liberty and Liberation

In this chapter I shall start to distinguish between the nineteenth-century liberal and the libertarian views of freedom. Concentrating mainly on the former tradition, I shall suggest that liberals have accepted certain moral, social and economic constraints on freedom as necessary for a healthy society, and that libertarians reject most of these constraints as incompatible with true freedom. I shall then examine the nature of social influences and obligations in the light of these two views.

It will be convenient for the purposes of this chapter to take as the spokesman for the nineteenth-century liberal tradition John Stuart Mill, whose *Essay on Liberty* was published in 1859. In many ways, Mill was a more radical and progressive champion of freedom than most of his liberal contemporaries. His advocacy of the positive value of spontaneity, originality and individuality indicate that he was not merely concerned to establish the right to what Sir Isaiah Berlin[1] has called 'negative liberty'—the individual's freedom from interference with his actions by others. However, I shall argue that in general the liberal tradition seeks to mark out for the individual a limited sphere of freedom from interference, whereas the libertarian tradition promotes a programme of action for 'positive liberty'—self-determination, self-direction and control of his own life by the individual—which it often refers to as 'liberation'.[2]

Mill was primarily concerned to define the proper limits of authority over individual freedom of belief, of life style, of behaviour and of association. He saw authority as taking two major forms: that of law, and that of 'public opinion' (i.e. social prescriptions backed by social sanctions). He gave his definition of the limits of authority in one simple principle:[3]

> that the sole end for which mankind are warranted, individually or collectively, in interfering with the liberty of action of any of their number, is self-protection. That the only purpose for which power can rightfully be exercised over any member of a civilised society, against

his will, is to prevent harm to others. His own good, either physical or moral, is not a sufficient warrant.

The phrase 'against his will' indicates the kind of constraint Mill saw as objectionable. He distinguished sharply between attempts to exhort, advise or persuade people into courses of action, and attempts to coerce them. He saw legal and moral coercion as necessary and beneficial in questions affecting social and moral obligations of one person to another or others. The law and public opinion should enforce the duties the individual owed others, and Mill assumed these could be authoritatively deduced and catalogued, in statute and in social convention. However, once these duties had been discharged, the individual should be left free to choose his own way of life. 'The only freedom which deserves the name, is that of pursuing our own good in our own way, so long as we do not deprive others of theirs, or impede their efforts to obtain it.'[4] Indeed, Mill insisted that the health and vigour of any society depended on giving citizens their freedom, and encouraging them to use it; and he deplored a tendency by the state and public opinion to lay down conventional modes of behaviour for every situation. 'In our times, from the highest class of society to the lowest, every one lives as under the eye of a dreaded censorship.'[5] 'A state which dwarfs its men, in order that they may be more docile instruments in its hands even for beneficial purposes—will find that with small men no great thing can be accomplished.'[6]

With this definition of the constraints on freedom, Mill's analysis of the forces which restricted men from positive, self-governing action was strictly limited. It suggested that all men of talent and intelligence would, in a society of wise laws and tolerant opinions, be free and prosper, and find the expression of their potentialities most suited to themselves. The weakness of Mill's argument, of course, and one which is all the more apparent to us now because of the nineteenth-century context in which he was writing, was that freedom from coercion by law and opinion did nothing to provide the *opportunity* for men to develop the faculties they possessed; and the social, political and economic situation of the time was such that most men were condemned to a life of relentless toil in order to survive. Yet Mill wrote as if economic necessity and subjection to the laws of the market were not a form of compulsion but rather the essence of freedom.[7]

it is now recognised, though not till after a long struggle, that both the cheapness and the good quality of commodities are most effectually provided for by leaving the producers and sellers perfectly free, under the sole check of equal freedom to buyers for supplying themselves elsewhere. This is the so-called doctrine of Free Trade, which rests on grounds different from, though equally solid with, the principle of individual liberty asserted in this Essay. Restrictions on trade, or on production for purposes of trade, are indeed restraints; and all restraint, *qua* restraint, is an evil.

Mill also made it clear that he defended the individual's right to 'a more showy or costly style of living' than his fellow citizens, to spend 'a very large income' as he pleased, to work so as 'to earn by superior skill or industry more than others can without it', and so as to gain 'a larger remuneration for a more useful service'.[8] He disapproved of attempts by public opinion to control or veto extravagant spending, or by fellow workers to deter the industrious through 'a moral police which occasionally becomes a physical one'.[9]

In this Mill is, under the guise of defending individual freedom, in fact simply presenting an argument for those who have certain economic advantages at a particular point in time to be allowed to gain the maximum benefit from those advantages. It is true that this arrangement has traditionally been called 'free' (as in the expression 'free enterprise') but often those who experience its effects do not see it as such, particularly when they are in a disadvantaged position. A man might say, 'Because of my competitors' tactics, I was compelled to go bankrupt', or 'because of the surplus of pigs, I had to sell at a miserably low price' or 'as the market was so bad, I sold up against my will'. People also use expressions like 'wage slavery' to describe the exploitation involved in low wages. Inequalities in relationships lead to compulsions of many kinds, even where the transaction is 'free' in the sense that there is no external restraint in the form of a law controlling the terms of the relationship. For instance, if women depended completely on men for financial support, and there was no opportunity for them to earn their own living, a situation in which men chose their wives could not be accurately described as 'free', at least for women, for many of them would be economically compelled to marry the first man who chose them.

Libertarians argue that economic forces have created a social order in which law and morality are used to justify constraints on individuals which distort and obscure their potential. They suggest that the only true freedom lies in conscious, active, committed resistance to social, political and economic controls. It is difficult at this point to do justice to the complexity and variety of libertarian thought, and to the radical break with the liberal tradition represented by Marx's philosophical writings. These matters will be discussed in the next chapter. However, for the purposes of this chapter, it is convenient to select, as a representative of modern libertarian thought, Herbert Marcuse, whose *Essay on Liberation* was published in 1969.

Marcuse asserts that the effort to achieve liberation must overcome 'the global dominion of corporate capitalism'.[10] He argues that economic forces give rise to much stronger and more insidious mechanisms of social control than Mill's analysis would suggest. He states that capitalism's repressive influence over individuals has been gradually and imperceptibly established through the adaptation of human nature to the requirements of technological production and consumption.[11]

The so-called consumer economy and the politics of corporate capitalism have created a second nature of man which ties him libidinally and aggressively to the commodity form. The need for possessing, consuming, handling and constantly renewing the gadgets, devices, instruments, engines offered to and imposed upon people, for using these wares even at the danger of one's own destruction, has become a 'biological' need . . . The second nature of man militates against any change that would disrupt and perhaps even abolish this dependence of man on a market ever more filled with merchandise.

He argues that capitalism gives rise to apparent political stability by establishing a 'false harmony' between people with economic advantages and people without them. Because the advantaged call the tune, the disadvantaged tend to adapt, to accept the rulers' definitions of their needs and of the permitted means of satisfying them. Thus 'a social system reproduces, by indoctrination and integration, a self-perpetuating conservative majority.'[12] The controls inbuilt into this system are so strong that we cannot meaningfully discuss the notion of changes in it within the context of liberal concepts of freedom such as Mill's. 'Consequently, the struggle for changes beyond the system becomes, by virtue of its own dynamic, undemocratic in terms of the system, and counter violence is from the beginning inherent in this dynamic.'[13] He suggests that the youth protest movement is producing a total rebellion of sufficient force to overthrow the whole of the established order. Liberation will come through the leadership of a self-appointed intellectual elite, which will free the majority from the dominion of capitalism, and enable them to reach a new perception of the common interest. The revolutionary movement would be founded upon the New Man emergining in youth culture, 'who would speak a different language, have different gestures, follow different impulses; men who have developed an instinctual barrier against cruelty, brutality, ugliness.'[14] In his vision of a socialist Utopia, people would be tender and compassionate, no longer ashamed of themselves, and would see production as a form of creation. The positive freedom this process of liberation would bring about would produce a transformation in the nature of all social relationships.

Marcuse therefore sees the forces of our present economic system as controlling and constraining individuals in a sense which is much stronger than that employed in ordinary language. For although, as we have seen, it is common to speak of economic disadvantage in terms of compulsion and, in extreme cases even of coercion, none the less this is not normally recognised as grounds for supposing that all a disadvantaged person's behaviour is determined by his economic situation. Most people think of themselves as under economic compulsion mainly during working hours, and as free during leisure and holidays. Thus a man who wins the football pools, retires from work, buys a house by the sea, and spends the rest of his days equipping it with the very latest gadgets and adornments would generally consider himself, and be considered to be, free from economic necessity. But Marcuse's notion of domination through consumption would imply that such a man was still repressed and controlled, because he was still behaving according to the demands of his economic conditioning, his 'second nature'. This would continue to be the case even if to his dying day he congratulated himself on his good fortune, and attributed all his new advantages to his material comforts.

To deal with these difficulties, we need to analyse in more detail the nature of the influences on behaviour which can lead us to describe a person's freedom as having been limited. Mill recognised many influences on behaviour, but he insisted that only some of these could be defined as constraints on liberty. These consisted in the use of threats or punishment to induce actions other than those the agent would have chosen of his own volition. Such constraints were exercised both by government and by public opinion, the latter by opinion at large and opinion in social groupings, among those who meet face to face. To ensure liberty, there were needed defences both against encroachments by the state, and against coercion by intolerant opinion.[15]

> there needs protection also against . . . the tendency of society to impose, by means other than civil penalties, its own ideas and practices as rules of conduct on those who dissent from them; to fetter the development, and, if possible, to prevent the formation, of any individuality not in harmony with its ways, and compels all characters to fashion themselves upon the model of its own.

Mill deplored this tendency as much as the tendency of government to intervene in matters of private beliefs and behaviour, and argued that the control of individuals' actions by custom and formal rules of conduct was as great a threat to liberty as state regulation.

Mill's conclusions indicate that he considered that any form of influence which did not directly threaten punishment, either official or in the form of 'the punishment of opinion', was not an infringement of liberty. This allowed him to argue that a man should show concern about others' actions if he considered them wrong, or as damaging to their own wellbeing, even if they affected only themselves. In demonstrating this concern by attempting to influence them to change their behaviour, he would not be infringing their liberty unless he tried to compel them to act differently, under threat of punishment.[16]

> disinterested benevolence can find other instruments to persuade people to their good than whips and scourges, either of the literal or metaphorical sort . . . . Even education works by conviction and persuasion as well as by compulsion, and it is by the former only that, when the period of education is passed, the self-regarding virtues should be inculcated. Human beings owe to each other help to

distinguish the better from the worse, and encouragement to choose the former and avoid the latter.

Mill's definition of constraints on liberty is unsatisfactory at this point, for ordinary language recognises many other influences as reducing individual freedom. We have already seen that economic dependence is often perceived as a form of constraint; but this does not simply apply to the case of someone in an economically advantageous position using that advantage against another who is forced to act out of economic necessity, because he is starving or has debts to meet. It seems to apply also to the use of economic advantage to influence behaviour in a certain direction, even where no actual hardship would result from an alternative course of action. Consider the case of the artist and his patron. If the artist is penniless, clearly the patron can use his influence over him (to commission a flattering portrait for instance); and here a clear and crude constraint stems from economic necessity. But even if the artist is in reasonable circumstances, and has no debts, the patron's power greatly to improve his circumstances and remove the danger of future debts enables him to exert an influence over the artist's output; he can, for instance, get him to produce more of a certain kind of picture by paying him more for these than for others. In so far as the artist is rewarded for painting pictures other than the ones he would paint without the patron's influence, we might well want to say that his artistic output is constrained by the patron's influence, and that he is not free in the same sense as an artist who does not depend in any way on a patron is free.

It seems therefore that various kinds of dependence in relationships limit freedom in ways not directly related to punishment, but to other forms of influence. These limitations are brought about both by depending on others and by having others as dependants; they also apply to situations of mutual dependence. Take the case of an adult daughter living with her ageing parents. They own the house, therefore she depends on them for accommodation, but they are in failing health, so they depend on her for physical assistance. Both sides are constrained both by their own dependence and by the other's dependence on them. From the daughter's point of view, she is forced to adopt a style of life other than the one she might choose if she could live alone, because of both her need for accommodation and her responsibilities towards them. From the parents', they are constrained to live where their daughter can get work. Neither side is free to live the life they might independently choose.

Mill would probably have classified this example above as one of reciprocal moral obligations or social duties, and would have described their force as 'socially obligatory'. He suggested that those who failed in such duties should be considered 'fit objects of moral reprobation, and, in grave cases, of moral retribution and punishment'.[17] However, he gave no satisfactory account of the nature of social duties or of the force of moral obligations. How, for instance, does the duty of a daughter to her parents differ from a duty incurred by contract, or a civic duty like driving with due care and attention? It would seem that there are important differences between the ways in which we treat failures to meet different types of obligations. We are much more likely to be severely critical or punitive towards someone who fails to meet his obligation to help a seriously injured victim of a road accident (even if he is a stranger) than we are towards someone who fails to meet an obligation to be of assistance to a mildly ailing kinsman. Similarly, where there is a conflict between two obligations, such that only one can be met, we do not regard them as both equally obligatory, and the failure to meet one as necessarily a moral failure.[18] Such situations arise frequently, and it is generally considered that a man should fulfil his most urgent obligations to those who most need his assistance, even if he has to neglect other obligations in the process.

Mill does not discuss the effects of obligations on liberty, presumably because of his narrow focus on coercion in matters affecting only the individual himself. However, it is clear that not only does society's enforcement of obligations limit freedom; so do the obligations themselves. This is true of all kinds of obligations, from the most general moral responsibilities towards our fellow men to the most trivial implications of everyday relationships. My duty to rescue my fellow citizen from danger of death (even if he has brought this danger upon himself) restricts my freedom, as Jean-Baptiste Clamence found for himself in Camus's novel, *The Fall*. But so does my duty to visit my parents every Christmas. In the case of the former duty, the obligation to act under it is very strong, and the penalties, from public opinion at least, of failure are considerable. But in the latter case the obligation is a weak one, and failure to meet it may not be taken seriously. Yet often a trivial duty like this is much more restrictive than a serious duty, in that it prevents many more activities which might otherwise have been undertaken. I can rescue a drowning man from a river and still be free to choose what to do with the rest of the day; but my Christmasses for the rest of my parents' lives are committed.

Mill also failed to give us any satisfactory account of influence through persuasion. He simply stated that since rational argument is necessary to the process of reaching true conclusions, we should never regard the attempt to persuade by argument as an infringement of liberty.[19]

> the only way in which a human being can make some approach to knowing the whole of a subject, is by hearing what can be said about it by persons of every variety of opinion, and studying all modes in which it can be looked at by every character of mind.

This point of view placed great faith on men's opportunity, ability and willingness to understand arguments from different points of view, and reach their own rational conclusions. Provided that there was freedom of speech, so that all opinions could be expressed, persuasion would be a means towards more men forming right judgments of their own free choice.

This account may be adequate for the rather limited number of cases where rational persuasion is used by a friend, or another person regarded as an equal, to influence someone's behaviour in a certain direction. Here we would agree with Mill that attempts to persuade leave him as free to decide on his own course of action as he was before they were applied; and that rational argument to another as an equal is a mark of respect for a person's liberty rather than an infringement of it. But the same is not true where persuasion takes the form of a more powerful person attempting to influence the behaviour of someone over whom he has some power, or where there is an important element of mutual dependence. The artist's patron already mentioned is in a particularly strong position to convince the artist of the merits of a particular style of painting, because in the last resort he is known to be in a position to reward the artist for following that style. Experiments in social psychology suggest that relatively small rewards are more effective than relatively large ones in such a process, for the latter are easily construed as bribes and, even if acted upon, do not persuade the actor to change his opinions; while smaller rewards, being less obvious justifications in their own right, require rationalisation in the form of the invention of some 'better' reason to justify a change of behaviour, and thus may end by succeeding in changing the actor's mind.[20] In the example of the daughter living with her parents, they would be in a stronger position to persuade her not to have a love affair than a friend would be, because their arguments would tend to remind her, even if only indirectly, of her obligations towards them and her dependence on them.

The question of exactly at what point persuasion becomes a constraint on freedom is not an easy one. An extreme position on this issue is taken by the behaviourist, B. F. Skinner, who argues that all persuasion is a species of control, and that the apparent distinction between actions that are freely chosen and actions that are done under compulsion is an illusion. Skinner suggests that the only difference is that in the case of an action we think of as freely chosen, the environmental conditions which give rise to the action are not made clear and specific enough to be understood, whereas in the case of an action taken under constraint they are. So when we 'change someone's mind' by persuasion, all we are doing is changing the way they behave, by offering them 'reinforcements' (usually covertly) for behaving in a different way. We could do this more honestly, reliably and efficiently, he argues, if we offered clear and specific rewards for behaving differently, but, in order to preserve the illusion of freedom, we tend to prefer weak forms of control. 'Rational' persuasion is a weak form of control; hence 'the "changer of minds" can escape from the charge that he is controlling people'. Skinner concludes that 'the apparent freedom respected by weak measures is merely inconspicuous control'.[21]

This argument rests on a number of fallacies. First, persuasion does not consist simply in a process of 'reinforcement' which offers the subject advantages for changing behaviour. *Rational* persuasion depends on rational argument, on steps leading from premises to conclusions. It depends, to be successful, on the demonstration that certain conditions lead to certain consequences. Otherwise, if the argument does not hold, then rational persuasion cannot take place. We could, of course, simply offer some tangible reward for a different form of behaviour without explaining why we consider it advantageous; but this would not be persuasion. To give a dog a bone when it obeys us is not to persuade it of the virtues of obedience. Even Skinner gives some tacit behavioural support to this point of view by attempting to present arguments which lead to the conclusions he wishes us to draw; to follow his own maxims, he would need only to flatter us into agreeing with him.

Second, from the point of view of the subject, to act in a certain way because one has been persuaded that it is a wise or good or prudent way to act is not the same thing as to act in a certain way because one has been influenced by someone in some other way. If another person has persuaded me to stop smoking, I can give an account of the reasoning behind my decision to change my behaviour in terms of how I believe it will affect my own future wellbeing. I can account for my choice of a different mode of behaviour in terms of my own motives, without reference to the motives of anyone else. If I have simply given up smoking in response to an offer of a large sum of money, I cannot say that I have been persuaded to stop smoking, or persuaded that there are good reasons for me to stop smoking. There may or may not be good reasons, but I know nothing of them. I have to account for my change of behaviour in terms of the reward that has been offered to me, and in terms of someone else's motives for offering me that reward.

However, the much more difficult case, which Skinner's account does nothing to help us resolve, is that of the man who changes his behaviour in response to the offer of a small reward, and later convinces himself that he was acting for some other motive. A slightly different version of the same problem is the man who acts under the influence of propaganda or subtle advertising techniques; he is 'persuaded' to act in a certain way by a combination of selected information and emotional stimulation. Without necessarily claiming that he is acting out of rational motives, such a man would certainly claim to be acting freely, and to be choosing to do what he does. This is another variation of Marcuse's problem of capitalist domination, of the psychological conditioning of the perception of needs and their appropriate satisfaction. Such behaviour modification techniques are not the prerogative of political manipulators and advertising men; they have been deliberately employed by psychiatrists and social workers. Similarly, the parents in our earlier example might well employ their powers of persuasion so extensively and effectively as to convince their daughter that she did not want to have a love affair.

The tendency of classical liberal philosophers like Mill to under-estimate problems of this kind stems from their confusion of a resentment of coercion (i.e. a wish for negative liberty) with a desire for positive liberty (self-determination). Because men generally resent interference in the form of overt controls over their lives, particularly controls which involve threats of punishment, it does not mean that they necessarily desire to be self-directing, in the sense that they want to take personal responsibility for basing all their decisions on rational conclusions which they have independently reached. It is perfectly logically consistent to say (as many implicitly do) that they want to be free from interference and coercion, but they do not want to think for themselves. They are quite prepared to be cajoled and rewarded into behaving in certain ways—this is simply being well adapted to one's environment—but they do not want to be bullied. Self-determination, which Mill described as 'the only freedom worth the name', is not the natural order of things which follows logically from negative liberty, but rather an ideal which requires very special conditions for its realisation.

However, it does appear that we can at least make a meaningful distinction in the vast majority of cases between actions which are freely chosen (in the sense of decided upon under motives of self-direction) and actions which are not free in this sense. For it is only rarely that we are likely to need to use a hypothesis of 'unconscious motivation' to explain the influence of other people on a subject. If we ask someone to account for a change in his behaviour, and he is willing to answer truthfully, he is very likely to be able to name the external influences on him. Thus, in the case of the small reward, he would not be unaware of its influence, though he might understate it; in the case of the propaganda or advertising, he might fail to give due weight to his emotional response, but he could give some account of its impact on his feelings; and in the case of the parental domination, she might not acknowledge the extent of their influence, but at least she would be aware that it was there. In such cases, therefore, we could certainly get evidence about the motives leading to a change of behaviour, from which we could go on to discuss whether the behaviour was self-directing, and whether the person exercised a free choice according to this standard of positive liberty. But there are only certain circumstances in which we would want to do this.

What I want to suggest is that self-direction is a consciously chosen ideal of conduct which it is only meaningful to discuss in the context of someone's having made a claim to be living according to its precepts. The ordinary man does not claim to be self-directing in most of his everyday life, and nor, I suspect, does the philosopher, unless perhaps he belongs to a particular school of existentialism. It is meaningless to talk of someone as being free or unfree from the ordinary influences of economic life, family relationships or trivial civic responsibilities so long as he fully expects to act in a way which is strongly influenced by his employer's demands, his newspaper's prejudices, his wife's preferences and his church's proscriptions; as meaningless, in fact, as it would be to try to assess the behaviour of the young Jean-Paul Sartre according to the standards of orthodox Catholicism.

However, most philosophers of liberal views tend to do just this, implicitly if not explicitly. Mill certainly did so, to the extent that he roundly condemned all forms of behaviour (in matters of individual conscience and taste) which were conformist and derivative. A similar attitude is conveyed in Stanley I. Benn's article, 'Freedom and Persuasion'. Writing of the problem of persuasion by mass-communication techniques, he argues: [22]

> whether a man is really master of himself or whether he is being
> interfered with, does not depend solely on the kind of influence
> another man exerts . . . it depends *also* on whether it would be
> reasonable to expect him, in the given conditions, to withstand
> influence of that kind.

But reasonable according to whose standards? There is not one universal standard of sales resistance, which is a moral imperative to all, housewives and philosophers alike. It is only reasonable to expect a man to resist an irrational argument if he claims to be a rational man. An irrational man who claims to be rational is far more politically dangerous and morally questionable than an irrational man who has the honesty to admit that he acts as he does because of the advertisements he watches and the colour supplements he reads.

However, while few men claim to be rational and self-directing all the time, most people claim to have the power to be so, to distinguish between occasions on which they are being so and occasions when they are not, and that they are, in fact, rational and self-directing on some occasions. It is certainly important that people should be able to do so, if they wish to, on some occasions, though there might be some disagreement about which the most important occasions for such exercises in self-direction are. But there also do seem to be occasions when a man is generally expected to be rational and self-directing, in the sense that he could be expected to be judged as if his actions were those of a free self-directing agent unless he could give very good reasons why they should not be judged in that light. These are occasions which concern serious moral obligations (of the kind discussed earlier) and legal obligations. It is not enough for a man who drives past a fellow citizen bleeding to death in the gutter to say that he was acting under an obligation to take his wife shopping; or that he did not stop because to do so would be inconsistent with his image as a driver of his particular make of car; or that he was late for work at the time. Nor are any of these kinds of reasons considered valid ones for breaking the law by, for instance, failing to observe the speed limit. So in such cases Benn is right to suggest that we do normally expect a man to resist other influences on his behaviour, and that the standard we apply is whether it is reasonable to expect him, in the given conditions, to withstand influences of that kind.

However, a good deal of confusion arises from cases where a man who has failed to act as the law or a serious moral obligation requires later claims that, in acting the way he did, he was compelled to do so, or did so against his will. Usually such claims refer to strong influences on behaviour not immediately apparent to an outside observer. Sometimes these influences are interpersonal, as in the case of a man who has committed a crime and who claims that at the time of his action he had lost his power to make balanced judgments because of being under the evil influence of a powerful accomplice. An example of this was provided in the Charles Manson trial. A more common claim is that the influence was of a very strong emotion or physical feeling which temporarily destroyed the ability to form rational judgments or carry them out. Both these claims amount to saying that the subject was not in a position to be self-directing at a time when he should have been.

These claims are difficult to assess because there is a good deal of confusion about the nature of compulsion, even in less problematical cases. John Plamenatz pointed out in his book *Consent, Freedom and Political Obligation* that there was no necessary self-contradiction implied in such statements as 'I was compelled to come to this decision', or 'I was forced to choose this rather than that'.[23] What such statements often claim is no more than that the subject acted from a motive from which he did not wish to act, even though he did have a choice; that he was acting from what Plamenatz calls 'undesired motives'. In many situations, men distinguish between their motives, and the desire to act from certain of them (desired motives) and not from others (undesired motives). The situation in which a man acts from a motive from which he does not wish to act is quite a different form of compulsion from, say, someone who is physically forced to do something by a group of stronger opponents, or someone who is overcome by a non-human agent like a wild animal or an avalanche, for in such situations he would have no choice at all. But it is also often different from the case in which a man does something under threat of punishment or pain. For in this case the man does have a choice; he may choose to suffer pain or even death rather than act as someone requires him to act. But in the first example, nothing more is being claimed than that the subject reached his decision to perform a certain action reluctantly, and would have preferred in other circumstances to act differently. This does not necessarily imply that he was not in a position to be self-directing; though it may do so. A person who is 'forced' to abandon a plan to go out for the evening because of a headache is acting from an undesired motive, but the compulsion that derives from an ordinary headache is certainly not sufficient to impair rational judgment or self-direction. Similarly someone who says he was compelled to act dishonestly out of loyalty to a friend is not usually claiming that this absolves him from moral responsibility for his actions.

The real difficulty arises when someone who has behaved criminally or has failed to meet a serious obligation later claims that he was physically or mentally ill and hence 'not himself' at the time in question. Here there is much room for disagreement. Did the middle-aged housewife steal the piece of cheese from the supermarket because she wanted to save up her housekeeping money to buy a new coat (desired motive), or was she unaware of what she was doing because she was in the grip of menopausal anxiety (undesired motive)? Such questions can also be posed about what Mill regarded as being usually 'self regarding behaviour', such as drinking. Although the decision whether or not to drink is generally considered to be one in which there is no obligation on the drinker to choose according to principles of self-direction and rationality, the same is not true if he is driving; and it is often held not to be true if he has reason to believe that drinking makes him behave antisocially. But what if he claims to be an alcoholic? He could argue that he did not make a free choice to get drunk on a particular occasion (and thus cause damage, or a car accident). He only did it because he was in the grip of his addiction. He really wanted to act from motives of sobriety, but he fell into temptation, against his will. How do we understand such a claim? The ordinary (non-alcoholic) man is disinclined to recognise the force of physical dependence on alcohol as sufficiently compelling to be counted as similar to an external force like an avalanche. He might reluctantly acknowledge that the onset of withdrawal symptoms could be taken as a threat, similar to a threat of pain or punishment. But he would probably be most likely to put the alcoholic's behaviour in the same category as that of any other person who, because of a strong desire for something inconsistent with his social duties, behaves irresponsibly. Medical and psychiatric opinion is sometimes more ready to accept the first or second claims than is ordinary opinion.

Disputes over such questions may often arise because people who act criminally or irresponsibly are seldom ready to admit to motives of greed, hedonism, selfishness, lack of concern for others' feelings, or cruelty; and because people are more ready to attribute these motives to others than they are to claim them for themselves. On the other hand, it is clear that a man who disclaims all undesired motives (whether they are afflictions like illness, or the unwanted influences of other people) it is proclaiming himself to be a free, in the sense of a self-directing, man. Someone who insists that he only drinks to get drunk, only steals for gain and never acts out of a sense of duty, but only from his own true feelings, positive or negative, about his fellow men, is asserting his positive liberty. However, few people consistently make such claims. One fictional exception to this rule is the hero (in the full sense of the word) of Ken Kesey's novel, *One Flew Over the Cuckoo's Nest*, Randle P. McMurphy. He was psychiatrically classified as a psychopath for making such claims and acting on them. Another such is Meursault in Camus's *The Outsider*, who explained having shot a man dead in terms of feeling tired and thirsty, having the sun in his eyes, and having been prevented by the man from getting to a river to drink. He was found guilty of murder without extenuating circumstances, and executed.

We should not suppose that such things as social obligations, family relationships, illness, disability or economic necessity are necessarily to be seen as constraints on liberty. They only come to be experienced as constraints if they prevent someone from doing something he desires to do. One man may do work that he hates only because he has a family to keep: another may do the same work because he enjoys the job. Only the former is acting from an undesired motive; for the latter, work is self-determined and self-fulfilling. But there is a third category of behaviour, which is that of the man who neither wants to work nor wants not to work. His motives for going to work are, in Plamenatz's term, 'neutral'. His freedom would not ordinarily be said to be restricted by his work, since, although he does not particularly want to work, he does not particularly want to do anything else either.

Such a man is certainly free in Mill's sense, but he is equally certainly not liberated in Marcuse's sense. For Marcuse's definition of liberation implies that a man does everything that he does because of a positive desire to do it; this applies to all his realms of activity.[24]

> Released from the bondage of exploitation, the imagination, sustained by the achievements of science, could turn its productive power to the radical reconstruction of experience and the universe of experience. The Form of freedom is not merely self-determination and self-realisation, but rather the determination and realisation of goals which enhance, protect, and unite life on earth. And this autonomy would find expression not only in the mode of production and productive relations but also in the individual relations among men, in their language and their silence, in their gestures and their looks, in their sensitivity, in their love and hate.

There are two important points about this description of liberation. First it is necessary for Marcuse to stress the positive quality of all liberated behaviour, its perpetual commitment to certain ideals, because unlike most philosophers and almost all ordinary people he insists that *all* behaviour which does not challenge capitalist values is constrained in the sense of being a reflection of false needs and false consciousness, a reflection of social and economic conditioning. Thus, within the world of everyday life apparent distinctions between desired, neutral and undesired motives are misleading since all take place under the domination of a repressive political system. Actions which are apparently free, spontaneous and self-directing are not really any such thing unless they are undertaken as part of a rebellion against this system. Thus liberation comes to be related to freedom only in this very specific sense of freedom from the yoke of capitalism.

But, equally importantly, liberation, in the sense of breaking out of this yoke, is defined by Marcuse in terms of certain specific forms of behaviour rather than simply in terms of an escape from restraints. When he talks of enhancing, protecting and uniting life on earth, these goals do not necessarily follow from the release of capitalist restraints; they are ideals in their own right. It is clear that Marcuse sees these ideals as being the ends of liberation, and that release from restraints is for him merely the necessary means for achieving these ends. It is also clear from what he says about the necessity for a minority group, the intellectual elite, to impose its will on a (conditioned) conservative majority that he does not see either negative liberty (freedom from restraint) or positive liberty (self-determination) as ideals which are part of the ends of liberation.

It could be argued that all Marcuse is saying here is that once a man is in fact released from constraints, including those of which, through long usage and adaptation, he has become unconscious, he will experience great feelings of spontaneity, creativity, compassion for his fellow men and universal goodwill. Similar if much more modest claims about the psychological effects of self-direction have certainly been made by others. For instance, Plamenatz wrote: [25]

> It seems highly probable that actions from desired motives are nearly always accompanied by such an emotion (of pleasure) and those from undesired motives by such another. This latter is usually called a feeling of frustration, but it is more difficult to find a convenient name for the former, since none appears to be in everyday use. Perhaps, all things considered, it will be least inconvenient to call it a feeling of spontaneity, provided that it is understood to be an emotion and nothing more.

But this claim does not imply that such feelings have any particular significance, political or otherwise, or that they necessarily lead to other actions, revolutionary or compliant.

Marcuse is also certainly not alone in suggesting that acts which are apparently the same are to be understood quite differently according to the spirit in which they are undertaken. His assertion that liberated art is qualitatively different from the tame art of commercialism, for instance, is perfectly comprehensible to the ordinary man. It was Mill, after all, who said that 'it really is of importance, not only what men do, but also what manner of men they are that do it'.[26] Ordinary language agrees with Mill and Marcuse that there is a difference between what is creative and what is merely conventional, and that in life if not always in art, the spontaneous is generally to be preferred to the routine, the original to the hackneyed, and the novel to the stale. However, it is not clear to the ordinary man that the youth protest movement has a monopoly of these advantages, in life or art.

In the next chapter I shall consider the philosophical origins of the libertarian notion of liberation, and attempt to clarify the differences between this view of freedom and the one put forward by liberals like Mill. I shall also analyse libertarian criticisms of the failure of the present order of society to deal with human needs and problems, and the libertarian claim that its solutions are consistent with the promotion of individual freedom.

3
The True Nature of 'the Social Being'

The libertarian notion of liberation suggests an opposition between the 'true' self of each individual and the demands of the social order. It insists that only by repudiating formal definitions of social obligations, and the conventional expectations of others, can individuals be truly free. Yet libertarian writers have not turned away from the problems of social organisation; on the contrary, they have tended to be utopian in their visions of a better society. They have suggested that personal liberty can be reconciled with the ideal of full and spontaneous participation in public affairs, once the evils of the present order are abolished. The self is not necessarily at odds with its social role; this fragmentation of the individual is a product of particular social conditions. Only true freedom, however, can permit reintegration and allow the development of a meaningful awareness of others' needs.

The major difficulty that such theories have to overcome is the suggestion that men are essentially aggressive, greedy, exploitative and cruel. Traditional liberal thought (such as Mill's) assumed that without a system of reciprocal obligations, enforced by some superior power, life would be, in Hobbes's phrase, 'nasty, brutish and short'. Those who wish to construct a society upon the principle of individual freedom attempt to counter this by attributing brutish features of people's behaviour towards each other to the distorting effects of inappropriate social controls. In the absence of these, they claim, man's true nature would unfold itself, and he would display quite other, less dislikeable characteristics in relation to his fellow men. These claims have been pursued not only in literature and philosophy, but also in a number of experiments, on a small and large scale, designed to show that where relationships between individuals are defined in ways fundamentally different from those of our traditional structure of society, men can behave in much less brutish ways towards each other than those who hold political power would have us believe.

Varieties of libertarian thought

Yet among those who have claimed to have discovered the recipe for a social or political utopia there has been remarkably little agreement, and their accounts of the true nature of man, the necessary conditions for its realisation, and the fundamental evils of traditional society have been extremely various. In this chapter I shall only be able to indicate some of the main themes of their arguments which are relevant to questions of freedom and social obligation. I hope in later chapters to show why one particular version of the libertarian tradition has come to the fore in recent debates about social control and the Welfare State.

The libertarian tradition stems from the writings of political philosophers who saw definitions of social obligation as serving the ends of the ruling class, and as supporting an unequal distribution of power and wealth in society. Their primary concern was with political obligation— the relationship between the individual and the state—rather than with personal obligations between individuals; but they traced the fundamental evil of both to the same source, the ownership of property. If individuals ceased to own and possess, all their relationships, both public and private, could freely assume their natural form.

Yet within this agreement about the source of distortion in relationships, there was great divergence about the natural form that would emerge when property was abolished. For instance, at the end of the eighteenth century the English writer, William Godwin, argued that all attempts at organisation and co-operation were to be avoided, and that if men as individuals simply followed their own wishes, a better society would automatically emerge. Since men had no innate ideas, they were infinitely adaptable, and would tend to choose rational behaviour, and to avoid conflict with others. 'Perfectibility is one of the most unequivocal characteristics of the human species, so that the political as well as the intellectual state of man may be presumed to be in a course of progressive improvement.'[1] Rulers used the myth of man's corrupt and unregenerate nature to keep men ignorant and perpetuate vice; in fact, men were infinitely capable of responding to rational argument, and all vice was eradicable, since it was 'nothing more than error and mistake reduced to practice and adopted as the principle of conduct'.[2] Once property disappeared, men's needs would be seen to be simple and few, and would soon be provided for by the progress of mechanised industry. Godwin also anticipated an end to the institution of the family, which he saw as simply a means to subjugate women and children, for the sake of perpetuating property ownership.

Godwin thus showed no particular favour to the ethic of work and social duty, and in looking forward to an age of leisure gained through fully automated productive processes, he anticipated twentieth-century libertarians. But the characteristic nineteenth-century utopian constructions of a society free from exploitation were, unlike his, essentially co-operative and work-centred. For instance, Proudhon's ideal society was based on the workshop, in which small communes would produce for their own needs, and trade with others—in kind, since money would be abolished. Unlike Godwin, Proudhon was pessimistic about men's abilities, as individuals, to make rational choices. He believed that punitive sanctions were necessary to enforce obligations, and that social organisation should promote work as the 'first attribute, the essential characteristic of man'.[3] He advocated the retention of the traditional family structure, and a subordinate position for women. Thus the abolition of property did not for him involve a total withering away of differentiation in social roles, and the irrational side of man's nature still required social controls to ensure the performance of co-operative duties.

Marx's much more complex analysis of the relationship between property and social obligation clarified the conceptual basis of the break with the liberal tradition over freedom. The liberal tradition had analysed social situations in terms of the constraints upon individual freedom imposed by others' needs. Marx insisted that men were only 'naturally' uncooperative and hostile because of the dynamics of the capitalist system; liberal concepts of freedom were thus appropriate only for market societies. The notion that economic freedom resided in the individual's right to buy and sell without restraint could not be applied in the same sense both to owners of property and to those who had only their labour to sell. Marx argued that a man who was forced to sell his labour for a wage was renouncing his humanity—he was in a state of alienation. Like Proudhon, Marx believed that work was a basic need for men, and a process of self-affirmation, in which he came to know himself and others. Social relations are based on productive relations, and societies are 'totalities of relations of production'.[4] However, man's true nature can never be realised in a capitalist society because of productive alienation. In selling his labour for wages, he finds that[5]

> the work is external to the worker, that it is not part of his nature, that consequently he does not fulfil himself in his work but denies himself, has a feeling of misery, not of well being, does not develop freely a physical and mental energy, but is physically exhausted and mentally debased . . . His work is not voluntary but imposed, forced labour. It is not the satisfaction of a need, but only a means of satisfying other needs . . . Finally, the alienated character of work for the worker appears in the fact that it is not his work but work for someone else, that in work he does not belong to himself but to another person.

Marx argued that alienated work could only diminish freedom, by strengthening and enriching the forces (machinery and money) by which the worker was enslaved, and that the worker's alienation extended to all other spheres of his life, because the world of objects which he created 'stands opposed to him as an autonomous power'.[6]

Yet in spite of this process, Marx insisted that men still possessed within them all the human potentialities to overcome the destructive forces they had created. As members of the political community, men were social beings, exercising the kind of co-operation required for true freedom and development. What each man had to do was to reject his 'untrue' life as an alienated worker, and bring into being the potential he had as a citizen. Society was not a corporate abstraction confronting and limiting the individual; 'the individual is the *social being*. The manifestation of his life—even when it does not appear directly in the form of a communal manifestation accomplished in association with other men—is therefore a manifestation and affirmation of *social life*.'[7] Man's 'true' nature would be revealed after the workers' revolution had overthrown the capitalist system. Once the division of labour had been abolished, he would acquire 'all-roundedness' through humanised, unalienated work. The state itself would become superfluous in a classless society where individuals related themselves totally and positively to their fellow men.

All these theories argued that the abolition of property and the consequent redefinitions of political and economic obligation would result in fundamental changes in social and personal relationships. The other main strand of libertarian thought is primarily concerned with the latter kind of relationships, and with illustrating the falseness of conventional obligations. It distinguishes between a true and a false self, not in terms of the individual's relations with society as a whole (his political relations), but in terms of his day-to-day interactions with others. It emphasises the need for liberation in the personal sphere before the ends of political revolution can be accomplished.

Writers of this school (and particularly the existentialists) give much attention to the impossibility of finding true expression for the individual's personality within conventional definitions of social roles. The expectations embodied in role prescriptions operate as scripts for performances which can never reflect a person's real feelings, but only a sort of pantomime of the part society has given him. The result is that people are not really committed to the way in which they behave; their alienation consists primarily in a sense of detachment from what they do, in an awareness of themselves as apart and separate from their social role performances. Commitment can only be present if people control their own decisions, including making their own rules about their conduct, and reaching their own definitions of their obligations to others.

The central problem for this type of individualism is to show how the sum total of each person's commitment to his own standards of behaviour amounts to a viable social order. In the absence of generalised norms of conduct, would not civilised society collapse? Would not the weak and sick be neglected or exploited? Would not every duty to others be overlooked or flouted? The answer to these questions given by this version of libertarianism is that the rejection of conventional obligation does not necessarily imply neglect of others' needs; on the contrary, it may entail a very stern version of the dutiful assumption of social responsibility. A strong and chosen commitment to others at a point of crisis (for instance, volunteering for military action or joining an armed resistance movement) may for the individual involve the overthrow of conventional expectations, and the abandonment of a prestigious social role. The notion of duty implies that we act from motives under which we would not, in other instances, have chosen to act. But a true sense of duty, as opposed to the false or conventional sense, entails the recognition of needs in others which they cannot meet alone, and a commitment to solidarity with them. It would appear to be part of what we mean by describing a man as free and self-directing that he should be able, in some circumstances, to override his instincts towards self-preservation, and to take action to protect others in need. Our rules for moral conduct certainly attempt to encourage this; we try to organise society in such a way as to ensure that, in moments of crisis or emergency, people will recognise such obligations, feel moved to fulfil them, and to act accordingly. However, recent libertarian critics of our social order suggest that in everyday life, conventional definitions of social duties produce very different effects. Instead of clarifying the nature of our obligations to others, they obscure and mystify them, suggesting that some serious moral commitment exists, when in fact all that is happening is obfuscation, exploitation and the suppression of one or more personalities, usually in the name of harmony and co-operation. Nowhere is this process more marked, according to writers like R. D. Laing, than in the modern family. Using examples of parents with schizophrenic offspring, Laing shows how they employ a welter of dark hints, obscure threats, pleas, teasings, tantrums and lies to bind their children to them, to suggest overwhelming obligations, based on mythical needs or nameless dangers. True needs, real feelings, genuine crises, are precisely what do not emerge from such processes. Generalising from these families, Laing describes 'normal' family life as essentially a falsification:[8]

one has to pretend first not to feel the passion one really feels, then, to pretend to passion one does *not* really feel, and to pretend that certain passionate upsurges of resentment, hatred, envy are unreal, or don't happen, or are something else. This requires false realisations, false de-realisations, and a cover story (rationalisation). After this almost complete holocaust of one's experience on the altar of conformity, one is liable to feel somewhat empty, but one can try to fill one's emptiness up with money, consumer goods, position, respect, admirations, envy of one's fellows for their business, professional, social success.

Laing sees conventional psychiatry as society's last line of defence against the truth.

Laing's colleague, David Cooper, goes further than this in suggesting that the family serves as a model for every social institution in an exploitative society. Because 'the family specialises in the formation of roles for its members rather than laying down the conditions for a free assumption of identity',[9] and because of the concentration of power in the hands of parents, family socialisation creates a form of alienation in every individual, based on an internalised family structure of relationships. Until they systematically abandon these modes of experience (through the 'death' of the internalised family, and often, Cooper argues, by going mad) people cannot be truly aware of themselves or others. He suggests that once individuals are 'reborn', they can become involved in alternative models of 'living arrangements'. These are based on small communes, whose members relate to each other in a spirit of trust, openness and honesty, and decide their priorities in terms of perceived needs rather than formal obligations. Since the exclusiveness of the narrow nuclear family has been abandoned, the love and support such groups would give each other would be inclusive; it would be restricted neither by considerations of property nor of fidelity; it would therefore be more flexible and more appropriate than the assistance given by family members to each other.[10]

> [it] means that love relationships become diffused between members of the commune network far more than is the case with the family system, and this means of course that sexual relationships are not restricted to some socially approved two-person man-woman arrangement; above all, because this strikes most centrally at repression, it means that children should have totally free access to adults beyond their biological parental couple.

Cooper's insistence that individual rebirth, involving as it does a rejection of the hierarchical, alienating and suppressive elements of family socialisation, is a necessary precondition for any effective economic, social and political revolution is based on the observation that nearly all previous revolutions have given way to new forms of control and domination, in which individuals have had no more personal freedom than before.[11]

> for me it is a revolutionary act if in the course of months or years a person transcends the major bits of his micro- and macro-social conditioning in the direction of the spontaneous self-assertion of full personal autonomy which *in itself* is a decisive act of counter-violence against the system.

> even the most secure families crumble when someone longs hard enough not to belong and generates sufficient revolutionary

counter-violence to destructure the mendacious structure and introduce a saboteur truth. At this point I find a subtle but luminous equation of madness and political victory.

The logical steps by which Cooper makes this equation are left somewhat vague. Political power does not reside in the forms of institutions, but in their use to coerce or control people. To take the example of political oppression in South Africa (Cooper's country of origin), it is certainly true that the state is highly paternalistic in structure and is consciously based on the notion of the family, with the ruling white elite as the father, and the black population as the unruly and irresponsible children. But it does not follow from this that an overthrow of the family form will overthrow the political system. A rebellion by black children against their black fathers would hardly further the cause of liberty for the African population. Indeed, since *apartheid* ensures that most urban black workers are separated from their families, this particular source of oppression is notable by its absence. It is the ability and willingness of the government to use violence against the black population that constitutes the reality of political oppression.

Furthermore it is difficult to see how even the general abandonment of the institution of the family, and the creation of a sense of small-scale communal responsibility for the meeting of personal needs, would necessarily lead to a more satisfactory solution to wider social problems. The fact that communes provide a better therapeutic milieu for the experience of a psychotic breakdown than many families or most psychiatric hospitals is not evidence of their suitability either for revolutionary resistance to political oppression, or for post-revolutionary social organisation. It is quite unclear how such communes would produce the goods and services to meet basic needs, let alone build irrigation dams or power stations. Like Marcuse, Cooper identifies the constraints on personal freedom with alienating aspects of capitalist structures; but what seems least credible in the accounts given by Cooper (and indeed by Marcuse) of a non-alienated society is the notion that it could be based on the products of super-alienation. For Cooper is really arguing a kind of psychiatric equivalent of Marcuse's concept of the genesis of the New Man; a road to socialism via madness rather than via economic alienation. The self must experience total separation from the social role: the person must cease to function as a social being. It is only through the experience of a chaotic non-existence, the total fragmentation of consciousness, the out-and-out rejection of the 'reality' of the world into which one has been socialised, that a truer alternative can be created. The state of super-alienation thus becomes, by a kind of double-negative, converted into a positive rebirth, a new beginning. Since both Cooper and Marcuse write in a style that is abstract, polemical and rather grandiose, this process often appears to be a sort of conjuring trick, executed with more grandiloquence than dexterity. We are left feeling that they have made a leap in the dark which those who have neither their faith nor their experience of these phenomena cannot really be expected to follow.

Participation and freedom—the therapeutic community

As an illustration of the complexities of any attempt to reconcile personal liberty with a sense of social responsibility I would like now to discuss the 'therapeutic community'. A number of experimental attempts have been made to construct a social system out of the relationships between inmates and those who care for them in residential institutions. They are relevant as examples for the purposes of this chapter because they have been concerned with precisely the sort of people that Cooper is describing: those who have reached a point of alienation at which they can no longer sustain any pretence of performing a conventional social role or meeting society's expectations. Therapeutic communities attempt simultaneously to create a new system of social relationships to replace the old, institutional, role-differentiated hierarchy of the hospital ward, and to enable the emergence of a new identity in the individuals undergoing treatment. Both aims are pursued by trying to encourage patterns of interpersonal communications, between individual patients and staff members, which are free, open and honest. All participate equally in the day-to-day running of the community and in decision-making. Thus people who have reached a certain point in a career of disruptive, disturbing or self-destructive behaviour may, in the supportive environment of a very strong group, confront each other with the futility, dishonesty and despair of their existences, yet feel sufficiently secure to change. As part of a system of relationships which is focused on interpersonal communication and caring, they can abandon their old, defensive perceptions of themselves and others, and temporarily submerge themselves in the group identity which is based on the unit's therapeutic ideology.

It has not proved easy to give equal emphasis to the pursuit of all these aims in therapeutic communities. Many early experiments concentrated on the task of de-institutionalising the regimes of chronic wards in mental hospitals.[12] These tended to lay stress on promoting more democratic decision-making processes, and more permissive, egalitarian relationships. However, as specialised units were set up to deal with behaviour problems, with recidivists and addicts, significant alterations in their ideologies became apparent. In her study of Maxwell Jones's unit, the Henderson Hospital, Rapoport found increasing emphasis upon communalism and on reality confrontation.[13] These latter aims seem to have actually superseded the original ones in later developments, such as Synanon. Elements of hierarchy and authoritarianism reappear to create the degree of control felt necessary to support the individual through the limbo of the loss of his old identity, until he is ready to build up a new identity, largely based on the unit's ethos, but constructed out of the new expression it has enabled him to find for his feelings, and his new relations with the other members of the community.

One essential feature of such regimes is the total power of the group over the individual. He is denied privacy, any area of his life which is to be outside the purview of the group. Every action, however apparently insignificant, is 'fed back' into the group by others; every remark or gesture is material for group discussion or criticism. In some cases, sexual activity is forbidden, not because it is disapproved of *per se*, but because it constitutes pairing which detracts from group processes. Other regimes allow sex, but insist that the details are discussed at groups.[14] A student's first hand account of one such unit gives the flavour of such an experience.[15]

> The residents are expected to share everything from possessions to
> feelings . . . and there is no area which is sacrosanct . . .
> Reality-confrontation is perhaps the overriding value. Residents are
> made aware, in forceful terms, how they are affecting others, and must
> not deny the validity of any observation, by laughing it off or arguing.
> Total honesty is mandatory, and anything less will be met with anger
> and derision . . . Cleanliness and politeness are expected at all times.
> Any infringements of these standards will result in all the residents
> being summoned by a bell, and specific misdemeanours, such as
> cigarette ends, will be pointed out until someone accepts
> responsibility. All residents are expected to look for these deviations
> from the high standards and to 'pull each other up' on them . . .
> Sanctions for bad behaviour . . . may take the form of wearing a sign or
> being demoted down the hierarchy, and are known as 'learning
> experiences'. During my stay . . . a resident felt that he had deviated
> from the ideals of the community, so made himself a sign spelling out
> his problems and wore it round his neck for several days.

This form of group dictatorship (made tolerable only by the fact that other members of the unit are people in various stages of recovery from similar problems) stands on its head Goffman's famous account of total institutions. Goffman pointed out that the individual in mental hospitals, prisons and so on, defined himself by taking a stance against the regime; he derived his sense of identity from small or large acts of resistance against the 'total' demands for conformity with institutional standards which were imposed on every area of his life. Yet therapeutic communities are far more total in their demands. The 'mortification' of the self which Goffman describes in conventional hospitals is carried much further in some units; induction procedures may be less formal in Jones-style communities, but in some drug-treatment centres they include searching and removal of personal possessions. Above all, what Goffman calls 'contaminative exposure' of every aspect of the individual's life is much greater, for there is no privacy, and *every* aspect of behaviour is treated as 'symptomatic'. There can thus be no question of the development of protective friendships or loyalties between community members, or an anti-institutional culture; each weakness will be picked upon by the group as ruthlessly as hens peck an injured one of their number (to use McMurphy's analogy). Nor is there any room for what Goffman calls 'adaptations'; the individual cannot 'work the system' to his own advantage, or withdraw, fight or even become a model inmate. There is simply no escape from the demands of the group.

It is clear, therefore, that such therapeutic communities hold personal liberty of no account; they set no store by self-determination, or the right to privacy; they allow no opinions to be held in secret, no individual peculiarities to be harboured, no furtive resentments or wistful desires. All must be known, every deception, every defence revealed, so that the old persona can be ruthlessly destroyed. If such is the process by which the total fragmentation of an alienated consciousness must be achieved, before the reconstruction or 'rebirth' of the individual can occur, it sounds very unlike the accounts given by Cooper and Marcuse; and indeed the methods pursued in therapeutic communities owe little to the philosophical tenets of existentialism. If anything, their theoretical antecedents lie more in the direction of behaviourism and learning theory; the demands they make on the individual are in the name of *reality*. Community members are constantly being confronted with their behaviour, and made to accept responsibility for the effect they have on others. Far from rejecting the values of wider society, 'deviants' in most communities are encouraged to reject the values of their subculture. For instance, in Synanon the 'reality' of the drug addict role is presented as pathetic and disgusting rather than exciting or rebellious, and clean living is offered as the only satisfactory way of life.[16]

We are no longer drug addicts. We were all addicts, and when we were addicts we talked about dope. We are trying to do something else. We are trying to learn how to live like human beings . . . My problem wasn't drugs, even though drugs made me sub-human. What I needed, and still need, is to learn more about proper living.

We offer you life as an adult in comparison to the life of a snivelling, whining dope fiend from the gutters of New York.

Above all, however, the factor that eliminates individual liberty in therapeutic communities is group pressure. The group insists on the most onerous form of reciprocal obligation—the obligation to be absolutely open and honest with all one's fellow group members all the time, to share everything, and to put one's loyalty to the group above any partisan feelings or self-interest. This is not, as Cooper and Marcuse describe it, a consequence of rebirth; rather it is a precondition. It is imposed on the individual until he can provide evidence of having fully absorbed the group's standards, and of being completely willing to meet their expectations of him. Only then will he be judged to be ready to develop a self of his own.

The success of these methods may come as no surprise to students of social psychology. The power of the group, and particularly the small group, to alter perceptions, attitudes and behaviour in line with its own consensus has long been claimed from experimental evidence.[17] The important question is whether such group pressures are compatible with the degree of honesty and openness which therapeutic communities also aim to achieve. Psychological experiments have found small groups to be notoriously bad at tolerating ambivalence, at enabling the free expression of feeling, or allowing conflicts of perception and opinion. Can the individual under such pressures be free to be 'honest' and 'true' to himself? What therapeutic groups (at least of the older Martin and Jones type) claim to have achieved is the creation of a democratic and permissive milieu in which some degree of ambivalence and conflict is the norm, and where the categorical, defensive rationalisation, the preference for consensual attitude over felt response, which is the mark of experimental groups, is precisely what is rejected. It is certainly the claim that such groups produce a sense of greater intimacy, spontaneity and honesty in relationships, and that these generate high morale, support and mutual trust, which explains the fact that many non-problematical members of the community are volunteering themselves for various group experiences.

However, even in the Jones type of regime, the element of control in the group's relations with individual members is quite specific. Rapoport noted of the community meetings at the Henderson Hospital that, 'While it is recognised that treatment occurs here, and that there are powerful social forces at the disposal of treatment aims in such a group, the principal aims of the community meetings are those of social control.'[18] If this is true there, it is very much more true of some of the other units. Indeed, some of them make the element of control so explicit that time is set aside, taken out of the mainstream of the regime, for the expression of feelings which resist group pressures to conform. Thus at Phoenix House, a unit for treating drug addiction, there are encounter groups three times a week at which all the rules of the community are suspended so that all the emotions and tensions about the very controlled regime can be released. All the rules about not swearing, not defending themselves, keeping cool and behaving 'as if' they were happy are abandoned, and residents scream at each other about their resentments of the injustices, pettinesses and betrayals of the community life, and their feelings of loneliness and despair. Only by allowing for the separate expression of such feelings can the control of the totalitarian, all-seeing, all-reporting, all-criticising group be tolerated.

Such examples prompt questions about the true nature of the feelings of security, trust and intimacy of less overtly brutal therapeutic groups. Do these reside in the democracy and permissiveness of their ethos (as Jones suggests) or are they rather a reflection of the total submergence of the self into a 'group personality'? Recently writers have made explicit comparisons between the techniques of brainwashing and those of therapeutic communities. It has been pointed out, for instance, that communist methods of indoctrination are broadly similar. 'Thought reform consists of two basic elements; confession, the exposure and renunciation of past and present "evil", and re-education; the remaking of a man in the communist image.'[19] It is the combination of total control over the individual with denial of the validity of his past, his old self, and the insistence that he participate in his own resocialisation, under pressure from an all-powerful peer group, which is so characteristic of brainwashing techniques, and has prompted questions about the ethical justification of some therapeutic methods.[20]

Privacy and participation

What therapeutic community experiments suggest, therefore, is that members of small-scale face-to-face groups and communes can achieve a high degree of mutual responsibility, and that this is maximised by encouraging full participation in group activities. A commitment to honesty and openness can lead to a sharing of perceptions and a confrontation with others' feelings and needs, which in turn creates a shared group identity and purpose. In so far as participation is voluntary, in the sense that all are at liberty to leave at any time, this achievement reconciles freedom with social responsibility of a high order, at least on this small scale. Furthermore, the glimpses it is possible to get of the social and political organisation of communist China suggest that there at least it has proved possible for an enormous country to produce a remarkable unity of purpose, and concerted economic progress—with the minimum of overt coercive control—on the basis of small communes. The face-to-face pressures in the communal group have achieved a level of enthusiastic participation which is self-directing and yet also reflects a dedication to the wider aims of society as a whole, and the thoughts of Chairman Mao.

However, the nature of the Chinese achievement draws attention to the absence in such societies of one kind of personal freedom which has been characteristic of Western cultures. Our concept of freedom gives great importance to the right to privacy and to private relationships. There seem to be important links between this notion of privacy and the ideal of an exclusive love relationship. Western cultures have recognised a passionate kind of love for one other, which is stronger than any other feeling, and ultimately, if it is not allowed expression, can destroy all the compassionate concern in other relationships. Our institutionalisation of privacy in exclusive relationships is based partly on respect for passionate feelings, and partly on fear of them; on the recognition that thwarted passion can make men coldly indifferent to the suffering of their neighbours, and violently hostile to those they see as obstacles to their desires. Conflicts between passionate love and obligations to others have been the theme of much tragic literature, and the view that man's most intense emotions are potentially destructive of all his dearest principles and finest standards is an explicit element in tragedy from the Greeks to Shakespeare, from Oedipus to Othello.

Yet Western culture has also attempted to harness the passionate side of individuals' natures, and use it for compassionate ends, thus providing a very intense form of care and support. This is the ideal of the nuclear family: to mobilise the emotions in an exclusive love relationship to serve the dependency needs of the children of that relationship. It is not clear whether therapeutic communities have achieved a true inclusiveness in relation to all humanity, or have simply transferred the family kind of exclusiveness to the small group. (Selection and induction procedures suggest the latter may be the case.) Either way, the difficulties of sustaining inclusiveness and compassion in a Western individualistic culture are similar, in the group or the family. Passionate love seeks a single object, an exclusive intimacy, and if baulked by the inclusive demands of others, looks outside the group or the family, and may leave in search of what they cannot provide.

The notions of privacy and exclusiveness are highly correlated with the kind of liberal consciousness which was characteristic of the nineteenth century, and is still an important element in our notions of personal freedom. Mill's liberalism was centrally concerned with the identification of a private area in which a man's thoughts and actions would be immune from the interference of others. This was distinguished from the public sector of his social obligations, which was governed by consensual, conventional rules of conduct. These were rules which all men must endorse, and agree to be bound by, irrespective of their group or class loyalties, or their local affiliations.

Thus we seem to have two conflicting notions of personal autonomy: the liberal tradition's idea of a sector in each individual's life, marked off as his area of private concern; and the libertarian tradition's concept of the individual as free to engage with others in evolving a communal, participatory, inclusive pattern of social relationships, which constitutes a self-directing group, and which is not bound by other, external rules of conduct, but in which no individual can claim the right to keep any part of himself or his relationships outside the group's activities.

If we now return to the wider political perspectives of the earlier part of this chapter, we can see that these two traditions give rise to different notions of political participation and obligation. The liberal ideal is of a society composed of enlightened individuals, capable of rational decision-making and self-determination. Their enlightenment is derived from their all-round education and first hand knowledge of a number of social issues. This ideal is most nearly realised in societies with a large middle class which, in accordance with de Tocqueville's precepts, is active in numerous political, communal and voluntary civic organisations. Membership of a multiplicity of different groups and organisations exposes individuals to numerous points of view. However, they form their own political judgments as private individuals, balancing the perspectives derived from their cross-cutting loyalties and affiliations. Liberals thus see democracy as flourishing where informed individuals participate equally in national political issues, and reach a national consensus on the essential priorities of their society.[21]

Liberals see two major threats to the kind of freedom permitted by this type of democratic participation. First there is the tendency of 'extremist' political views to arise where individuals belong only to groups that reinforce a single, simple view of social problems and their solution. Liberals explain the success of communist parties in retaining the loyalties of large sections of the working class in terms of their ability to create organised structures which affect their perceptions of every aspect of their daily lives, by 'having them belong to party-controlled unions, live in workers' co-operative housing, belong to party-aligned sports and social clubs, attend cultural or musical activities sponsored by the party or the unions and read party newspapers and magazines.'[22] This form of political activism produces demands for sudden, dramatic social change, accomplished by authoritarian methods, inconsistent with liberal notions of freedom and democracy. Second there is the tendency towards the development of a 'mass society'. If individuals do not exercise their powers to make their own decisions on political issues, then democracy will mean little more than the government of everyone by all the others' opinions. Mill and de Tocqueville drew attention to this danger of the growth of a form of public opinion which regulates every kind of behaviour, and which imposes a drab uniformity on private as well as public life, so that originality and spontaneity are feared and suppressed. Here again, the excessive power of the group over the individual's exercise of his own judgment is seen as giving rise to an evil, in this case an exaggerated 'other-directedness'[23] which reduces men to anonymous members of a mass.

Libertarians attribute these features of the 'mass society' to weaknesses in the liberal concept of freedom. As we have seen, they suggest that liberals make a false distinction between private freedoms and public obligations. If we allow any of our obligations to be defined by an impersonal, external authority we shall suffer a form of alienation. The mass society is a reflection of mass production, mass consumption, mass education, mass communication and a hierarchical, bureaucratised society. It is a reflection of the concentration of power in a ruling elite, whose excessive authority leads to the powerlessness of the masses. The liberal notion of a balance of power, and of the middle class as holding the balance, is rejected. The top group is seen as 'increasingly unified, and often . . . wilfully co-ordinated', the middle levels as 'a drifting set of stalemated . . . forces', the bottom as 'politically fragmented, and . . . increasingly powerless'.[24]

As a consequence of this analysis, libertarians draw different conclusions about the forms of resistance against authority required to bring about freedom and a new notion of social obligation. They argue that the powerless, and particularly minority groups in the most disadvantaged positions, cannot possibly gain recognition for the autonomy they seek by participation within the democratic process. These questions will be the subjects of the next chapter.

4

'Alternative Realities'

One of the major difficulties in any discussion of the libertarian notion of liberation is whether it provides concepts which can be usefully applied to pre-revolutionary society. The earlier political philosophers of the libertarian tradition tended to reserve their descriptions of liberated behaviour for the post-revolutionary utopia. More recently, writers like Marcuse have identified groups within capitalist society which, by virtue of their active resistance against its constraints, they see as models for liberation. Rebellion and protest are presented as in themselves liberated, or giving rise to liberated behaviour. But how does this analysis of resistance against the social order affect our understanding of social deviance—of behaviour classified as breaking laws or other rules of conduct? Are deviants liberated in a sense that conventional members of society are not?

This question arises to a large extent because vociferous protest groups have emerged among people who have been traditionally treated (either blatantly or subtly) as inferior or sick. These protest groups have emphasised the common features in their situations, even though the differences are equally obvious. In some cases these are people who have suffered both material disadvantages and stigma, like the homeless or claimants of social security; in others, their disadvantages have stemmed from inequalities of obligation in relationships, like women; in yet others they have been regarded as deviant, and have been punished, treated or repressively tolerated, like homosexuals. Very often their group activity has centred around the assertion of their identity as a valid one, as the expression of an authentic mode of being a person; thus they demand recognition of that identity by society, and that they should not be treated as inferior because of what they are. Claimants, women and homosexuals are all in their different ways insisting that the characteristics that make them unlike others should not be seen as misfortunes, handicaps, weaknesses or impediments, but rather as expressions of themselves as people, living their own lives. Such groups encourage their members to define their differences from others rather than to affect conventional attitudes, or 'pass' as members of the majority; they support the development of an identity which challenges others either openly to declare their prejudices, or to grant them full acceptance.

The fact that minority or disadvantaged groups have taken such action to assert the authenticity of their way of being has attracted the attention of philosophers and sociologists. In particular the issues raised by the formation of groups of this kind have been discussed within the context of sociological theories about social deviance. This is partly because the interactionist approach to deviance is particularly interested in analysing the effects of official interventions by authorities like the police, the courts, the medical profession and social workers into the lives of people who are subsequently given labels like 'criminal', 'inadequate' or 'mentally ill'. But it is also because interactionists have tended to concentrate much of their attention on behaviour about whose definition there is a good deal of dispute—where the accounts given by these official agencies of what happens and the motives that lie behind what happens are very different from the accounts given by the participants themselves. In particular, they have been interested in examples of behaviour defined by the participants either as self-expressive or simply as pleasurable, but defined by the authorities as deviant.

It is the contention of this school of sociologists that we cannot hope to understand such behaviour without a full investigation of its 'social meaning' to those who participate in it. By this they mean the significance given to their behaviour by people who take part in activities which are condemned or banned by wider society, but on which they place a different value. Such groups enable individuals within them to construct an interpretation of their experiences which is contrary to the interpretation given by the rest of society. Thus for instance, using an example of the kind of group I have already mentioned, a homosexual group whose slogan is 'gay is good' enables homosexuals who might otherwise feel guilt and shame to construct a concept of themselves as normal, natural and healthy, in spite of contrary opinions by the majority of others.

However, these groups are not studied in isolation. Another interactionist theme is the effect of attempts by the majority to impose its definitions of their behaviour upon 'deviants'. Where a large number of people are behaving in ways that are disapproved, the processes by which some of these are singled out for punishment or treatment have considerable repercussions upon the social organisation and self-definition of the rest who have not been so labelled, and upon their relations with wider society. Interactionists thus tend to be particularly concerned with forms of behaviour which invite official interventions, either punitive or therapeutic, and with the consequences of such interventions.

It is worth noting at this point that interactionist sociologists give attention to all the many different kinds of behaviour which attract social disapproval or official intervention, and insist on grouping them all together under the title of 'deviance'. This seems to be connected with their interest in the libertarian theme that all unconventionality and unorthodoxy is a form of protest, and potentially a source of liberation, or ultimately of revolution. However, by emphasising what these forms of behaviour have in common (that they are condemned and subject to intervention), they may obscure important differences. For instance, they may fail to distinguish between purposeful protest, which develops a critique of the established order and alternative modes of action or organisation, and behaviour which is simply contrary to society's rules.

In this chapter I have selected one particular form of behaviour which has been studied by sociologists of this school—drug use. It is selected mainly because Jock Young's book, *The Drugtakers*, is both a comprehensive analysis of this form of behaviour and a full account of how the interactionist approach is applied to such a topic. It also specifically raises issues about liberty and liberation. At the end of the chapter I shall return to the wider question of how the activities of minority groups asserting their rights to full citizenship can be understood in relation to liberation. In the meantime, the example I have chosen serves mainly to focus attention on the method of analysis of this particular school of sociologists.

(Before embarking on this, it may be worth noting that drug use would seem to be an example of the type of action over which Mill would have argued that (apart from a consideration of its effects on others) neither law nor opinion should have sought to impose controls. He declared himself opposed to interventions 'where the object of the interference is to make it impossible or difficult to obtain a commodity'[1] on the grounds that they were intolerable constraints on the liberty of the buyer.)

In considering the effects of official interventions into the field of drug use, Jock Young gives the example of increased police action in an area with a high incidence of marijuana smoking. He suggests that such interventions increase the segregation of drugtakers from others who do not share their values, increase their differentiation from others, increase the secrecy of their activities, make marijuana scarcer, thus attracting professional suppliers, increase identification between marijuana users and heroin addicts and increase public concern about drug use, creating a 'fantasy crime wave'. Young's argument is thus that increased police interest in marijuana use has the effect of redefining this activity in such a way as to make it conform more closely to the stereotype of a crime, to lead to closer links between marijuana users and hard-drug users, and to increase the dangers of creating a professional distribution network.

In the field of addiction to hard drugs such as heroin, he suggests that characteristic medical and psychiatric reactions to the individual addict amplify his deviance also. They tend to treat addicts in hospital environments, where decisions are taken for them, and to use clinical definitions of addiction as a form of sickness with a pronounced tendency towards relapse. Hence responsibility for his behaviour is removed from the addict, and he is given a sick role. The prestige and authority of the treaters are used to influence the addict in the direction of believing that he is not acting freely in using drugs, but rather is in the grip of a physical or psychological compulsion, which he cannot be expected to understand or control without expert assistance. The addict thus ceases to be a free agent; and no demand is made of him to choose to stay off drugs, nor are any good reasons given to him why he should do so. Young points out that the most successful methods for treating drugs have involved insisting that the addict takes responsibility for himself, that he has the power to choose to give up drugs, and that there are good reasons and possible means for doing this.

In all this Young is taking a line very consistent with that of Mill, that interference with the liberty of the individual, besides being undesirable in itself, is also apt to have undesired consequences. But his arguments go much further than this, for Young is also concerned to explain the origins of drug use, and its 'social meaning'. This leads him to make a number of assertions about the part played by drugs in the movement towards liberation among young people and about the nature of social control which are much more questionable.

Young quotes Marcuse's account of the dominion of corporate capitalism through the creation of false needs, but suggests that the values of productivity and organised, routinised consumption are constantly being covertly challenged and contradicted by other values. He quotes Sykes and Matza's description of 'subterranean values':[2]

> the search for adventure, excitement and thrill is a subterranean value
> that . . . often exists side by side with the values of security,
> routinization and the rest. It is not a deviant value in any full sense, but
> must be held in abeyance until the proper moment and circumstances
> for its expression arrive.

But as Young points out,[3]

> the world of leisure and of work are intimately related. The money
> earned by work is spent in leisure time. It is through the various life
> styles which are evolved that men confirm their occupational status . . .
> The inter-relationship between formal and subterranean values is
> therefore seen in a new light; hedonism, for instance, is closely tied to
> productivity . . . a man is justified in expressing subterranean values if,
> and only if, he has earned the right to do so by working hard and being
> productive.

It is necessary for those who control productive resources to represent the enjoyment of an exciting leisure as one of the semi-automatic rewards of being particularly productive.

In a stable, rural, subsistence economy, necessity strikes its own natural balance between work and leisure. Escape from toil is usually accomplished through religious ritual or in festive revelry. But situations of increasing affluence, extensive geographical and social mobility, urbanisation and alienated work give rise to difficulties in establishing norms for leisure hours which satisfy social needs. Offering an explanation for the emergence of a drug cult, Young writes:[4]

> I suggest that this occurs when the culture to which a group belongs becomes inadequate for solving their particular desires and problems. People have certain aspirations for their social world: sexual, economic, expressive, etc. Their culture attempts to provide solutions to these particular problems and when there is a disparity between people's aspirations and their means of achieving them a situation occurs which sociologists term *anomie*. In face of this contingency, people tend to create new means of achieving their aspirations or will alter their desires to achievable ends . . . To explain then the use of a new drug such as LSD or the new use of an accepted drug such as alcohol, we must first explain the rise of a subculture of people who are using this drug. And to explain the rise of subcultures the most potent concept is that of anomie.

This anomie is specifically related by Young to the process by which[5]

> the growth of bureaucracies in almost every sphere of social life have enmeshed the workaday world in a system of rules which have precluded to a large extent the possibility for the individual to express his identity through his job. The high division of labour and rationalisation of occupational roles have made them inadequate as vehicles of personal desires and expressivity.

As a result individuals and groups experiencing anomie turn to leisure and to subterranean values for means of self-expression. But Young insists that such actions are conscious and deliberate choices, even in the case of hard drugs.[6]

> People accept socialisation into drug culture because they find the cultures attractive in terms of solving problems which they face; they do not 'catch' drug addiction, they embrace it.

> A person becomes dependent on a drug to the extent that—in his reckoning—efficiently produces effects which he judges as valuable. . . . his dissociation is a matter of choice rather than bowing to the inevitable. Moreover, his disdain for society is of an articulate and ideological nature. He evolves social theories which uphold

subterranean values as authentic guides to action, and which attempt to solve the problem of the domination of the ethos of productivity.

Thus Young asserts that groups who use drugs as 'Doors in the Wall' (in Huxley's phrase) to 'step out into a world free of the worries of workaday life' are not acting asocially.[7]

> It is fallacious to think of these episodes as escapes from reality; rather we must view them as escapes into *alternative* forms of reality. For social reality is socially defined and constructed and the world of subterranean values, however ambivalently it is viewed by 'official' society, is as real as the world of factories, workbenches and conveyor belts.

He points out that what seems objectionable to non-members of such subcultures is their refusal to defer gratification or pay a price for pleasure in work and self-discipline, and that 'the social reaction against a particular form of drug-taking is, in general, proportional to the degree to which the group involved embraces values which are hedonistic and disdainful of work.'[8]

When Young asserts that drugtaking subcultures construct an 'alternative reality' which is 'beyond the ethos of productivity', it is not clear what kind of claims he is making for that reality. He is clearly saying that this is an area of behaviour from desired motives, freely chosen. He frequently insists that non-drug-users must recognise the drugtaker's actions as meaningful and chosen within the integrity of his personality. But does Young want us to conclude that drugtaking is part of a *successful* attempt by bohemian youth to break out of the anomie of modern, mechanised, routinised existence? Is he inviting us to see such actions as *liberated* in Marcuse's sense? It is important to answer this question, because in order to give any specific meaning to the claims of Marcuse's *Essay on Liberation* we need to be able, in examining a piece of behaviour, to say whether it is liberated or not, and what it is that is liberated or unliberated about it. It is also important to understand whether Young is saying that the 'alternative reality' of drugs is to be taken any more seriously than, say, the alternative reality of surfing or sun-worship. For it is a fact that some young people have chosen to remove themselves from the field of productive work and conventional leisure pursuits to concentrate all their energies on surfing or on sun-worship, and it may well also be the case that to treat these practices as deviant in the sense of being either criminal or insane would have most deleterious social consequences. But to say all this is to do no more than to agree with Mill that much more is to be lost by needless interference in harmless individual eccentricities than is to be gained. Young insists, along with Marcuse, that the major social evil of conventional, formal society is its tendency towards the repressive dominion of formal, work-orientated definitions and conventional, consensual modes of thought and behaviour, and that the anomie produced by such repressive formality must necessarily lead to the rebellious counter-definitions and subterranean subcultures among the young. He invites us to see drugtaking as a form of assistance. He therefore owes us some account of how successfully drugtaking would overcome such repressive dominion if it were left to its own devices by the agents of social control.

Let us suppose for a moment (and the weight of evidence in Young's book is in this direction) that he is inviting us to see drugtaking as liberated behaviour in Marcuse's sense; that is, as a kind of action undertaken from desired motives, in protest against the restrictions of a repressive culture, giving rise not only to spontaneous feelings of wellbeing and freedom, but also to a significant form of protest and revolt against corporate capitalism. (In assuming this I am not testing either Young's or Marcuse's hypotheses solely in these terms, as will become clear later.) Now clearly there is no sense in which the mere act of drugtaking is, in itself, a rebellion, either effective or ineffective, against anything. People have taken drugs in almost every culture, and some cultures approve or even sanctify such acts in certain circumstances. As Young points out on more than one occasion, the physical effects of the substances themselves are so neutral as to require interpretation and socialisation before they can be experienced as meaningful at all; so if their use is to be interpreted as desirable, rebellious and liberating, this must depend on the cultural context of their use. Thus it is for Young to show us that this is how most, or at least many, drugusers interpret them, and then that they actually produce or are accompanied by these effects.

He argues that drugtaking is characteristic of groups of people who have rejected the work ethic and conventional aspirations, and have developed alternative aspirations, centred on pleasure, free time, play, expressivity, communication and understanding. But to establish that their behaviour is liberated in Marcuse's sense he would need to show that they had *actively rejected* the former values and aspirations, and not simply abandoned them as unobtainable, and that they had *actively embraced* the latter, rather than drifted into a group whose norms and values they subsequently adopted. To say that drugtaking is chosen behaviour, and seen as a means to the solution of problems of anomie, is certainly not enough to establish it as liberated behaviour in Marcuse's terms, for such a description would cover the case of a young person who drifted out of employment, drifted into a bohemian area, drifted into the company of drugtakers and thus drifted into the habit of taking drugs. In fact it seems very probably that this is how a great many, if not most, drugtakers embark upon this form of behaviour. Young does not offer any evidence that the drugtaker's choice of his drugs is any more committed than the straight person's choice of his car or deep freeze; and this possible lack of strong commitment might help to explain the considerable drift out of as well as into this life style. Drugtaking attitudes and habits could be as derivative and changeable as any others.

However, it could be argued, following the logic of the 'Door in the Wall' analogy, that it is not the original taking of drugs that constitutes the rejection of the workaday world and commitment to an alternative; rather it is the effect of drugs, in producing alterations of perception and improvements in communication and understanding, that constitutes both the liberation and the alternative reality of drug use. This seems, at first sight at least, to give considerable importance to the drugs themselves (as used by subcultures anyway) in the process of entry into this alternative, liberated experience. But if the successful negotiation of a trip into alternative reality depends on the drug itself, then the existence of the other 'world' which lies beyond the ethos of productivity and workday values depends on the supply of available drugs. Without these, the subculture ceases to be liberated. This would seem to represent a dangerous dependence by the liberated world on the repressed one. With the exception of marijuana, virtually all drugs commonly used are sythetic substances, whose manufacture and sales originated from a commercial market in the medical and therapeutic field. Cocaine was introduced as a cure of opium addiction, which was fairly common in the nineteenth century because of its widespread use in medical practice; heroin was introduced to cure cocaine addiction; and other drugs like physeptone and methadone have been used as cures for heroin, and have also proved addictive; yet all continue to have medical uses and to be manufactured and sold quite legally.[9] Barbiturates and amphetimines were used as treatments before they were taken over by the young. The supply of all these substances thus depends on a commercial market.

Furthermore, where drugs have been strictly controlled and supplies have thus been greatly limited, as has been the case in the USA, the dangers of dependence by drugtakers upon their suppliers becomes more overt and explicit. This kind of situation, where commercial suppliers can no longer use legitimated channels like medical prescription, gives rise to black markets, run by professional racketeers and strong-arm men. Instead of depending on loopholes in formal distribution of drugs, young people have to resort to this source of supply, indicating their vulnerability to exploitation by the most overtly ruthless and greedy type of moneygrabber. If we are to understand liberated behaviour, as Marcuse does, as a serious challenge to corporate capitalism, this dependence would seem to be a considerable weakness. Drug users who buy from organised criminal suppliers are necessarily acting from undesired motives, for the supplies are usually expensive and often of poor quality. They also are creating, by this behaviour, a market for a particularly ruthless form of commercial exploitation; to be exploited is the very antithesis of liberation.

On the other hand, it might be suggested that for the most part, the members of bohemian cultures are not as dependent on drugs for the creation of their alternative reality as the foregoing analysis would suggest. It might be argued that drugs are only 'Doors in the Wall' in the sense of points of entry; after this, the subculture becomes more essentially concerned with alternative values and life styles than with the experiences of drugtaking. Here again, however, this argument would have to deal with the difficulty of the dependence of this subculture on the wider culture which is dominated by commercial production and consumption. Commercial interests are very quick to respond to any new life style, and to produce a marketable manufactured version of the characteristic symbols of it. Thus the needs relating to subterranean values—self-expression, play, intimacy, communication, etc.—are in turn subjected to the formal values of commercialism and consumerism, even if the values they promote are difficult to reconcile with the productive ethos. As the new group becomes a market for its own particular industry, its norms can come to be importantly determined by those who supply it. The best example of this is pop music; commercial companies now control a great deal of what was once a spontaneous expression of youthful creativity, and the mass media serve to forge links between suppliers and those who form their market, to reinforce this dependence, and to interpret the values of consumers in terms of the ethos of producers. The youth market becomes similar to established consumer groups like housewives.

Elsewhere, Young recognises this process.[10]

> commercial interests soon realize that groups such as the hippies, who have developed strong subterranean traditions, are not only a new market for leisure goods, but excellent innovators in the fields of music, design, clothes and fashion . . . For the leisure industry, like the mass media, is constantly in search of the new and just as the media perform a symbolic defusion of alternative realities, commerce delivers a more subtle blow—it buys the *style* of revolt lock, stock and barrel. [It becomes simply] a new mode of consumption and part of the good life.

But since Marcuse agrees that this is precisely how the most sophisticated form of repressive domination by the capitalist world takes place, this admission would seem very damaging to the notion that it is the bohemian life style that is liberated.

In view of these difficulties, let us now assume instead that Young is *not* inviting us to define drugtaking as liberated in Marcuse's sense. In other words, let us assume that he sees drug use simply as an activity, not necessarily as a spontaneous free activity. We can now examine the implications of Young's claims about 'alternative reality' in the light of this assumption. Here at once we are struck by the contrast Young makes between drugtaking, as an alternative form of reality, and 'escapes from reality'. He is at pains to insist that drug use is not a form of escapism, but rather the construction of something real but different; he adds that 'many authors such as Huxley would argue that the world behind the

Doors in the Wall is more substantial and realistic than that of the formal world'.[11] But if drugtaking is seen as simply a reaction against the values and behaviour patterns of the formal world, without any larger claim about it being a liberated choice of behaviour, then any behaviour that is a reaction against this formal world must be seen as creating an alternative reality, or a world beyond the ethos of productivity. Thus foreign travel, or the collection of beermats, or astrology or any other absorbing interest which is outside the scope of the workaday world constitutes the construction of alternative realities. If this is how we are being invited to understand the use of this phrase, no objection can be made; but how then is escapism to be defined? It is hard to think of any form of activity that could be described as escapist (in the sense of getting away from the workaday world) which would not involve creating an alternative reality. For every kind of activity has its own language, imagery, modes of perception and system of values; and thus no activity could succeed in providing escape from workaday reality without creating an alternative one. Young's distinction thus becomes meaningless.

In the end we come to recognise that we can best understand Young's notion of an alternative reality in terms not of any kinds of activities, such as drugtaking, refusing to work or conflicting with the authorities, but rather in terms of subcultures with different values and aspirations from those of the consensus (as expressed for instance in the mass media and in official policy). It is certainly true that drugtaking subcultures do have different attitudes and lifestyles; but if this is all that is being claimed, then we must recognise that no very special case is being made for drug users or for drug use as compared with other activities and the subcultures which surround them. It amounts to saying that the subcultures surrounding drug use should be seen as similar to religious sects, or small political parties, or fanatics of a new sport, or devotees of a new art form. If this is all that is being claimed, then it is simply misleading to speak of an 'alternative reality' as if drugtakers lived in a separate world, insulated from the influences of the same social, economic and cultural forces which affect us all, whether we are Plymouth Brethren, members of the National Front, exponents of Kung Fu, or Pre-Raphaelites. For even the subcultures surrounding activities which are escapist (to use this word in its ordinary sense) do not succeed in absolving us from responsibilities to other human beings, and particularly to our fellow citizens, still less do they make us immune to the influence of others. So it is unscientific for those who analyse such subcultures to invite us to suspend our powers of sociological and economic analysis in respect of such subcultures by describing them as if they were outside the realm of these influences.

(Indeed, one might well question the use of the term 'subculture' to describe a group of people who share as many of the activities, attributes and attitudes of wider society as drugtakers do. The fact that they have certain distinctive habits, perform certain different rituals, use different language and wear different clothes, hardly seems to qualify their groups for this status. In other ways, they use the same facilities, expect the same rights and enjoy the same benefits as other citizens. We would be unlikely to use the term 'subculture' in connection with judges or clergymen because of their distinctive habits, beliefs or clothes; its use in connection with drugtakers therefore seems questionable.)

It only remains for us to consider how the foregoing analysis of drug use helps us evaluate Marcuse's concept of liberation. It is quite possible, of course, that Marcuse would not accept that drug use was ever liberated. But very similar difficulties occur if we try to analyse any other form of behaviour which at first sight seems to constitute a reaction against the domination of market values. As soon as we come across an example of such behaviour which is uncommitted, which lacks spontaneity, which is merely modish, or worse still, completely insincere, we are forced to question whether this activity is *per se* liberated. Similarly, every case of a person who claims to be liberated and subsequently accepts a well-paid job with ICI, or applies for admission to a mental hospital, casts doubt on the validity of his claim.

These difficulties seem to stem from the fact that feelings of anomie and dissatisfaction with the dominion of consumer values do not logically lead to any particular action; someone who experiences anomie at work or during his leisure hours could react to such feelings in any number of ways. These include the 'escapist' activities mentioned but also many other reactions which may even intensify alienation and social control. For instance, one way of dealing with anomie and frustration is to become converted to an authoritarian religion like Mohammedanism, which exercises strict constraints on behaviour and recognises certain religious dignitaries as virtually infallible authorities—witness the Black Muslim sect. It could be argued, of course, that the only activities which could claim to be considered liberated are those which actually challenge the dominion of corporate capitalism. But here again an enormous number of people—many artists, drugtakers, criminals, religious fanatics and political groups of all shades of opinion—claim to be doing just that. Again, it could be suggested that we restrict the term liberation to those which successfully challenge capitalism, but until capitalism falls it will be difficult to see which these are.

This is not to say that we cannot recognise some actions as creative, spontaneous, loving, compassionate and hence liberated in Marcuse's sense. On the contrary, these words have an established use, and can be meaningfully employed to designate actions which are distinguishable from those which are jaded, stale, derivative or hackneyed, mean, intolerant or lacking in compassion. We might well want to describe such actions as liberated, at least in the sense of liberated from convention or formality. However, we would want to say that the motive for liberated actions of this sort need not be rejection of capitalist values, at least not in any conscious sense. Furthermore, people engaged in the workaday world, under the dominion of corporate capitalism, may act sponaneously, humanly and compassionately, even in the course of their workaday existence. When this occurs it is certainly distinguishable from the routine actions required by workaday processes and stands out, indeed, in contrast to what is normal in commercial behaviour. But the performance of an action which is liberated in this sense does not give the person who does it a new status, outside or beyond the workaday world. Someone who behaves in a spontaneous, liberated way is not thereby 'saved' from the reality of production and consumption, and transported to some alternative reality. He may, and nearly always does, relapse the very next second into that mode of behaviour again. This does not mean that he is not altered by the experience of behaving in a free and spontaneous way; it means that the change in him does not free him from the influences of his everyday environment and relationships.

Thus we recognise spontaneous, creative, compassionate and human behaviour by their spontaneity, creativity, compassion or humanity, and not by the social context in which they occur. No group, party, clique or faction has a monopoly of these qualities, even though some unquestionably have more of them than others. To reach any other conclusion than this would be to run the risk of a very dangerous form of intolerance, and a very arrogant form of interference in others' liberties. For if we are to believe, as Marcuse seems to invite us to believe, that particular groups can be seen as liberated in his sense by virtue of their political stance and life style, and that the whole of the rest of society is to be seen as lacking in the qualities of liberation by virtue of their repression by corporate capitalism, then liberation becomes a process of conversion to one particular set of values and patterns of behaviour. Freedom in its fullest sense is thus defined in terms of particular beliefs and denoted by specific actions, and the process of liberation becomes the imposition of these on the rest of humanity. In this way liberation becomes the enemy of liberty, and Marcuse's values can only triumph at the expense of Mill's. Those who are concerned about freedom in the narrower sense defined by Mill will therefore see it as their business to defend themselves against the exponents of liberation.

It appears, therefore, that as with other attempts to elaborate a notion of positive freedom, Marcuse's concept of liberation ends by proving difficult to reconcile with freedom from constraint. But in this particular case there seems to be a confusion which adds to the inconsistency of his thesis. For his unsubstantiated claim throughout is that the groups whose protest and rebellion against conventional definitions of relationships he is describing are necessarily seeking to overthrow the entire social order, and replace it by one based on their own. His use of the term 'elite' is significant here; it implies that such groups claim a right to impose their ideas on others. However, most of the groups discussed at the start of this chapter reject elitism, and are asserting rather the right to be treated as free and equal citizens, to be recognised as fellow human beings. This may indeed lead them to criticise the hypocrisy and falseness of the lives of the majority, and to suggest that a new social order, based on the values of spontaneity, compassion and humanity in relationships, would be the only way of ensuring that all people are truly accepted as equal, whatever their mode of being. But this is not the same as insisting that others adopt a particular life style, patterns of behaviour or beliefs, which are claimed to be superior because they derive from a successful escape from the (unconscious) yoke under which all others labour. Those who claim that their interpretation of their own experiences ought to be treated as valid by the majority must presumably be willing to enter into a dialogue on which they accord an equal respect to others' interpretations of their own experiences. Their reality will then be a genuine alternative, rather than a rival orthodoxy.

To say this is not, of course, to deny the possibility that the only way open to a minority to assert its identity may be by force. If the majority persistently refuse to treat a minority group as equal citizens, and refuse to recognise its right to choose its own way of life, then this may well be the only solution for that group. But if the values represented by such a group are love, compassion and creativity, they will presumably use this only when other methods have failed; and they are unlikely to assume that these same values and priorities are entirely absent from the lives of members of the rest of society by virtue of their participation in the economic and political order. Instead of annexing these values to themselves as the prerogative of an elite, they will see them as the legitimate aspiration of every citizen, and identify their aim as the creation of opportunities for their fellow citizens to find expression for them.

5
Freedom and Social Control

Libertarian writers have pointed out that no satisfactory concept of freedom can emerge until we have developed a proper understanding of the controls exercised by the social system. They have argued that nineteenth-century liberals gave a distorted picture of the constraints on individual freedom, because they assumed that our laws, our economic organisation and our family structure reflected obligations between people which were by common consent necessary and in the interests of all. Making no such assumption, libertarians insist on an analysis of the purposes, methods and consequences of all our institutions for social control.

Recently, interactionist sociologists have developed such an analysis from a broadly libertarian standpoint. The perspective they have adopted has been based on studies of social deviance and society's attempts to control it. Their writings have been persuasive and influential, but also potentially misleading in a number of ways, and particularly in relation to the role of state intervention as an element in social control.

Before starting on a critique of their analysis, it is necessary to establish an important point about social control and the individual. It is wrong to suppose that this problem can be understood by treating each man as if he was to be seen only as a seeker after liberty; for the same person, even if he is an ardent libertarian, is also a constraint on the freedom of others. Everyone, in so far as he enters into relationships of any duration with others, creates obligations in others to himself, as well as in himself to others. Only relationships which are *ud hoc* once-for-all encounters escape this fate. This is the essential difference between a sexual encounter and a love affair; between taking part in a game of football with a group who happen to meet in a park and membership of a football team; and between the mutual support given by a group who happen to find themselves in a situation of common disadvantage (such as being kept waiting for hours in a social security office) and the organisation of a protest or resistance group.

This is not of course to say that the spontaneity of each of the first examples in the above pairs makes it always preferable to each of the second examples. To say that any lasting relationship creates obligations is not to say that it necessarily creates the sense of burden and constraint. While it may well be true that the *feeling* of acting because of an obligation is nearly always slightly frustrating, and sometimes extremely frustrating, many relationships that create strong obligations do not give rise to any such feelings at all. For instance, husbands and wives are not under lesser obligations to love and support each other during the early years of their marriage than during the later years; yet few couples feel constrained and burdened by this as strongly during the former as during the latter, and fewer still (except in the novels of Thomas Hardy) resent their obligations as soon as they incur them as much as they resent them later. Presumably this is because the happiness and hope which accompany the taking on of such responsibilities overshadow their onerous nature, the advantages of the arrangement far outweighing its duties. Similarly, anyone who has played in a football team will only have to compare the experiences of being a member of a winning team with those of being a member of a losing one to be aware of how much greater the feeling of obligation is where relationships are not leading to desired results. A run of defeats is sufficient to make obligations willingly accepted seem intolerable burdens, and colleagues who once seemed as amiable as they were skilful can quickly be revealed as tedious, petty and bad-tempered as well as possessing two left feet. Finally, even obligations which are by common consent burdensome may, if undertaken willingly and purposefully, lead to a sense of satisfaction and achievement. Thus, while few parents would want to have a maladjusted child, some adults cheerfully take jobs looking after maladjusted children, often for small financial rewards, and a few have made such tasks their life's work. Many mothers would rather help run a playgroup for ten children than look after their own one in isolation; and being a social worker with the elderly is regarded by some as preferable to looking after their own parents.

There is even a sense in which all relationships, however short term, can be seen as an *interference* with others. Even interventions which are intended to be entirely friendly and helpful are often interpreted in this way, even by those who understand the motives for them perfectly. Thus, for instance, one sometimes hears a conversation something like this:

A I wish I could tell X that his suspicions of Y are quite unfounded. Y likes him very much.

B Don't interfere.

A But I only want to help.

B Yes, I know. But it's better not to interfere. Let X find out for himself, he'll appreciate it more when he does.

Such information-giving by A as an equal, with no attempt to usurp X's right to form his own opinion, is still construed as interference by B. To some extent this may be a relic of the ethic of conduct which saw independence as the major social duty, and presumed that any action accomplished without help was somehow morally superior to one which required assistance. But on the other hand even help can be misconstrued or, if it achieves its end, that may turn out to be undesirable in itself. However, this should not lead us to think that we should not offer people help when it is within our power to do so. If assistance is a form of interference (if not in Mill's sense then at least in the limited sense that it introduces a new factor in someone's life that they have not necessarily desired) then all this shows is that we should be suspicious of maxims like 'It's always wrong to interfere'.

It is important to clarify these points, because there are some very considerable confusions around them in the discussion of social policy and interventions in the field of social problems. For instance, interactionist sociologists have made some very useful studies of how particular pieces of behaviour come to be defined as social problems, and especially of how official agencies select these from the much wider number of possible targets for their attention. However, they tend to overstate the extent to which those people whose behaviour is not selected as a suitable target for official intervention are left 'free' (from interference, control, deviant labels or whatever) by virtue of such official neglect, and the extent to which behaviour ceases to be a social problem if it escapes the notice of these authorities; hence they tend to overstate the ill-effects of interventions.

Interactionists pride themselves on not falling into the error of the structural functionalist school, of giving society's rules and procedures, as embodied in the legal code and the administration of justice, a status of objectivity in the definition of social problems which they do not deserve. But it is making a very similar mistake to suppose that if the arbitrary and selective procedures of official agencies do not catch an act in their net, then no social problem exists. For it is not only the official agencies who are in the business of defining acts as socially problematical, and while unofficial labels cannot be attached with the authority of official ones they can certainly be made to stick, and can strongly influence attitudes in the process. The interactionists often emphasise the fact that subterranean and subversive values and behaviour are virtually universal; but so are formal roles. Thus, while we are all potential deviants, we are all potential agents of social control as well. Most of life consists of attempting to influence the behaviour of others and to evade others' influence in about equal parts; and in this process of influencing and avoiding influence we alternate between formal and informal roles and values. As parents, kinsmen, neighbours and members of organisations, we tend to be more often engaged in activities that emphasise formal rules of conduct and uphold social obligations. In our pursuit of relaxation and pleasure we are often keen to escape both from the requirements of our own formal roles and obligations, and from contacts or confrontations with other people in their formal capacities. If we go out to get drunk, we are anxious not to encounter not only the police (as official agents of control) but also our boss, our neighbours and our maiden aunts. Nor is our anxiety to escape from formal relationships necessarily in direct proportion to the *illegality* of our activity; we may be quite happy to meet friends and workmates while we are in a pub, drinking after hours, but keen to avoid anyone we know if we are out with someone else's wife. From this example it seems that people sometimes fear unofficial definition of their behaviour as deviant more than they fear a formal label.

Interactionists seldom do more justice to these complexities than did their predecessors. Phillipson and Roche point out that although such sociologists may sometimes define deviance in terms of nonconformity or rule-breaking in general, they tend to 'limit inclusion to activities which are formally banned on a society-wide basis'.[1] 'Thus although the terminology used [rule-breaking and rule-enforcement] would seem to widen the field of study considerably, in practice the deviance perspective ends up focusing on similar issues to the earlier "social problems" school.'[2] This considerably weakens the force of some of the arguments interactionists use. For instance, Becker states that he now rejects his original formulation of a category of 'secret deviance' for undetected acts.[3]

> If we begin by saying that an act is deviant when it is so defined, what can it mean to call an act an instance of secret deviance? Since no one has defined it as deviant it cannot, by definition, be deviant . . . secret deviance consists of being vulnerable to the commonly used procedures for discovering deviance of a particular kind, of being in a position where it will be easy to make the definition stick.

Once we recognise that social control is as universal as secret deviance, such statements become relatively meaningless. Every action we do is capable of being interpreted as a breach of one of our obligations to someone somewhere, even if only in the negative sense that in doing something for someone we are failing to so something for someone else; and even the isolate who does nothing for anyone but himself can be accused of failing to honour his obligations to all his fellow citizens as a participant member of his community. (Isolates are, in fact, particularly vulnerable to labelling by public opinion.) Thus the only way that Becker can give any particular meaning to this statement is to concentrate his attention on state definitions of deviance by official enforcement agencies, and to treat all other forms of rule-breaking and social control as entirely different in kind.

However, this leads to a distortion of the processes of social control, and hence to a distorted view of the relations between freedom and authority. The treatment of official controls as entirely different in their nature and effects from unofficial controls leads to the kind of split between two 'worlds' which was criticised in the last chapter, where a misleading attempt is made to suggest that the processes by which state agencies recognise, define and attempt to remedy what they see as problems are entirely different from these processes as carried out by non-official persons. To take another example from Young's book: he argues that subcultures of drug users regulate drugtaking in important ways, including the enforcement of standards of hygiene. For instance, he states that heroin addicts in Central London,[4]

> alarmed by the publicity given to the early deaths of their fellows, have begun to use disposable equipment and sterile water for injection. This is an interesting example of the way in which drug subcultures, providing they are cohesive and fed the right information, can considerably control the worst effects of drug abuse. Unfortunately, the rapid rise of heroin addiction in this country tends to undermine any extensive and consistent subculture of addiction so that many new addicts are inadequately socialised by their elders and the lore of drug use is not transmitted adequately.

The language Young uses to describe these processes is sufficient evidence of similarities with processes that occur either in the context of the educational system (socialisation, transmission of lore) or in the medical sphere. In fact, he elsewhere describes the workings of subcultures as an alternative and superior way of controlling the ill-effects of drugs, which is more likely to be effective in achieving some of their aims than the interventions of the law and the medical profession.

Thus, while it is obviously true that only someone with official authority can define behaviour as problematical or deviant in any official sense—and there are many consequences of official definitions and treatments which do not follow from unofficial ones—this should not lead us to assume that these consequences are greater constraints on freedom than are the consequences of unofficial processes. Such an assumption would, for instance, deny most of the claims of women's liberation movements, for while some of their protests concern official limits on women's opportunities, incomes and rights, the majority are about constraints on women's freedom which stem from the ways in which men interact with them in the most informal and intimate situations. If women can argue that their lack of freedom can stem more crucially from their socialisation as daughters and their situation as wives and mothers than from their legal status and rights, then we must look as closely at such processes in any discussion of freedom as we do at the activities of official agents. For as Becker says (but does not further analyse), 'Elites, ruling classes, bosses, adults, men, Caucasians—superordinate groups generally—maintain their power as much by controlling how people define the world, its components and possibilities, as by the use of more primitive forms of control.'[5]

What sociologists and other social scientists could thus be expected to help us better to understand are those interpersonal, group and societal influences on behaviour which make us something less than the free agents that Mill and his fellow liberals desired us to be. They could describe the actual mechanics or dynamics of the processes by which others use individual or corporate power to control us and change our behaviour and attitudes. Yet so far their models have seldom attempted such explanations except about patterns of influence on a very small scale. For instance, social psychology concentrates on laboratory experiments with small groups, and has certainly produced some theoretical 'laws' from these; but it has not produced analyses of a similar precision of wider social influences. Studies of the nuclear family, too, have given rise to theories about systems of communication and their effects on members. The anthropologist, Gregory Bateson, and his colleagues advanced the hypothesis that parents who repeatedly gave a child two conflicting messages on different levels, and forbade him to leave the family, might eventually drive him mad.[6] However, in spite of the apparent precision of the 'double bind' hypothesis, it has proved very difficult to test.[7]

On a slightly larger scale, Elizabeth Bott's research produced a theory about the direct effects of marital partners' social networks on their conjugal role relationship.[8] She suggested that a close-knit kinship and peer-group network gave rise to segregated conjugal roles, whereas loose-knit networks led to joint roles. Her pioneering study has led to other research into the influences of networks, and recently Boissevain has claimed to be able to predict the outcomes of social situations from an examination of the characteristics of the social networks of the participants.[9] He argues that a precise analysis of the number, type and patterns of relationships of individuals in conflict with each other can enable us to explain the outcomes of such confrontations. Although he provides only one full example of such an analysis, this seems an important attempt to introduce some precision into an account of the forces affecting social behaviour, and to frame a testable hypothesis about wider influences on individuals.

Until we have some such hypotheses, it will be difficult to measure the relative power of official and unofficial relationships as forces affecting individual's actions, or to show how these operate as constraints on freedom. In the meantime, we can only try to take some account of all of these influences in considering questions on the freedom of those defined as having social problems. The deviance perspective tends to be limited and misleading because, even where it does not concentrate its attention on individuals who have already been labelled and segregated from non-official influences (as criminologists did for years by studying prison populations), it often concentrates instead on groups which have become relatively isolated from other members of society (as interactionists do now by studying subcultures of drugtakers, sex offenders and delinquents). Where segregation and isolation have taken place (either through official action or by voluntary withdrawal), individuals and groups tend to perceive the issue of their freedom as depending crucially on specific agents of social control rather than on their families, neighbours, workmates or the community at large. Nor is it adequate to suggest, as Robertson and Taylor do, that there has been a historical trend towards greater social 'gaps' (i.e. lack of commonly known norms and shared community membership) between the person controlled and the controlling agent;[10] for this rather vague concept cannot help us analyse the conflict between a schizophrenic daughter and her parents, or a confused old lady and her village neighbours. Even where such 'gaps' do develop, they may well be the end products of attempts by families, friends and neighbours to influence behaviour rather than the results of nebulous historical processes.

What I am therefore suggesting is that freedom in relation to social problems and their treatment can best be analysed in the same way as freedom in any other context; by looking at the actual pattern of relationships between the people importantly involved. Since any pattern of relationships must necessarily create obligations and constraints which influence actions and restrict choices, this applies to situations where someone's behaviour is alleged to be problematical as much as to any other situation. What we have to do is examine the relationships to see what these requirements are and what the participants characteristically feel about them. We can then ask a number of questions about them. Should such relationships exist at all? Does anybody gain any advantage from them? What are their effects, not only on the parties, but also on others not directly involved? Are they fair, as between the parties? Does each party understand his obligations, how can he meet them, how can he change them and under what conditions can he escape from them?

This form of analysis should enable us to begin to unravel the very common confusion involved in trying to assess whether or not an intervention by an individual, an authority or the state into a relationship or set of relationships constitutes an infringement of liberty. At least one factor in such an assessment must be whether or not the parties in this relationship both freely agreed to the terms of it, and whether both share a common interest in its continuing in its current form. For if the relationship was established on terms which are so advantageous to one party and so disadvantageous to the other that it constitutes a situation of power and privilege for one party over the other, then we cannot make the same kind of case against intervention in it as we could if it was freely and equitably entered into. For instance, we should be less inclined to describe slavery as a natural condition, as Aristotle did, or to justify the ownership of slaves as a right, the interference with which would be an infringement of liberty, as many eighteenth-century writers did. We should also be less inclined to assert with Mill that it is an infringement of liberty to interfere with a man's freedom to have great wealth and to spend it as he pleases. For these 'freedoms' are gained at the expense of others, and the case for their continuation is thus a case for a set of relationships based on privilege and power, in which freedom for some is gained through their ability to place constraints on many. Similarly, the case against intervention in family life often rests on the freedom of more powerful members (usually husbands in relation to wives and parents in relation to children) to exercise their power without restriction.

However, one of the problems of analysing this element in situations is that power and privilege seldom parade themselves as such, and are more often to be found disguised as necessary protection, responsibility, duty, leadership, initiative or organisation. This is particularly true of the economic sphere, where the powerful and privileged nowadays seldom distinguish themselves by shows of strength or conspicuous waste but present themselves rather as making an exceptional contribution to national prosperity by virtue of their outstanding intelligence, foresight, organisational skills, creative energy, ability to communicate and courage in taking risks. So successful are they in achieving this legitimation of their position that the hierarchy of power and privilege in society is very widely regarded as reflecting a gradation of merit, measured according to these admirable criteria. Thus they are in a strong position to argue that a 'free market', which allows them to maximise the benefit of their advantages, is in fact not only the most efficient economic system, but also fair and advantageous for all; so that even today the arguments for private education and medicine, for example, are presented in terms of 'freedom of choice', as if those deprived of using scarce medical and educational resources were in some invisible way the beneficiaries of a system which allows their more fortunate fellow citizens to enjoy the liberty to corner them. Yet in spite of the very obvious fact that a free market situation gives advantages exclusively to those who already have them, or are in a position to make them, it is still widely regarded as our most fundamental liberty to maximise our earnings and to spend our money as we choose. We are ready to sacrifice a great deal for these freedoms; we are also ready to suppose that a society which allows these freedoms is likely to be a better society than one which does not.

The processes of production and their influence over patterns of consumption are by far the most clear, efficient and generalised controls on behaviour in our society. More than any other force, they determine its shape, order its priorities, regulate its routines, bestow its benefits, and impose its penalties. In ways too numerous and obvious to dwell upon, they pattern and mould the whole social system, so that prestige and power depend ultimately on control over productive resources or the means of consumption. Hence it is not surprising to find that one of the ultimate standards by which social behaviour is judged is its contribution to, or at least consistency with, productivity; nor is it surprising to discover that one of the most widely employed arguments for constraints on individual liberty is that they are necessary for the maximisation of productivity.

The difference between the economic forces that control social behaviour and other forces lies in their apparently automatic reinforcement of values connected with productivity, and their opportunity for swift punishment of the habits of idleness. The world of industry has been so organised that, in accordance with Skinnerian principles, it becomes clear and obvious that to earn more it is necessary to produce more, that the person who does not pull his weight should not expect to prosper, and that the most highly skilled and productive deserve most rewards. Unlike the sphere of morality or even that of the criminal law, there is, in the wage structure, an inbuilt system by which positive valuation can be conveyed to the worker who conforms to expectations of him, who behaves as he is required to behave. Hence there has traditionally been seen to be little advantage to be gained for employers by reinforcing the work ethic with exhortations (although this has happened in post-war Japan) because to do so would merely draw attention to the fact that the whole system is being organised by people who stand to gain more from their workers' exertions than the workers themselves do. Instead, the work ethic is presented as deriving from an organic-corporate notion of industry, in which the employer's and the workers' interests are interdependent, and both will benefit each other by maximising production, while the business of exhortations and threats is left to the mass media and the politicians, who simultaneously reinforce this consensus view, by praising high productivity and condemning strikes. It is a measure of the success of employers in propagating this view of industry that few people ever question the necessary connection between income and work, or doubt the validity of 'free collective bargaining' as a method of determining the economic measure of a man's worth. Of all the forms of state intervention in the economic process, wage fixing is the least common and the most unpopular, as the Conservatives found to their cost in the early months of 1974. The wage structure can therefore be seen as the most effective method of controlling behaviour in our society, and hence one of the least resisted; for strikes are almost always about the level of wages of a particular group, and very seldom against employers' rights to control productive resources.

This effectiveness of economic controls helps to explain the very slow, halting and chequered history of the development of state intervention into the operations of the economic system. For not only have employers fought against 'infringements of their liberty', but also many workers have resisted interventions into processes which had been so ordered as to create an apparently obvious interest for them in behaving according to employers' definitions of their obligations. It has only been very gradually, as state interventions in the form of taxes and subsidies, nationalisation and joint ownership, safety regulations and anti-pollution restrictions, have been seen not to be as destructive of efficiency or as productive of servitude as employers threatened, that these measures have received much popular support. But even now to achieve this much, they have to be presented as consistent with the economic freedoms which reside in the existing distribution of power and prestige; and the few interventions which have been made have not significantly altered the balance of advantages between different sectors of society.

What I am suggesting is that these controls exercised through industrial processes are so widespread and powerful that they are very unlikely to be successfully overcome or offset by any power less than that of the state itself. The same could well be said for other very powerful influences which shape behaviour: the traditional distribution of power between men and women, between adults and children, between majority groups and minorities, whether in race, religion or custom. It could also be said of many other less common forms of exploitation in the field of consumption—the exploitation by commercial interests of damaging dependence on tobacco, alcohol and certain drugs, for example.

However, it does not follow automatically from this suggestion that the state ought to intervene in all these matters immediately and unquestioningly. For as we all well know from smaller-scale examples, interventions that are not properly planned and thought out can have all sorts of unwanted results. An intervention to try to prevent exploitation may not be effective; it may even increase it; or it may result in the victim being exploited by someone else, or the exploiter finding another victim or another form of exploitation; or both may turn on us and exploit us instead; or we may have misunderstood the situation—the 'victim' may be a masochist, or he may really be controlling the 'exploiter' by some form of subtle manipulation. Alternatively, attempts to end exploitation may cause a stalemate, a fight or a war, a revolution or a counter-revolution, any of which might possibly be more destructive in their consequences than the exploitation itself. For all these reasons, we need to take a very critical look at the form of any proposed large-scale intervention, to make sure that its overall effect is likely to be beneficial to anybody, let alone the majority.

This applies even more strongly to state interventions in the lives of citizens, for the state, by virtue of its great power, can itself become an exploiter in a number of ways, and can do so on an enormous scale. It can be excessively punitive and cruel; it can overregulate and overcontrol; it can reduce scope for choice and decision-making; it can standardise and routinise; it can be unjust and partial; it can create excessive dependence; it can mystify, complicate and confuse. Such effects are evils in their own right, and the fact that the state may produce them in order to try to abolish or offset other evils, such as the evils of capitalism, is not in itself a sufficient warrant for doing so, unless they can be shown to be substantially lesser evils for substantially larger proportions of the population than would result from noninterventions. In any case, the state has a duty to try to minimise such effects, whatever its motives for intervention. And of course, interventions may simply reinforce other evils, by intensifying injustice, inequality and exploitation, both public and private, whether practised by large corporations, by local authorities, by groups or by individuals.

Any state, therefore, which was equally concerned for the welfare of each of its citizens would be constantly trying to discover the best ways of intervening in their lives to ensure that no one of them was so disadvantaged in relation to another, or several others, or all the rest, that he was being exploited by their power over him. Wherever it could intervene to end such exploitation without itself causing more exploitation (either by itself or by someone else) in the process, it would do so. The pursuit of the maximum liberty of the largest number of citizens would thus be a process of the optimisation of relationships, so that as many as possible of the connections between men and their mutual obligations to each other, would be seen by them as fair and advantageous to all parties, as productive of valued results, and hence as freely entered into. Such interventions would be likely to be liberating, in the sense of giving rise to the increase of spontaneity, creativity, compassion and humanity; and if we see both negative liberty (freedom from interference) and positive liberty (self-direction) as being essentially confusing and confused ways of expressing a concept which is partly connected with means to those and other ends and partly with the ends themselves, they would also be consistent with liberty.

The Welfare State and all the other arms of government intervention have been claimed by governments of all political parties at different times and in different forms to be instruments of such benevolent interventions in the interests of every citizen. However, it takes only a little consideration of this claim to recognise that, however well intentioned a government might be, it would be an enormously difficult aim to achieve. For while there are certain standardised or institutional forms and methods of oppression, domination and exploitation, in so far as these ultimately take the form of relationships between individual human beings, there is an enormous range of possible expressions of such relations. Thus even if satisfactory forms of intervention are found to abolish the worst forms of generalised exploitation in formal institutions like the political structure, the organisation of industry and the family, there would still remain an enormous field of potential oppression. People contract obligations in their friendships, become slaves to their voluntary good works, are caught in the net of their recreations. Even the behaviour by which we seek to break out of the holds of our formal relationships often subjects us to new bonds and responsibilities, to lovers, fellow addicts or partners in crime. The longer we live the more we are held in a mighty web, connected by an intricate pattern of invisible threads to this person or that institution; our position as much determined by the relative strengths and tensions of the strands that hold us as by our desires, breaking some only to become more firmly or directly held by others. It is to the subtleties of this web, and of interventions into its intricacies, that I wish now to turn.

6

'Perfect Respectfulness' and 'Painful Nearness'

.

At this point we can start to consider the third major element in this book. How do attempts by one person to give assistance to another affect that other's freedom? What I hope has become clear from the foregoing rather lengthy analysis of liberal and libertarian notions of freedom is that we can only meaningfully discuss the question of someone's freedom in the context of all his social relationships, and his situation within society as a whole. Equally, we can make sense of an alaysis of his assistance only if we see it in terms of this network of relationships. The offer of help is perceived by its receiver in the context of his family ties, his friendships and his neighbourhood contacts; it is also interpreted in accordance with his perception of his social role, and its position in the social system. In this chapter, I hope to show that the notions of personal assistance and friendship suggested by the nineteenth-century view of freedom and social obligation formed the basis of Victorian social work; and that a changing view of the position of the individual in relation to others, and to the social order, undermined the moral assumptions on which early social work was built.

Such issues seem to me to be best examined in the fairly detailed context of actual social situations; and for this reason I now want to set aside the rather abstract and philosophical analysis I have followed up to this point, and use instead a method derived from the study of literature. In so far as the novel represented an attempt to work out within the literary form the emotional, social and moral implications of human relationships, an examination of some of the complex situations analysed in novels may enable us to analyse different views of assistance and of the nature of the web of relationships and obligations in which individuals are held.

The characteristic nineteenth-century view of that web is vividly conveyed in the novels of that era, and as reflected in the works of Jane Austen or George Eliot, for instance, portrays a much more subtle and intricate picture of the nature of social obligations than is represented by the works of philosophers like Mill. The essential nature of that view was that it defined the individual and estimated his worth in terms of the way in which he responded to all his social obligations; it saw him as an integral part of the web of relationships that contained him, rather than as struggling against it, as most modern literature does. Lionel Trilling has pointed out the extent to which, in the golden age of the English novel, a man was seen as existing meaningfully only as part of his society; his development was known only through the social influences on him, and he was thus represented as completed in society, not complete in himself.[1] Even as late as Conrad, the novel illustrated the virtues of 'an uncompromising commitment to duty, a continuous concentration of personal energies upon some impersonal end, the subordination of the self to some general good.'[2] Such an ethos emphasised honour, service and the acceptance of the social order. 'Work is the sure means of keeping oneself sound and whole, worthy of one's own respect, true to one's own self.'[3] The class structure was seen as a necessary condition for personal authenticity, the means to knowing one's 'station and its duties'.

One important feature of this view was that it made very few distinctions between public and private virtues, between the qualities required for the honourable discharge of civic duties and those needed for the successful conduct of intimate relationships; it thus suggested that the good and honourable citizen was simultaneously an admirable and amiable spouse, parent or companion. Jane Austen conveyed this view least ambiguously in her novel *Mansfield Park*. The heroine, Fanny Price, is characterised by her simplicity, modesty, singlemindedness and sincerity; she never deviates from the path of duty or allows her affections or antipathies to influence her conduct and her judgment. Neither her love for Edmund Bertram, her guardian's honourable younger son, nor the flattery of her admirer, the sophisticated Henry Crawford, can deflect her from behaving in the way she sees to be right. Ultimately it is Henry's lack of principle and serious social purpose that betrays him and leads him into the disaster of a loveless adultery with Edmund's sister; and it is the same fickleness, the same preference for brilliant performance over solid morality, that disillusions Edmund about Henry's sister Mary, and then leads him to turn instead to Fanny, whose patience and virtue are rewarded with his love. Unlike Jane Austen's other novels, *Mansfield Park* comes down unequivocally on the side of duty and serious-mindedness; it judges moral issues categorically, and, like Fanny herself, prefers the upright dullness of obligation to the sparkling freedom of the uncommitted. The old rural order, hierarchical, peaceful and unchanging, with its traditional family and community structure, is favourably contrasted with the greater social mobility of the metropolitan world where relationships lack formal definition, and all is liberty, fluidity and change.

Fanny Price was the forerunner of a line of Victorian heroines, implicitly if not always explicitly Christian, who appeared throughout nineteenth-century literature in writers as dissimilar as Dickens, Charlotte Brontë and George Gissing. Even in settings as drastically different from the elegance of Mansfield Park as Dickens's London and Gissing's *Nether World* of the slums, they share many of Fanny's characteristics and principles. While they are retiring, modest, simple, undemanding and with a certain proneness to ill-health, they possess great reserves of moral courage, an inner conviction in their own mission in life, a strong sense of their identity, and devotion to principle, allied with an eagerness to enter into relationships with others in which their commitment to moral improvement can find expression. As Trilling puts it, they pursue an ideal of 'intelligent love', the notion that 'the finest and deepest relationship that can exist between human beings is pedagogic' and 'consists in giving and receiving of knowledge about right conduct, in the formation of one person's character by another, the acceptance of another's guidance in one's growth'.[4] The positive duty to form such relationships and to fulfil the obligations arising from them was a much higher priority for these women than the pursuit of any personal ambition; they set no store by individual freedom, but only by the opportunity to participate in a process of moral influence which would ultimately improve and uplift both parties in the relationship.

It is not difficult to recognise in such women the originals of nineteenth-century social workers. For instance, the heroine of Dickens's *Bleak House,* Esther Summerson, although created some twenty years before the full flowering of Victorian social work, would in many ways recommend herself as much as a social worker today as then. As described by A. E. Dyson,[5]

> She is highly observant . . . and extremely intelligent . . . She is also
> given a high degree of self-knowledge and unusual gifts of
> self-sacrifice . . . Her instinctive sense that there is something wrong
> (with others) co-exists therefore with suspended judgment, and a
> willingness to let them speak for themselves. In all this, Esther's tone is
> entirely without malice. Indeed her morally aware but unmalicious
> intelligence is sufficiently a rarity to make of it, in so far as it is really
> Dickens's, a virtuoso display.

It was precisely this combination of qualities which women like Octavia Hill brought to early social work. Like Esther, she first felt the power of personal relationships as an adolescent, taking responsibility for other girls, less fortunate than herself, in a school. From this beginning she developed an approach to people based on an ideal of friendship; that true charity consisted in giving people 'not alms but a friend'. 'By friendship she meant giving all her resources to the common pool of daily life in which she shared as an equal.'[6] The defining qualities of this 'respectful' attitude to people, however humble, are well illustrated in the details of Esther Summerson's encounters with others' misfortunes.

Esther's approach to relationships is defined by its contrast with those of other characters in *Bleak House;* the arrogant retreatism of an outmoded ruling class, which has forgotten its responsibilites (the Dedlock family); the self-centredness and conceit of Harold Skimpole and Mr Turveydrop; but above all, the self-aggrandisement and self-justification of the good works practised by Mrs Jellyby and Mrs Pardiggle. Even before she had observed the latter's 'mechanical way of taking possession of people', Esther had turned down the offer to become involved in her charitable activities.[7]

> I was not sure of my qualifications. That I was inexperienced in the art of adapting my mind to minds very differently situated, and addressing them from suitable points of view. That I had not that delicate knowledge of the heart which must be essential to that work. That I had much to learn myself, before I could teach others, and that I could not confide in my good intentions alone. For these reasons, I thought it best to be as useful as I could, and to render what kind of services I could to those immediately about me, and to try to let that circle of duty gradually and naturally expand itself.

Yet within these self-imposed limits, and acknowledging her youth and inexperience, there is a great deal to admire in Esther's approach to people in various kinds of distress; she is, in fact, the embodiment of Octavia Hill's spirit of 'perfect respectfulness'. There is her sensitivity in weighing the consequences of intervention in the tragic decline and fall of the young Ward of Chancery, Richard Carstone, and her tact, skill and courage when she finally does intervene; but she is even more impressive in the face of the ultimate forms of human suffering, illness and death. Not until Richard is dying does she make a link of common humanity, the same link as with the crossing sweeper, Jo, and conveyed with the same compassion and gentleness as to the bereaved mother, Jenny. It is only where her own feelings and emotional needs are directly involved, with her guardian and suitor, John Jarndyce, that her behaviour is (to modern eyes at least) neither creditable nor credible.

It was the essentially moral analysis of human problems and conflicts which gave women like Esther their sureness and courage in helping others; it was the same factor which limited the scope and extent of their interventions. In *Bleak House,* since the inner conflicts of ambivalent characters like Richard Carstone and Harold Skimpole are presented in terms of strength and weakness, right and wrong, duty and self-indulgence, the purposes of Esther's efforts to help them are strictly defined. The doctrine of Free Will forbade that another should pre-empt the choice between good and evil actions; it would be impossible and wrong for Esther to try to usurp their right to choose, even if it led them to make the wrong decision. Esther's 'perfect respectfulness', like Octavia Hill's, was based on the principle that the only form of help morally justified is that given by moral equals to each other. (Even the mutual sympathy of the impoverished brickmakers' wives or the help given by the starving Nemo to Jo comes in this category.) Mrs Pardiggle's charity, dispensed from a stance of moral superiority, is portrayed by Dickens as not only evil but also ineffective. The Victorian social and moral code was based on equal obligation for all to honour their commitments to each other, and to do so freely, by choice, or to suffer the punishments of the law or of opinion.

This characteristically Victorian concept of social obligation as universal and reciprocal, with its concomitant emphasis on public virtues, and on the assessment of a man's character and worth in terms of his performance of his social role, is by no means dead. In his analysis of the work of a modern country doctor, *A Fortunate Man*, John Berger presents a picture of an individual at the centre of a very similar web of obligations, living an essentially public life, yet committed to a very personal, intimate service to others from strong principles about their human dignity as individuals, and as responsible equals. Berger describes the doctor's relationship with those he serves as implying that 'he should recognise his patient as an ideal brother . . . by the doctor presenting himself to the patient as a comparable man'.[8] But in spite of the emotional demand for fraternity, the doctor is separated from his patients by as wide and clear-cut a distinction of social class as that between Esther and Jo; the doctor's compassion and humanity are part of his social and professional role. This is in turn a function of his educational and occupational privileges; and Berger comments, 'It is by virtue of the community's backwardness that he is able to practise as he does.' The doctor 'can strive towards the universal because his patients are underprivileged.'[9] He ends by asking, 'Is he not an outdated nineteenth century romantic with his ideal of a single personal responsibility? And in the last analysis is not this ideal a form of paternalism?'[10]

The accusation of paternalism against this whole approach to problems in human relationships stems from several of its facets. First, the very concept of service which is central to it implies privilege, and involves the repayment to fellow men in compassion for advantages they do not have. Second, as we have seen, it is didactic; for all that the parties are treated as moral equals, one has a lesson to teach, the other one to learn. Third, the lesson is about how to live in society or how to die in it; acceptance of the order and structure of the world as God-given are as much a part of this approach as they were in Job's final submission to Jehovah's will. This does not mean that social change is ruled out; Dickens, for instance, satirises the fossilised world of the Dedlocks, where the chief threat to the social order is through 'people (ironmasters, lead-mistresses, and whatnot) not minding their catechism, and getting out of the station into which they are called—necessarily and for ever, according to Sir Leicester's rapid logic, the first station in which they happen to find themselves.'[11] But it does mean that changes should take place on a human, personal scale, and should be related to people's personalities and abilities, rather than to some impersonal end of progress, whether technical or political. All Dickens's worst villains are either trying to be something they are not, or else without any established social station. The young men he presents as admirable are all (like Alan Woodcourt) earnestly following an appropriate trade or profession; the most estimable of his older men are established in a role that fits their personality. Furthermore, while Dickens is ruthless in his satire of those institutions he saw as corrupt and malevolent, like the Court of Chancery, there were many more of the formal modes and social duties which he unquestioningly endorsed; the requirement to work to the fullness of one's powers, to see each task through to its end, to fulfil one's primary obligations to parents and to children, and, in the case of women, to be submissive and obedient wives.

Towards the end of the nineteenth century many of these values were coming to be questioned, and the novel reflected this process faithfully. Of all the moral and aesthetic presuppositions of the earlier more optimistic period, the one that was subjected to the most critical scrutiny was the notion that the individual could reach his fullest self-expression through a social role, and as part of the formal structure of society. The web of obligation and influence, extending outwards through the family to the formal and institutional sinews of the state, began to be perceived instead as a deadening and destructive constraint, unjust, distorting, cramping the potential creativity, joy and spontaneity of each person. Instead of a search for the fullest and most meaningful participation in the social order, life was presented as an ambivalent struggle, now for a satisfying role, now for an escape, a refuge from the torments and demands of the formal world.

In his preface to the first edition of *Jude the Obscure* (1894), Thomas Hardy wrote that the novel was about 'a deadly war waged between flesh and spirit'. In fact there is some reason to suggest that it would be as accurate to describe it as a conflict between natural man and civilised man. Jude, an orphan, bent on escaping through education from his limited existence as an assistant in his aunt's village bakery, is frequently surprised—ambushed—by passions of which he was unaware, and for which he was therefore unprepared. They appear to him as obstacles to what seem his 'nobler' aspirations—learning, social improvement, ordination, etc. Yet after he has made his impulsive and disastrous marriage to Arabella, parted from her, and been jilted by his cousin Sue, he comes to realise that these ambitions are 'purely an artificial product of civilization'.[12] At this stage he opts instead for 'true religion'; but after the torments of his continued relationship with Sue, and when this reaches its climax with the death of their children, he is convinced that even religion consists of 'old husks and prejudices', and finally that 'natural instincts are perfectly healthy'.[13] But even then Jude is confused and contradictory; his maxim is applied to Sue rather than himself; it is her instincts he trusts, rather than his own. He cannot bring himself to be angry or resentful towards her, and he still adopts an absurd code of 'honour', caricatured in his second, drunken marriage to Arabella: 'I'd marry to W—— of Babylon rather than do anything dishonourable'. And he is still afraid of himself and his feelings. As he parts from Sue, he begs her, 'You have been my social salvation. Stay with me for humanity's sake. You know what a weak fellow I am. My two Arch Enemies you know—my weakness for womankind and my impulse to strong liquor. Don't abandon me to them Sue, to save your own soul only!'[14]

Earlier, in his only moment of real dignity, Jude addresses his fellow artisans at Christminster; 'I was perhaps, after all, a paltry victim to the spirit of mental and social restlessness, that made so many unhappy in these days!' He is able to claim at this point, 'I doubt that I have anything more for my present rule of life than following inclinations which do me and nobody else any harm, and actually give pleasure to those I love best'.[15] Worn out by his attempts to win esteem or even acceptance in the world of learning, and able to eke out little more than existence in his trade, Jude seeks refuge in the intimacy of his relationship with Sue, which in turn is shattered by her guilt at the children's death.

The principal target of Hardy's critical assault is the notion of a 'sacrament of marriage'. He argues in his second preface (1912) that 'marriage should be dissolvable as soon as it becomes a cruelty to either of the parties—being then essentially and morally no marriage'.[16] With one eye he looks back to a past where marriage was jollier and less intense than in its Victorian manifestation. Widow Edlin says:[17]

> Matrimony have to be that serious in these days that one really do feel afeard to move in it at all. In my time we took it more careless; and I don't know that we was any worse for it! When I and my poor man were jined in it we kept up the junketing all week, and drunk the parish dry.

But with the other eye, Hardy looks forward to a companionate marriage of which Jude and Sue's relationship is an imperfect expression. Jude feels that it should be asexual; he feels guilty about his physical desire for Sue, and when eventually she allows him to make love with her, he is afraid that 'perhaps I spoilt one of the highest and purest loves that ever existed between man and woman!'[18] Sue is even more ambivalent and vacillating in her expectations of their relationship. Although she claims to be a free spirit, 'more ancient than mediaeval', and rejects Christianity, she is anxious to conceal this from everyone except Jude; het it is Jude she constantly teases and torments, and ultimately deserts, proclaiming that

'we should mortify the flesh' and that 'we ought to be continually
sacrificing ourselves on the altar of duty'.[19] In returning to her husband,
Phillotson, she claims to be acting from motives of religious submission
and obedience, fulfilling her sacred vows.

It is not clear whether Hardy wished his readers to understand Jude and
Sue's failure to establish a bond of mutual love and trust solely in terms of
the cruelties of a society that preferred loveless marriage, and the physical
sacrifice of women, to unmarried partnership and harmonious
co-operation between the sexes. Certainly, for a modern reader it is
difficult to understand it only in this way. We are inclined to agree with
Jude that Sue is not what she wishes to seem, 'outside all laws except
gravitation and germination', but rather 'quite a product of civilization',
having 'nothing unconventional about her'. Jude's early impression of her
as 'an urban miss' is only filled out by his realisation that she has not a
'passionate heart'. It seems much more likely that Sue's permissive
'townish' upbringing and education left her with a larger residue of guilt
(in the Freudian sense) than even Jude (who thought his ancestor a felon
and his father a villain, and who avoided killing earthworms) possesses.
Her pseudo-unconventionalities, her shallow rebellions, her insistent
postures of 'modernity' and 'free-thinking', often seem no more than a
cover-up for a deep-seated guilt of a most irrational, punishing kind.

In his portrait of Sue, and in much else that he wrote, Hardy
anticipated Freud, as did D. H. Lawrence, writing in the next two decades.
Lawrence, too, portrays a deadly war between flesh and spirit which
reflects the dilemma of man in society, and the penalties of civilisation. In
Sons and Lovers, Paul struggles with himself over his relationship with
Miriam, his notions of love and marriage.[20]

> marriage was for life, and because they had become close companions,
> he and she, he did not see that it should inevitably follow that they
> should be man and wife. He did not feel that he wanted marriage with
> Miriam. He wished he did. He would have given his head to have felt a
> joyous desire to marry her and to have her. Then why couldn't he bring
> it off? There was some obstacle; and what was the obstacle? It lay in the
> physical bondage. He shrank from the physical contact.

But when Paul decided he did want a physical relationship with Miriam, it
was her intense spirituality, the separateness of her love from her bodily
experience, which led to conflict and failure.[21]

> He never forgot seeing her as she lay on the bed when he was
> unfastening his collar. First he saw only her beauty, and was blind with
> it. She had the most beautiful body he had ever imagined. He stood
> unable to move or speak. Looking at her, his face half smiling with
> wonder. And then he wanted her, but as he went forward to her, her
> hands lifted in a little pleading movement, and he looked at her face,
> and stopped. Her big brown eyes were watching him, still and resigned

and loving; she lay as if she had given herself up to sacrifice; there was her body for him, but the look at the back of her eyes, like a creature awaiting immolation, arrested him, and all his blood fell back.

The paradox represented by both Jude and Paul is that their greater compassionate awareness and sensitivity to the feelings of others, and particularly of the women they love, gives them a more subtle and complex view of their obligations to them; yet this awareness fills them with guilt immobilising them and making them ineffective. As Paul puts it,[22]

> They were so sensitive to their women that they would go without them for ever rather than do them a hurt, an injustice. Being the sons of mothers whose husbands had blundered rather brutally through their feminine sanctities, they were themselves too diffident and shy. They could easier deny themselves than incur any reproach from a woman; for a woman was like their mother, and they were full of the sense of their mother. They preferred themselves to suffer the miseries of celibacy, rather than risk the other person.

In 'Civilisation and its Discontents' Freud describes a very similar attitude to relationships, and accounts for it in terms of the development of a complex social structure. In his review of the methods by which men seek to reduce the pain of perceiving the futility and finiteness of human existence, he writes of 'that way of life which makes love the centre of all things and anticipates all happiness from loving and being loved'.[23] Characteristically, such men[24]

> make themselves independent of their object's acquiescence by transferring the main value from the fact of being loved to their own act of loving . . . The state which they induce by this process—an unchangeable, undeviating, tender attitude—has little superficial likeness to the stormy vicissitudes of genital love, from which it is nevertheless derived.

Initially, this approach to relationships is valued by civilisation (which Freud often refers to as 'culture'). 'But the inter-relations between love and culture lose their simplicity as development proceeds. On the one hand, love opposes the interests of culture; on the other, culture menaces love with grievous restrictions.'[25]

Thus as well as insisting on a human instinct of aggression and a death instinct, Freud saw civilisation's demands as being destructive and distorting.[26]

> it is impossible to ignore the extent to which civilisation is built up on *renunciation* of instinctual gratifications, the degree to which the existence of civilisation presupposes the non-gratification (suppression, repression or something else?) of powerful instinctual urgencies.

Culture behaves towards sexuality . . . like a tribe or section of the population which has gained the upper hand and is exploiting the rest to its own advantage. Fear of revolt among the oppressed then becomes a motive for even stricter regulations. A high-water mark in this type of development has been reached in our Western European civilisation . . . Object choice is narrowed down to the opposite sex and most of the extra-genital forms of satisfaction are interdicted as perversions. The standard which declares itself in these prohibitions is that of a sexual life identical for all; it pays no heed to the disparities in the inborn and acquired sexual constitutions of individuals and cuts off a considerable number of them from sexual enjoyment, thus becoming a cause of grievous injustice.

Furthermore, Freud refuses to resolve this conflict by placing social duty above individual gratification, or by giving the demands of civilisation any higher status than those of the religious code which he dismisses as 'superstition' and 'an illusion'. On the contrary, he explains the sense of social duty and the rigour of conscience in terms of the same childhood experiences which give rise to other irrational fears and beliefs. The superego 'simply carries on the severity of external authority which it has succeeded and to some extent replaced.'[27]

Aggressiveness is introjected, 'internalised', in fact it is sent back where it came from, i.e. directed against the ego. It is there taken over by a part of the ego that distinguishes itself from the rest as a super-ego, and now, in the form of a 'conscience', exercises the same propensity to harsh aggressiveness against the ego that the ego would like to exercise against others . . . . Civilisation therefore obtains the mastery over dangerous love of aggression in individuals by enfeebling and disarming it and setting up an institution within their minds to keep watch over it, like a garrison in a conquered city.

Yet:[28]

renunciation of gratification does not suffice here, for the wish persists and is not capable of being hidden from the super-ego. In spite of the renunciations made, feelings of guilt will be experienced . . . Renunciation no longer has a completely absolving effect; virtuous restraint is no longer rewarded by the assurance of love; a threatened external unhappiness—loss of love and punishment meted out by external authority—has been exchanged for lasting inner unhappiness, the tension of a state of guilt. The price of civilisation is paid in forfeiting happiness through the heightening of the sense of guilt.

The interaction between the public aspect of social obligation (civic duty and communal responsibility) and private, intimate relationships was thus a much more complex affair than the simple sincerity and integrity of the admirable characters in early Victorian literature. The requirements of an advanced and technical civilisation made the performance of social roles a much more limited means for expression of the personality; the division of labour moulded men into the narrow patterns of specialised occupations. Few men could any longer find authentic self-expression in the all-embracing humanity of Dickens's best professional men; or in the practical, honest, courageous omni-competence of Jane Austen's naval officers; or the calm assured mastery of Conrad's sea-captains. This same greater complexity demanded more self-control, more self-denial, a greater conformity with others' restrictive expectations, in the performance of public roles. Yet a greater sensitivity to, and awareness of, the private emotional needs of others in more intimate relationships had not been accompanied by a movement towards more varied and heterogeneous life styles and patterns of behaviour. If anything, the *mores* of family and social life had become more stiflingly rigid, more stuffily solemn and moralistic, less tolerant of diversity, less open to wider influences. Thus people like Jude and Paul, aspiring, intelligent working-class boys with a strong streak of idealism, were trapped both by the constraints of dull, unsatisfying jobs and the rigidities of formal patterns of relationships.

It was at this point that there occurred, therefore, that distinctively modern feature of self-awareness that Trilling calls 'the disintegrated consciousness'. With the passing of the age when something of the order, peace, honour and beauty of Jane Austen's great houses seemed available to all, when a man could commit himself to his social role in the integrity of his personality, there came a new age in which the individual sought some limited autonomy for himself in resistance against the pressures of wider society. He might choose to serve that wider power in ways that were prudent and necessary for his survival, but his true self was defined in opposition to it. The price of this separation of public role from private self was the disintegration of the person, fragmented between his social obligations and the pursuit of his individual identity. Trilling suggests that this is still the characteristic position of modern consciousness; avowing the objectives of the social order in our roles 'as householders, housekeepers and parents', but privately identifying ourselves in antagonism to it, and to the constraints it places upon our opportunities for self-fulfilment.[29]

These changes were not without their implications for the growing profession of helpers with personal problems, which had established itself mainly in the medical sphere and, for women who followed in the footsteps of Esther Summerson and Octavia Hill, in social work. Professional integrity rested on very similar grounds to the integrity of the personality; the notion that someone could commit his whole being to a social role, whose purpose was the moral improvement of other individuals; that in the intimacy of human contact, there could be an education of the emotions which would free the recipient to participate more fully in social life, to fulfil his social obligations more adequately; to reach more nearly to his own ideal of personal integrity. Yet such a view took a very narrow interest in the processes of influence, concentrating exclusively on the rational, didactic and moral aspects of the professional relationship. What the novels of Hardy and Lawrence hinted at was that the subtlest and most effective form of influence is not rational but emotional, that in the grip of the most powerful forms of emotional influence a man is not 'himself', in the sense of an autonomous, independent being, with fixed and impermeable boundaries, but rather a potential container for the passions of others. Lawrence's portrait of Paul in *Sons and Lovers* portrays vividly the young man's inner conflicts as he is unable to disentangle or even distinguish himself from the influences of his mother and his women friends. Even to Clara's husband, Baxter Dawes, 'he felt an almost painful nearness'.[30]

Freud, too, recognised this phenomenon. In his theory of transference and countertransference, he sketched the beginnings of an attempt to account for the emotional content in therapeutic relationships; but it is a curiously wooden and stilted theory, accounting for personal influences and feelings in a very impersonal way. His scientific interest in the phenomenon seems to have derived more from the observation of his colleague Breuer in full flight from the positive transference of Anna O than from a need to analyse his own reactions. As Philip Rieff writes[31]

> One cannot be certain, but partial clues—reproaches addressed to himself in his own case histories for his lack of overt sympathy, the haughty way in which patients are mentioned in his letters to Fliess—lead one to doubt that Freud was much involved in the pathos of those he treated. This may be one explanation for his strict disavowal of the counter-transference.

A much richer and more enlightening account of the impact of such emotional influences on a helper committed to the mid-Victorian mode of personal and social integrity is contained in the modern novel set in the 1860s, *The French Lieutenant's Woman*, by John Fowles. Charles Smithson, a man in the prime of life, intelligent, self-assured, with every prospect of succession to a title and a country estate, engaged to the young lady of his choice, full of the consciousness of his station and its duties, a gentleman in short, encounters Sarah Woodruffe, a young woman given over to grief and mourning on account of her desertion by a French naval officer she loved. Charles's attitude towards Sarah contains within it many of the aspects of medical caution in approaching neurotic patients, and especially women, After all, mid-Victorian relationships between men and women were not equal, let alone free; women, though idealised, were also suspect, because of their greater sensibility, their irrationality and their vulnerability; these things made close involvement dangerous. Such contacts, therefore, were surrounded by a set of formal rules (rather like those of a present-day professional relationship) of which sexual taboos were the most important. However, Charles believes that his moral principles are sound enough protection against these dangers; his firm sense of his identity gives him a feeling of emotional inviolability, and his belief in free will emphasises his choice in having a way, and a morally righteous way, out of every potential emotional involvement, however intense. Hence Charles is spurred on by his inquisitiveness about Sarah, whom he finds intriguing, mysterious, tragic and faintly attractive, and seeks to counsel her over her personal problems.

However, when she quickly makes an urgent request for an opportunity to confide more deeply the nature of her secret, he instinctively shies away.[32]

> Moments like modulations come in human relationships: when what has been until then an objective situation, one perhaps described by the mind to itself in semi-literary terms, one it is sufficient merely to classify under some general heading (man with alcoholic problem, woman with an unfortunate past, and so on), becomes subjective, becomes unique; becomes, by empathy, instantaneously shared rather than observed. Such a metamorphosis took place in Charles's mind as he stared at the bowed head of the sinner before him. Like most of us when such moments come—who has not been embraced by a drunk?—he sought for a hasty diplomatic restoration of the *status quo*. 'I am sorry for you. But I must confess that I don't understand why you should seek to . . . as it were . . . make me your confidant'.

Later, when they have discussed the emotional consequences for her of her love affair with the Frenchman, Charles again recognises a subtle change in their relationship.[33]

> [He] was overcome, as by a backwash from her wave of confession, by a sense of waste. He perceived that her directness of look was matched by a directness of thought and language—that what had on occasion struck him before as a presumption of intellectual equality (therefore a suspect resentment against man) was less an equality than a proximity, a proximity like nakedness, an intimacy of thought and feeling hitherto unimaginable to him, in the context of a relationship with a woman.

Yet Charles still felt he was in control of the situation, and of his feelings. At a later stage, when still more deeply involved, he sought to excuse his conduct to himself.[34]

> From the outset his motives had been of the very purest; he had cured her madness; and if something impure had for a moment threatened to infiltrate his defences, it had been but the mint sauce to the wholesome lamb. He would be to blame, of course, if he did not now remove himself, and for good, from the fire. That he would take good care to

do. After all, he was not a moth infatuated by a candle; he was a highly intelligent being, one of the fittest, and endowed with total free will . . . And so, leaning on free will quite as much as on his ashplant, he descended the hill to the town. All sympathetic physical feeling towards the girl he would henceforth rigorously suppress, by free will. Any further solicitation of a private meeting he would adamantly discountenance, by free will.

Yet this confidence is not allowed to survive for long. John Fowles's novel brilliantly depicts Charles's gradual disillusionment with his notions of personal integrity and social duty through his relationship with Sarah. He comes to see his whole existence, including his engagement to Ernestina and the prospect of his inheritance, as a complex, cohesive sham, part of a social system which maintains itself at the expense of individuals' truth to their real selves and feelings. The quality of proximity which he feels in relation to her contrasts so vividly with the alienation of his social role and the artificiality of his relations with Ernestina that he can no longer fulfil the expectations of his family and class. It was surely no coincidence that Sarah was an outcast, who had placed herself outside society, its obligations and its rewards. In his attempt to help her return into it, to accept a social role again, Charles is convinced of his own futility, and comes to share her fate.

The notion that the authentic expression of the true self is of the outsider, who resists society's demands on him, is more difficult to reconcile with ideas of constructive interventions in the lives of others than the Victorian notion of personal integrity and social cohesiveness. If the only relationships that can fully express human emotions and needs are those beyond the reach of the web of society's influences, then personal freedom and liberation must resist the encroachments of helpful people, especially those who represent the official ethos of participation in the formal world. But how then can we justify intervention in others' lives, and especially the interventions of professional 'helpers' and therapists? These are the subjects of the next chapter.

7

The Ethics of Intervention

The notion of intervention into the lives of others can be looked at as an interference with others' freedom; it can also be looked at as an obligation on every citizen, as part of the web of reciprocal social duties which itself constrains freedom. Thus in deciding whether to intervene to discover whether my neighbour's child's cries are the result of an everyday situation or of his cruelty or neglect, I am deciding partly whether I am entitled to interfere in his private family life, and partly whether I am obliged to do so to avoid the suffering of a helpless infant. Intervention, by involving me in my neighbour's life, limits both of us in some way; he is invited to make himself answerable to me, and I am offering myself as responsible towards his child. In the discussion that follows there is a possibility of both of us involving ourselves in personal obligations towards each other. Assuming that he has some problem with his child, I may undertake to offer him some assistance in his difficulties, and he may undertake to alter his behaviour in some way to the benefit of his child.

In Chapter 2 I suggested that some social obligations are serious and binding, and that among these was the obligation to intervene to save the life of a fellow citizen who was in danger of losing it. It is not impossible to think of exceptions even to this rule. There is not an obligation on *every* passer-by to go to the aid of a person injured in a road accident, irrespective of how many others there are, or his actual competence in medical matters. On the contrary, his duty is to ensure that he does not impede more expert helpers, and to stand by only to provide such support as may be necessary. On the other hand, when there is no one else about, and the victim's situation is desperate, then there is no excuse in incompetence. In a matter of life and death there is a moral obligation to help which overrides one's reasoned estimation of one's chances of succeeding. Thus in his novel *The Fall*, Camus's 'judge penitent' begins to doubt his own morality from the time when, after passing a girl on a bridge late at night, and a moment later hearing her throw herself into the water and call for help, he hesitates, thinks how cold the water must be, and walks on. It was not a question of how good a swimmer he was, for he made no attempt to rescue her. He simply turned his back on his obligation to her.

However, there are many other less clear-cut situations in which the ordinary citizen hesitates to intervene for other reasons. These include situations where, although there has been no request for help, and although the outcome of failure to intervene cannot exactly be predicted, a dangerous or even potentially tragic result, either in terms of physical or emotional damage, or of harmful effects on personality development or relationships, seems likely. Here the ordinary citizen, talking about a neighbour's household in which such a situation was developing, might say 'I'd like to help, but I haven't got the knowledge and skill', or 'my family commitments don't allow me the time to help', or 'they'd probably resent someone like me interfering', or 'they have to learn to stand on their own feet'.

It can readily be seen that all these reservations about intervention may, in some circumstances, be justified. The ordinary citizen may lack the particular combination of concern, skill and tact necessary to gain the trust and engage the commitment of his neighbour in avoiding the undesirable outcome. He may indeed have even more pressing obligations within his own household. It might even be the case that only a crisis could bring the neighbour to recognise what was wrong, and take steps to put it right, so intervention would be counterproductive. But none of these possibilities can exclude the danger that, because everyone can present themselves with similar arguments against intervention, no one will do anything about the situation, and the unfortunate result will occur. It is thus presumably at least partly to overcome such avoidance by ordinary citizens of potentially tragic situations that the roles of various expert helpers have evolved over the past hundred years.

In this chapter I do not propose to deal specifically with official interventions by representatives of the state's agencies. State interventions raise certain particular problems (which will be discussed in the second half of this book), both as regards the approach of the helpers themselves, and as regards the receivers of help. Instead, therefore, I want to concentrate on forms of help which derive more directly from notions of neighbourly assistance, and which, though they have become increasingly associated with expertise and professionalism, are not necessarily linked with state agencies. Obviously many of them have, particularly recently, been incorporated into official organisations, even though historically they developed outside them. But their principles have evolved largely independently of their role within the state's provision, and it is with the evolution of these principles that I shall be concerned. The occupations with which I shall be dealing are those Halmos has grouped together under the title 'counselling', and particularly social work.

One of the more paradoxical claims of these helpers has been that they have, as one of their absolute principles guiding their interventions into the lives of others, a principle of 'client self-determination'. Thus, for instance, Father Biestek asserts that 'a conscious, wilful violation of the client's freedom by a caseworker is an unprofessional act which transgresses the client's natural right and impairs casework treatment or makes it impossible.'[1] On the face of it, such a claim is absurd, and Biestek himself would appear to be contradicting his own maxim when he states later that self-determination must be limited, that some clients cannot make decisions for themselves, or cannot make sound decisions; thus the caseworker may have 'to assume an authoritative or executive role in order to protect the client from the very probable results of his own confused planning'. He adds that 'caseworkers are primarily interested in the skills whereby clients are helped to accept and adjust to the limitations of personal freedom arising from law and authority'[2] and that 'the natural right to make choices and decisions about one's own life does not extend to moral evil',[3] so that the caseworker has a duty to help his client keep the moral as well as the civil law. All this is hardly surprising in an occupation that systematically intervenes in people's lives to influence their behaviour—the surprising thing is that the claim of a principle of self-determination should have been made in the first place. What was the origin of this claim?

Nowadays, social work experiences doubts about the ethics of intervention. It feels torn between respecting the vulnerability of the insecure and confronting the destructiveness of the impulsive; between imaginative identification with the sufferer and the process of showing people how to live with suffering; between joining with clients in their search for personal identity and insisting upon the performance of their social obligations. But, historically, social work sprang from an age that saw little conflict between these tasks; for, as we have seen from earlier chapters, in the mid-nineteenth century, personal integrity and identity were seen in terms of honourably fulfilling a role in society. The rules of right conduct could be taught and learnt, and such instruction, if given in the right spirit, was always beneficial. The philosophical underpinnings of early social work were to be found in the writings of Mill and T. H. Green, who was himself not only tirelessly devoted to good works, but also a personal influence on many of the leading early social workers.[4] Green's organic view of personalities, families and communities (he and some of his social worker colleagues founded 'a society for looking at things as a whole') encouraged a notion of freedom in which self-realisation, the making of choices, was essential to the formation of a self, yet could be understood only in terms of the individual's participation in the 'moral organism' of society. Hence the rights to individual liberty were only justified as serving a moral end, 'in the sense that the powers secured in them are essential to the fulfilment of man's vocation as a moral being, that is, as a being who in living for himself, lives for other selves'.[5] Only personal relationships could affirm the unity of society, and confirm the moral status of individuals.

The way in which this concern for all members of society as moral beings, partaking of the same organic enterprise, expressed itself was mainly in the relationships between voluntary charitable visitors and the poor people on whom they called. The early social workers of the 1860s and 1870s were consciously counteracting the effects both of the harshness of urban life and of the degradation of the system of poor relief. They 'tried to give the people they wished to help the experience of consideration and politeness, of shared work and pleasure, of friendship and fellow-feeling, of being individuals of importance as such, that was being denied them in countless details of daily life by industrialising Britain.'[6] Una Cormack argues that 'the objective of the social workers was ultimately a kind of equality' but for most of them 'the equality they envisaged was one of feeling and friendship rather than finance'.[7] She produces quotations from many of the leading social workers of the time which emphasise their concern with the freedom and human dignity of those they visited. Octavia Hill echoed Mill in stating, 'Each man has had his own view of life and must be free to fulfill it . . . In many ways he is a far better judge of it than we, as he has lived through himself what we have only seen.'[8] Mrs Bosanquet insisted 'that poor persons shall not be visited unless on some definite errand, or unless acquaintance has been previously made with them; or, lastly, unless there is some special reason for believing that the visit will be acceptable.'[9] T. H. Green looked forward to the day when 'all honest citizens will recognise themselves and be recognised by each other as gentlemen.'[10]

Just as in literature the last decade of the nineteenth century marked the end of this optimistic conception of personal and social integrity, so in the political arena this period saw growing awareness of clashes of interests, open manifestations of class conflict, and an increase of political consciousness among the working class. In the face of these phenomena, which became more evident as the twentieth century progressed, the theory which underlay social work was forced to take account of fundamental conflicts between society's expectations of individuals (including the submissive acceptance of economic disaster and political turmoil) and individuals' demands for a decent life. But faced with such conflicts, social work was always ambivalent and unsure; it never recovered the certainty which it derived from the archaic model of the individual as a member of his community. It compromised and vacillated between analyses of individuality derived from the early works of Freud, in which the repressed id was assisted in its search for ways to express itself, and the neo-Freudian amendments to this analysis which emphasised the need for the ego to adapt to the demands of the culture. It asserted the rights of individuals to 'fair' and 'humane' treatment by governments, but seldom took sides with their organised, militant protests against injustice and inhumanity. Thus although the term 'client self-determination' derived from the 1930s, and from a period when American social work was identified with the 'liberation' of client groups, both in psychological and political terms, the next decade saw a backlash in which the claims of 'reality' were reasserted, qualifying clients' freedom almost out of existence.[11] Once self-realisation and the development of personality by free choice ceased to be (as it had been successively for Kant, Mill and Green) a moral aim, and became merely a psychological one, it had to be balanced against the counter-claims of social duty. Once self-determination ceased to be the constitutional exercise of the individual's resistance against the state's coercion (as it had been for Locke, Mill and de Tocqueville) and became instead the organisation of partisan rebellion against legitimated authority, it had to be balanced out against the counter-claims of law and order.

This dilemma is still present in social work and other counselling occupations today. The notion that the helper must be in some sense aligned with the individual's attempt to assert his identity, and to find a valid, true expression for it, is offset by an acute awareness of the necessity to limit such expression to socially acceptable forms, consistent with obligations towards and expectations of others. Robert Witkin poses the similar problem facing teachers of the creative arts in secondary schools as follows:[12]

While the teacher of the creative arts regards self-expression as fundamental, his understanding of self-expression embraces a number of disparate activities which forces him to recognise only some forms of expressive action as legitimate while viewing others as quite illegitimate . . . Thus an individual is said to be expressing himself, albeit in a wholly illegitimate way, when he kicks in a window pane or daubs a lavatory wall, just as surely as he is held to be expressing himself (in a legitimate way) when he paints a picture or composes a piece of music . . . The teacher therefore perceives in self-expression both a positive necessity and a disturbing threat. He sees it as both creative and constructive on the one hand and as destructive and anarchical on the other. Self-expression is the fruit of the tree that conceals the serpent. The teacher is moved by two conflicting impulses, on the one hand to encourage self-expression and on the other to stifle it. It is out of this dilemma that the distinction between legitimate and non-legitimate in self-expression emerges. What form this distinction takes in the case of any particular teacher is determined largely by his own values as they have evolved through his experience in his social milieu. What is certain, however, is that in so far as the nature of the expressive act itself remains shrouded in mystery, the ambivalence towards self-expression which dominates the teacher's praxis will also persist. The teacher's ambivalence spreads very quickly to the pupil who also comes to view self-expression with the same mixture of suspicion and fascination.

The same fundamental ambivalence towards self-expression (which was obvious in the theoretical literature of the 1950s, and is still reflected in orthodox American 'casework theory' of the Florence Hollis type) has since tended to divide counsellors into warring factions. In his book *The Modes and Morals of Psychotherapy,* Perry London identifies two opposing schools of thought, one of whose major points of disagreement is the value of the expression of self and of personal freedom. Although, as he points out, 'there is a quiet blending of techniques by artful therapists of either school'[13] so that in practice distinctions are not as contrasting as theoretical stances would imply, those whose methods he describes as 'insight therapies' are generally committed to promoting self-knowledge as a means to self-determination.[14]

By implication, it is the right of individuals above all else, to live as they choose . . . The supposition of all the Insight theorists is the same; that the self is valuable, that it is worthy of being known, and that its title to explication and intelligibility is its very existence rather than any behaviour it undertakes or performances it sets in motion . . . the moral goal this . . . finally serves—autonomy, freedom to experience the self, to enhance it, to gratify it, to unbind it, to give it rein to palpate itself and, so doing, to be fulfilled. It offers the ultimate justification of the individual.

It is easy enough to see why such an ideological commitment appeals to the counsellors themselves. As we have seen in an earlier chapter, the notion of a fragmented consciousness, of alienation from social roles, assumes that the self can only grow and flourish in opposition to society's demands. As a way of life for themselves and for their middle-class clientele, the notion of personal liberty entailed by this approach has an obvious attraction. What is much less clear is how it applies to their most disadvantaged and deprived clients, the traditional consumers of social work help. How do those who opt for this horn of the dilemma justify their libertarian stance in relation to the immature, the impulsive and the antisocial?

The simplest justification, which goes some way to meeting objections raised at once in the name of 'reality', is that of Alan Keith-Lucas; that in relation to social workers' assistance, client self-determination is not a right, it is a fact.[15]

Certain kinds of decision cannot be made by anyone other than the person about whom they are made . . . There is a kind of choice—to take help or not to take it, to get well or remain ill, to grow or to regress—that will affect the use a client will make of their services, but which they cannot make for him . . . It can be made by a man in prison as readily as by a business executive; in fact, since it is inevitable, it will be made by both.

Thus, whether or not therapists and social workers adopt techniques that allow for choice, ultimately clients will exercise it, if only by refusing to have anything to do with the help offered, and deciding instead to 'curse God and die'.

It is perhaps among people who cannot avoid contact with counsellors of one kind or another that the moral justification for recognising and supporting this freedom is most poignantly illustrated. The handicapped, the elderly frail and long-term residents in institutions are captive populations who may have to endure many years of personal assistance by social workers from whom there is no physical escape. David Soyer makes the point forcefully that clients have rights to their aspirations, however 'unrealistic' they may seem to social workers. He insists that they should be allowed not only to dream their dreams, but also to test them against reality, to risk failure and disappointment.[16]

> Within our client populations, there are those who for all their lives
> have been deprived yet over protected . . . Certainly, one of their
> deprivations is that they have never had the adventure of putting to the
> test of reality their adolescent 'dreams of glory' without first having
> soberly looked at the pros and cons with a social worker.

It is very arguable that the same restriction now increasingly applies to a sector of the non-institutionalised population on whom social work attention is heavily concentrated, and whose only escape from the repressive tolerance of non-judgmental controlled involvement is behaviour which, while it is certain to be classified as 'acting out', will at least have that very special quality of being something done for oneself.

Another important strand in the defence of client self-determination is the fact that the 'reality' occupied by the social worker, and whose claims he is pressing on the client, is no more immune from invasion by the client's definitions, perceptions and emotions than the latter's is by his. We have already illustrated an excellent case of such counter-therapy in Sarah Woodruffe's conversion of Charles Smithson to the existential position of outcast. Social workers who encounter clients in their worst moments of confusion, disorder and disruption soon learn (in one way or another) that any personal relationship that deals with strong feelings is a process of mutual influence in which neither's previous experience is necessarily binding upon the other. Janet Mattinson, in her book *The Reflection Process in Casework Supervision,* argues strongly against what was once the orthodox line in counselling. She quotes Ferard and Hunnybun's maxim that the social worker must stretch out a long arm to save his drowning clients, but be sure to keep both feet on the bank, and continues,[17]

> This message is paralysing in two ways. It is difficult to imagine the skill
> of being close enough to clients to be able to help them talk about their

fears and fantasies and at the same time remaining enough apart to be unaffected by those fears and by the actual behaviour of the client. And it assumes that the worker is another species, unlike his client and unlike the rest of mankind, non-introjecting, and always able to resist being pushed into a role, even by the most manipulative. . . . *'You can exert no influence, if you are not susceptible to influence.'*

However, the notion that clients' feelings may affect social workers' behaviour raises difficult questions about the nature of a process of 'unconscious' influence. Janet Mattinson writes of the social worker 'acting-out' feelings for the client of which the client is not aware, and says that the social worker is often not aware that he is doing so: 'the [worker's] capacity to react consciously will depend on the degree to which he is conscious of himself; what he picks up from the client unconsciously, he will react to unconsciously.'[18] However, the implication is never that this process *cannot* be known, but rather that the former social work orthodoxies cultivated defences against its recognition and use. The theory that the worker needed to control his feelings and keep a safe distance relied on a notion of persons as particularly impervious to interactive influences; it might even have increased their vulnerability to unwanted invasions by feelings and by its insistent refusal to recognise them. Charles Smithson's interaction with Sarah Woodruffe was an example of haughty disdain falling prey to intense passion. But the negative version of this can be even more destructive. As Janet Mattinson says:[19]

Psychological distance determined on the principle of safety and lack of involvement with a corresponding lack of recognition of increased exposure to only the most powerful projections, 'has the paradoxical effect of getting the worker unknowingly more deeply involved with the client's most negative features.' His conscious decision not to be involved will further blunt his capacity to look at the collusive nature of his behaviour. Action supposedly based on an 'objective' decision, because of the distance from which it has been made, is often a horrifyingly accurate reflection and confirmation of the client's worst fears.

Thus the worker's problem in becoming aware of the client's effect on him is really a part of the process by which both parties are seeking to know themselves better through their interaction. The assumption, to be sure, is that the worker starts with a more secure self-knowledge, and in a much less disturbed state; but this should enable him to feel safe to take on aspects of the client's experience, to 'become' something of the client for the client, even at the expense of short-term confusion and collusion.[20]

A worker who has walked into a trap and can then do something about it—can resolve something, can relinquish some aspect of his behaviour—is not only providing a more realistic model, but giving the client hope that he can do likewise. . . . Omnipotence is probably the most disastrous characteristic for any social worker, and too much reliance on technique, as opposed to response and then understanding what response is about, fosters omnipotence.

The fact that feelings are *shared* with clients as equal human beings, rather than as incomplete or immature 'cases', is thus crucial to their approach.

There is implicit in most recent writings from the insight schools of therapy a suggestion that failure to become aware of feelings, to know oneself, to share feelings with others, is in some sense a moral failure. This harks back to Freud, cutting through some of the hasty obfuscations by which his reviewers and interpreters obscured his original message. As Philip Rieff points out,[21]

For Freud . . . neurosis was no intruder, ruining the happy life of the emotions; it was not simply the objective symptoms manifested by the patient, but was, beyond that, an element of *character*, identical with the patient himself. It was the host himself—or rather, his moral character—that must be treated.

In some sense, the patient had chosen his illness; his symptoms were thus significant, a language which told, more clearly at first than the patient could himself, of the moral failures of his life. By insisting on the significance of seemingly meaningless, alien illness, psychoanalysis introduced a method of treatment which resided in knowing the worst, in trying to listen to what the patient had learnt to be deaf to in himself. It is this approach that other insight therapies have adopted and extended. As Perry London puts it, for the therapist insight becomes an end in itself, 'which, insofar as it does not relate to symptoms, forces a redefinition of his work; this new definition is one that casts him in the mould of a secular moralist.'[22]

For the counselling interactionists, the quest for greater honesty and self-awareness in the counselling relationship (as manifested in the methods of the school of Transactional Analysis as well as in psychoanalytical derivatives) can be justified as a means towards the client's achievement of more satisfactory personal relationships. But the most extreme form of the development towards moral rather than functional treatment is to be found in the existentialist approach. Here the notion of 'cure' or 'improved social functioning' is almost entirely replaced by an attempt to construct an alternative way of being, a new meaning to life. R. D. Laing's treatment of psychotic young people in communes which become new homes for them for an indefinite period, and where they often leave behind every vestige of their previous existence, exemplifies this. The counterpart to this in community work is the insistence on client groups reaching their own definitions of their problems, and seeking their own solutions, however politically or socially disruptive, rather than simply 'participating' in the management of their disadvantages by others more powerful than themselves.

Such examples are often selected as providing grounds for criticising the whole insight approach. For ultimately the notion that the counsellor's role is completely permissive, that all responsibility for exploration and discovery reside ultimately in the client, loses credibility in the face of the more blatantly ideological or political manifestations of client responses to therapy. The suspicion is at once aroused that the counsellor is being disingenuous; that he is rewarding and reinforcing certain responses more than others, and is thus shaping the client in his image. When the declared aims of intervention are so broad and client-centred, yet the outcomes are so often (if successful) stereotypical and predictable, the accusation that the counsellor is not acknowledging or declaring his covert aim comes to be made, and doubts about the genuineness of client self-determination grow. Furthermore, psychologists who have analysed examples of 'non-directive' therapy have found strong evidence that therapists can affect clients' behaviour by their differential responses to it without intending to or being aware of doing so.[23]

But even stronger criticism of all insight approaches to interventions stems from the accusation that they have, by concentrating on fostering awareness of the self, and of the significance of feelings, lost sight of the original justification for intervening at all. If lengthy processes of 'treatment' by these methods do not, to any very significant extent, change behaviour or relieve troublesome symptoms (and research suggests that, by and large, they do not), then surely the counsellor has practised upon his client a kind of confidence trick, using his discomfort from his symptom as a pretext for something which is ultimately unrelated to it? If the counsellor is concerned with freedom, should he not consider whether his intervention is justified at all, given that he has no serious intention of giving priority to the need that brings himself and his client together?

Those who advance such criticisms are normally exponents of methods of counselling which derive from learning theory, and which concentrate on changing clients' behaviour and alleviating their symptoms rather than understanding their motivations. Since behaviourist approaches require no hypothesis of a covert self which controls the client's behaviour without directly manifesting itself in it, their concept of self-determination is rather different from that of the insight schools. What they mean by a personality, or a person, is simply a pattern of behaviour which has been learnt at some time during a life history; but the significance of any part of that pattern cannot be related to an unseen inner 'core' of self, for such a notion is, in behaviourist terms, meaningless. Thus actions which other therapists might see as indicative of strong inner feelings, or ambivalence, or unconscious mental processes, they regard as simply learnt responses, which as such may quite easily have been adventitiously acquired through chance coincidences of environmental circumstances. They are, therefore, no respecters of symptoms, and their respect for persons is reflected in their determination to eradicate pieces of behaviour which their clients experience as troublesome or inconvenient. They would thus assert that freedom for their clients resides, not in making conscious their motives for behaving irrationally, but in freeing themselves from slavery to behaviour of whose irrationality they have become conscious.

Since, according to this view, counselling is a process of relearning responses to certain stimuli, it is more helpful for the counsellor to make his role as a re-educator quite overt, thus de-mystifying the whole process. The original behaviour therapists (such as Wolpe) worked by a method which was so didactic as to require little more than submissive obedience. However, later and more sophisticated exponents of these approaches have placed much more emphasis on engaging the client's co-operation in the processes of changing his behaviour, and, more recently still, writers like Lazarus have attributed almost as much therapeutic importance to the counselling relationship as have members of the insight schools.[24] Indeed, the behaviour therapists have sought to outbid their opponents in the matter of honesty with their clients, insisting that by discussing their plans, by jointly setting targets and devising programmes, fixing time limits and agreeing goals, they are the helpers who really *share* with their clients. Certainly, their treatment methods and aims are more readily comprehensible, more clear-cut and more similar to the medical model on which most clients' expectations are built, and thus the behaviour therapists have been able to develop a notion of a 'contract' between counsellor and client, where the agreed terms of the relationship are known to both sides, and open to either to challenge. Eclectic social workers have increasingly borrowed this notion from the behaviourists, and researches like those of Reid and Shyne[25] have suggested that the more purposeful and short-term work which this focus engenders is (like behaviour therapy itself) more likely to produce measurable changes in behaviour and alleviation of symptoms. By identifying problems precisely, by concentrating on specific tasks, by making help a step-by-step process in which the client can perceive and measure the gains he makes, this method seems particularly appropriate to individuals and families whose 'normal functioning' has been temporarily interrupted, and who are looking for a treatment which will restore them to what they considered a satisfactory life.

One difficulty concerning freedom which surrounds these methods is the concentration of power in the hands of the therapist. In spite of all that is said about the sharing involved in a contract for treatment, the responsibility for the regime of relearning which is decided upon clearly rests with the therapist in a way which is not the case in insight therapies. However much the latter may reinforce certain kinds of expression of feelings, the responsibility for the feelings themselves, and any action which stems from them, rests squarely with the client. The weakness of this method—that feelings do not necessarily entail any particular action or any action at all, so that the whole process may become one of wallowing rather than doing—is also its characteristic permissiveness. Whether or not such methods are really weak or disguised attempts to influence, change or control the client's actions, as the behaviourists would suggest, they leave the moral onus on the client, for it is precisely the step between feelings and action which is left for him to make (one reason why he often doesn't make it). But the behaviour therapist, who measures all outcomes in terms of action, must get the client to behave differently, and in doing so must accept a more directive role. Even if he agrees with the client on what is to happen, he still has to *tell* him what to do. As Perry London says, 'It is no more possible to shift responsibility for his plans to the patient by discussing the treatment in advance, than it is for a physician to shift responsibility by describing a variety of available medicines.'[26]

This should produce moral dilemmas for any counsellors who are as conscious of the success of their methods as behaviourists usually are, and if it does not it is more a tribute to the simplicity of their theories than to their perceptiveness about human problems. It means in effect that the kinds of decisions characteristically regarded as giving rise to the most painful dilemmas for any individual are transferred to the therapist instead. In so far as these are moral choices, it is difficult to discern the principles by which the counsellor makes these decisions, for in behaviourist theory questions about morality tend to be reduced to questions about behaviour. Yet the fact that behaviour therapists claim to be able to produce changes not only in behaviour itself, but also in attitudes and feelings about behaviour, means (if we accept their claims) that they are arbiters over the whole area of values, priorities, obligations and relationships as well as over actions themselves. Thus, for example, Wolpe, faced with deciding whether to change a homosexual's behaviour or his religious scruples about it, elected the latter course.[27] Behaviourists would argue that in other forms of therapy, decisions to try to influence the client in a certain direction are still largely made by the therapist, but covertly. What is just as important, however, is the basis for such decisions, and the account taken of the clients' value system. By and large, behaviourist versions of social and moral theory are highly simplistic, and contain assertions which are easily taken to be authoritarian and disrespectful of the client's resistances against the social order, his struggles to establish an individual identity, and the pain of his personal dilemmas. Conflicts of interest are banished in the name of effective functioning; thus Jehu dismisses the topic of 'moral behaviour' with the definition, 'This consists of the acquisition of certain rules of conduct and behaving in accordance with these rules.'[28]

This is not to say that behaviour therapists adopt an attitude towards their clients which is aimed at suppressing their more tiresome actions for the good of the community; on the contrary, it is for their clients' sakes that their behaviour is changed. The kinds of examples of treatment favoured by this approach concern actions which are apparently irrelevant and meaningless, rather than expressive of strong resistance to society's demands. The symptoms eradicated are usually more inconvenient to the client than to anyone else (like phobias). In this way, behaviour therapists can readily protect themselves against accusations of employing powerful techniques to enforce the community's will on the individual. But if the aim is simply to eliminate all behaviour which is not 'appropriate', not 'well adapted' to social functioning, a number of questions still remain. What is the purpose of social functioning? If maladaptive behaviour is meaningless and irrelevant, what is the meaning and relevance of adaptive behaviour? For the difficulty is that the same logic which makes symptoms meaningless (that they are merely behaviour patterns which happen to have been learnt) deprives any other behaviour of meaning. Learning theory can only explain how people learn to behave; it cannot provide any reasons why they should learn one pattern of behaviour rather than another. Hence behaviour therapists are forced to rely on vague justifications derived from a notional societal consensus (productivity, efficiency, law and order) or borrow from some other social philosophy, such as the utilitarian notion of the greatest happiness of the greatest number.

However, more often, because of their overriding therapeutic concern for the welfare of their individual clients they develop no social theory at all, but claim only to be helping their clients achieve more satisfactory personal relationships. Here, like insight therapists, they are defining the value of the client's behaviour in terms of its worth to him alone. Although they set no store by the notion of self-expression, their rationale for well-adapted behaviour is ultimately much the same as the insight therapists' for their ideal: that the individual is, by means of achieving it, freer to build a more satisfying world for himself. If challenged on the lack of a social basis for their approach, both tend to resort to an ethic of relationships that emphasises intimacy, empathy and involvement, and to suggest that where individuals can achieve this, they necessarily contribute to a world which, since it is constructed out of relationships, will be improved and enriched by this development. Thus Glasser, for instance, asserts that, 'The more people are able to gain successful identities, the more successful the identity society will be. The society will founder if too many people cannot become successful, cannot gain the involvement and the confidence that they are competent and worthwhile, loved and loving.'[29]

It therefore emerges that the arguments between these two approaches to counselling about their relative merits as individual therapies conceal a common weakness—their inability to relate their help to the wider social context of their clients' lives. This is a very important weakness, for it greatly reduces the relevance of counselling to many of the problems with which the helping professions have traditionally been concerned. In order to offer assistance to people who are socially deprived or disadvantaged, counselling requires a theoretical framework in which the client's existence, and his struggles to establish a valid identity and meaningful relationships, are all seen as taking place within the context of a significant social order. The equation of counselling with individual therapy, based as it is mainly upon models derived from private practice with middle-class clients, tends to accept characteristic middle-class alienation from social issues, and justify a position based on political impotence and moral irresponsibility.

As we have already seen, Victorian social work, from which a major part of modern counselling was largely derived, had no such weakness. It insisted that both the social and the moral evaluation of its clients' behaviour could be derived from the application of axioms of human conduct which were outside and beyond the individual himself. While this categorical form of judgment, when applied to problems like poverty and homelessness, may strike us now as absurdly moralistic and absolute, it clearly provided a comforting form of certainly not only to social workers, but also (to judge by the accounts of the work of Octavia Hill and others) to their clients. Modern counselling methods exist in a social vacuum; this is particularly unfortunate when clients are confused and anxious about the social significance of their situation, or in conflict with others about definitions of their social obligations.

In an attempt to remedy this deficiency, many social workers have recently become much more conscious of political issues, and have tried to evolve a rationale of practice which takes account of the social and economic factors in their clients' lives. Community work and welfare rights activities have been among the approaches promoted by this new awareness. However, such methods have tended to be sharply distinguished from, or even placed in opposition to, more traditional forms of counselling. For Octavia Hill, her consciousness of her tenants' needs for, and rights to, space for recreation and play led her quite naturally from casework into community work, and the quasi-political activity involved in the creation of the National Trust, without any apparent consciousness of conflicts between these forms of activity. Modern social workers are much more aware of dilemmas about the individual versus society, minorities against the majority, and the necessity for strategies of help for the underprivileged based on conflict and the vigorous assertion of rights. They are thus inclined to contrast counselling with political protest in terms of social control on the one hand, and liberation on the other.

Yet ultimately the Victorian social workers' position was not only tenable, but perhaps the only possible basis for meaningful intervention.

However repugnant some of its presuppositions about the nature of social obligation may now seem, it saw the social worker and his client as fellow citizens, as part of the same social order, as responsible to each other and to the rest of society for an important segment of their life—concerned with public duties—as participating therefore in a wider community in whose activities the only form of social significance available to individuals was to be found, and in terms of which everyone's existence had ultimately to be justified. It requires no metaphysical notions of the absolute or the spirit of totality to understand that every man is a member of his society, and the fact that nineteenth-century Idealism chose to express this notion in such misleading terms should not obscure its truth from us. Membership of society is, like client self-determination, not so much a principle as a fact. Whether we like it or not, we cannot escape from it. Without it, counselling is as socially irrelevant as any other activity, for both the duty and the right to intervene in others' lives rest ultimately on some notion of shared participation in a social order. And if the notion of common citizenship applies to non-official interventions by voluntary helpers, it applies even more strongly to interventions by official helpers in the name of the Welfare State.

Part 2
Welfare Institutions

Flattery and Dumb Service

I have considered our notions of freedom from the point of view of philosophy, sociology and literature before looking at the Welfare State in any detail, because it is important to see whether there are differences between the way we think about our own freedom and the way we consider the freedom of recipients of welfare provision. In this chapter I want to try to summarise the arguments of the first half of this book, and show how I wish to apply them to an analysis of our welfare institutions.

Attitudes to freedom have changed substantially since the mid-nineteenth century, when Mill wrote his famous essay. Mill was concerned mainly with the minimisation of coercion, though he was also keen to emphasise the positive value of originality and spontaneity. He saw the dangers of a society in which 'even in what people do for pleasure, conformity is the first thing thought of',[1] but he attributed this tendency towards uniformity and mediocrity to the 'tyranny of opinion'. He saw this form of collective despotism, the enforcement of a rigid code of behaviour for every social situation, as an exact parallel with political despotism—as the imposition upon the individual of another's will, under threat of punishment. He therefore made little distinction between political coercion and private influence, seeing both in terms of compulsion and being concerned to define their appropriate limits. In fact, his principle of individual liberty was the same for all forms 'of compulsion and control, whether the means used be physical force in the form of legal penalties, or the moral coercion of public opinion'.[2]

Nowadays we are much more aware of subtler influences which threaten freedom. Above all, we have come to recognise that most people who behave in the conformist way which Mill deprecated do so not because they have been threatened or compelled, either by the state or by moralisers, but because society has been so ordered as to reward them for conformism. Complex processes of production, and equally complex modes of consumption, are both managed with technical sophistication by experts who know all about how to get the most out of us as producers and consumers, and who make us all very much alike by giving us quite a lot of things we are happy to have, and telling us about a lot of other things we might have if we were prepared to do even more of the things they want us to do. The essence of this system is that the rewards are cumulative; at first they are rather small, and it is only after a fairly long participation in the process of acquiring the benefits of the affluent society that we can expect to amass all the comforts and status symbols it can offer. The smallness of the initial pay-offs serve to obscure the thoroughgoing nature of the dominion which this process gains over us; because at first we have to work quite hard to achieve any benefits, we are able to convince ourselves that we are really participating only for the sake of survival, in the absence of practicable alternatives. As the rewards grow larger, these in turn are rationalised in terms of our earlier sacrifices, and so on, until we are thoroughly willing and active members of the property-owning consumer democracy, convinced that we are only getting what we deserve, and that all we want to do is precisely what our employers and the advertising men require of us, and of everybody else.

Seen from this point of view, conformism in modern society has very little to do with the fear of punishment, either by law or by opinion. If fear does play a part at all, it is more to do with anxiety over remaining within the system, over continuing to participate, however small the rewards. Thus the least successful and least rewarded participants none the less often strive hardest to conform rather than be relegated to the status of non-participant; their fear is not of coercion by the rulers, but of those they perceive as excluded from the system, the rejects and outcasts, the predatory outsiders. One is reminded of the famous experiment in social psychology in which a cross-section of American men were paid a very small sum to administer what they believed to be electric shocks of increasing intensity to unknown subjects, who simulated reactions of growing agony. A very high proportion (62 per cent) obeyed instructions to deliver the whole range of shocks in spite of the recipients' extreme expressions of pain, and they afterwards successfully rationalised their reactions both in terms of only doing what they were told, and of the subjects deserving it.[3] Thus the experiment showed not only an extraordinarily high incidence of conformity with the expectations of authority, for very small rewards, but also a very punitive attitude to those disapproved of by authority (who were in this case being punished for giving wrong answers to questions). Powerful members of our society seem to have very little trouble in getting us to do as they want, and simultaneously to fear and castigate those who deviate from their requirements.

However, for many of the more liberal among us, what we know about our tendency towards conformity and its sources does not please us particularly. We still hanker after liberty and individuality, but in a more ambivalent way than Mill and his contemporaries did. We want to believe that there is at least a part of ourselves which we can keep safe from society's influences and its blandishments. This helps to explain the prevalence of a notion of the self which is separate from, and in opposition to, our social roles. We like to think that our true selves are not implicated in all the dirty business which we are forced to take part in to earn a living and to keep up with the neighbours. This means that we pursue two separate courses simultaneously: a private, inward journey to discover our real nature and means of expressing it, and a public, outward one, gaining such advantages as we can from what society offers, and not being too particular about the terms. It is a position that was first documented by Diderot in his description of 'Rameau's Nephew', a talented, sycophantic but unsuccessful court musician, obsessed with his social position, ever seeking after worldly success, yet keeping something of himself apart from his performance of his 'pantomime steps'—'he has no greater opposite than himself'. Hegel later described this form of consciousness as the 'Heroism of Flattery', a kind of self-preservation in which the self is disintegrated, by simultaneously prudently serving the power of society, but existing in a state of inner rebellion against it.[4]

The fact that we are aware of a self which can stand apart from the 'pantomime' of social role-playing makes us less certain of the binding force of social obligation than the Victorians were. For all his disapproval of interference in matters of individual conscience and taste, Mill exercised a categorical form of judgment on moral and social issues, and saw those who failed to meet their obligations—for instance to members of their families—as fit objects for punishment. But his interpretation of social duties went a good deal further than this, and he included acts of omission as well as commission in his list of offences a man might do against others requiring intervention and correction.[5]

> Encroachment of their rights, infliction on them of any loss or damage not justified by his own rights; falsehood or duplicity in dealing with them; unfair or ungenerous use of advantages over them, even selfish abstinence from defending them against injury—these are fit objects of moral reprobation, and, in grave cases, of moral retribution and punishment.

Today we would be much less inclined to bring moral standards, let alone sanctions, to bear on public behaviour, particularly in the commercial field; we rather assume that, since business and politics are complex enterprises involving the performance of certain sophisticated public relations operations which are relatively impersonal, the people fulfilling such roles are not necessarily acting 'in character', and may be 'really' quite different from the way they behave. Under these circumstances, we sometimes seem to expect little more of our industrial and political leaders than that they should keep within the criminal code. This has a number of paradoxical consequences—for instance, that we are less and less inclined to believe the things they say in public, yet we are reluctant to accept that they are deliberately defrauding us. President Nixon was able to confess at various stages of the Watergate affair to having misled the public on matters of fact without feeling it incumbent on him to resign from office, and his aides later said that they discussed the details of the cover-up in terms of 'management techniques'.[6]

Thus the tendency to see the performance of social roles as morally neutral territory, since it does not involve the 'true' self, while it frees us from the tiresome necessity of interfering in a moralising way in others' business, and of having them moralising in ours, does increase the trend towards the use of manipulation and control by reward in our public dealings with each other. Instead of trying to form clear judgments about others and their actions, we may tend to see them either as obstacles or as stepping-stones in our paths to our own ends, and be more interested in finding ways of dealing with them than evaluating their worth. This applies to behaviour and people defined as 'social problems'; we may be less condemnatory about illegitimacy or drunkenness than the Victorians, but also more inclined to look for ways of accommodating the social roles of unmarried mother and alcoholic, rather than helping them as people. Where we have no feelings of moral disapproval at all, but merely of embarrassment (as with physical handicap and old age) we tend to offer some form of compensation—financial or material—on the basis that if they are people like ourselves, they will accept this within their social roles, in the spirit of the Heroism of Flattery.

Economic inequalities and social injustice are another source of ambivalence. Like most Victorians, Mill believed unquestioningly in the efficacy of free trade and the market economy as the only means of increasing prosperity for all, and thus justified consequent inequalities in living standards and the distribution of power and resources. Modern consciousness no longer supposes that the free market is necessarily the best means to prosperity, let alone social justice; yet we continue to live in a society in which major decisions are shaped largely by commercial priorities, and where private business corporations are still the most powerful interest groups as well as the wealthiest. Once again, in the face of this dissonance, liberal consciousness can only split, dividing itself into attitudes and behaviour which are appropriate to the practical tasks of earning and consuming, and political opinions which reflect vague aspirations for a juster world. Yet nowhere is the difficulty of translating liberal opinions into effective action more painfully obvious than in fields like inequalities of wealth. Present-day liberal middle-class charities which claim to represent the interests of the poor start from the assumptions of structural inequalities in the industrial system without believing these to be morally or economically justifiable. They proceed to outline marginal changes in benefits which compensate individuals for these inequalities without supposing these to be adequate compensation. They produce no coherent political philosophy, they generate no vision of a better society, no concept of the poor person as a freer or more equal citizen. Since we can no longer find social or moral justifications for them, we are forced to reduce both economic privilege and economic deprivation to statistics, and to concentrate on elaborate technical devices for marginal redistributions which will eliminate the embarrassing lower reaches of our tables. The question of what sort of person a poor person is supposed to be in our society, or how he is to understand his poverty in relation to others' affluence, does not arise. Low wage earner and unsupported mother are simply factual descriptions of economic and social roles, which take their place alongside the roles of company director and merchant banker in a social structure that is constructed out of value-free sociology.

In reaction against the impotence and political irrelevance of modern liberalism, much more extreme forms of libertarian thought have had a considerable recent vogue. The defining characteristic of these writings, which helps to explain their popularity, is that they resolve the liberal dilemma in the most painless way; instead of pointing out the impossibility of political and social change without an organised overthrow of our economic system, they insist instead that liberal alienation from social roles is ineffective only because it is not thoroughgoing enough. If only we can make good our liberation from the last vestiges of allegiance to society's demands (as manifested in our obstinate tendency to earn large salaries and consume many products), we would simultaneously have achieved the revolution which would bring the economic system to its knees. The failure of modern liberalism thus is not its inability to translate subjective notions of freedom into political realities; it is its inability to escape entirely into the realms of subjectivity, creativity, play, joy and madness. Once our consciousness can allow us to overthrow our economic conditioning and our obedience to authority, the process of alienation will be complete, and a new society based on new freer relationships can be constructed from the wreckage of the old.

This type of analysis has been imported into the social sciences by sociologists of the interactionist school. They interpret particular features of 'deviant' youth subcultures in terms of an attempt to deal with tensions between the pursuit of the free expression of the self, and the demands of conventional roles.[7]

The problem which the bohemian faces is similar to that faced by industrial man in general. He, too, wishes to override his socialisation into the work ethic, to step out of the workaday world into the ecstasy of play. He too feels that his work role is of insufficient coherence and meaningfulness to provide a sense of identity. But whereas the average citizen wants balance (leisure at the right time and place, moderate at all times and commensurate with his productive capacity and status, and an identity, leisure-centred yet underscored by commitment to the work ethic), the hippie wants none of this. He seeks an undiluted subterranean experience and he wants it now. He believes that man is in essence a creative, expressive *and* hedonistic creature and, because of this, it is only in the realm of subterranean values that his true identity can be realised.

The hippie subculture therefore seeks experiences which 'make transparent the relative nature of seemingly absolute standards of conduct' and show 'contemporary man as alienated and social *mores* as mere games to be played'.[8] Writers like Young see these subcultures as constructing an alternative 'social meaning' to their members' existence, using their shared experiences as the basis for their redefinition.[9]

> The price they pay for this is in their eyes small, because not only are the material possessions which society has to offer not worth working for, but they are able through handouts from parents, working friends, national assistance, and part-time hustling, to remain well above the starvation line.

However, the 'social meanings' ascribed by these subcultural redefinitions are of somewhat limited significance. They are on a par with the redefinitions of Cooper's 'rebirth' process, a kind of group equivalent of his individual experience of pure subjectivity. To be sure, they are no less valid than anyone else's definitions of social reality, but nor are they any more so, and the fact that hippies still, as Young points out, depend on others for their subsistence makes them ultimately dependent on others' interpretations of the social meaning of their behaviour. In the last resort, the test of any interpretation of experience must be in terms of whether in a specifiable situation it produces certain results; in the case of a new interpretation of the 'social meaning' of behaviour, this test will presumably be whether as a result of it, certain changes in society, or affecting some members of it, takes place. Thus interactionists often seem to be describing little more than the state of mind of groups of young people. If they choose a subjective road to social change, this does not exonerate them from the task of producing objective results.

The appeal of libertarian writings to modern liberal consciousness, which has become ill-at-ease with itself, is to our somewhat guilty hopes that the basic split between ourselves as thinking and feeling beings and our performance of our social roles can be mended without the necessity of our having to give up our cherished notions of freedom, individual identity and self-expression. The libertarian approach suggests that this may be achieved without our actually having to do anything, except perhaps to stop working when we calculate that we can afford to do so, and to carry through to their logical conclusion whatever processes of alienation we have already embarked upon (either by going mad, or becoming a hippie, or both).

The claim of significance in terms of social and political change of these highly subjective phenomena rests on a tenuous link between the 'oppression' suffered by people who have become alienated at some stage of a conventional middle-class career, and the 'oppression' of people who have pursued an underprivileged career from the start of their lives. The notion is that because both are struggling against the domination of capitalism they are not only natural allies but even recognisably similar in their situations, and in the ways in which they may co-operate to resolve them. Thus Marcuse, for instance, quotes the joint student-worker rebellion in France in May 1968 as a possible precedent for a student-negro alliance in the USA, suggesting that the two groups have as common ground 'the total rejection of the existing society, of its entire value system'.[10]

However, such analyses obscure more than they clarify. In order to bring out the misleading elements in the equation, it is not enough to point out that the two groups are differentiated by their point of entry into the situation of oppression (poor people could hardly be said to 'embrace' poverty as a solution to the problems of alienation); nor is it sufficient to recognise that middle-class bohemians can usually escape from their situation if it becomes too uncomfortable; nor to acknowledge that there are, as yet, few if any organisational links between the two groups, and little sympathetic communication. The really important difference is that middle-class bohemianism can be seen as having developed out of a historical trend in the evolution of middle-class social roles. Socialisation into liberal middle-class values and behaviour nowadays presupposes a division between the expressivity and individual identification of the private self and the alienated performance of society's demands. Bohemianism therefore does no more than emphasise one side of this socialisation at the expense of the other, just as the conservative attitudes and behaviour of some stockbrokers and merchant bankers emphasises the conventional to the virtual exclusion of individual identity. On the other hand, socialisation into underprivileged roles (in so far as it is carried out by teachers, employment counsellors, bosses, other higher-class people and sometimes by parents too) is often a process which provides little, if any, scope for the expression of individuality, of feelings, of creativity, or of humanity. It is socialisation into a role of dunce, of drudge, of scapegoat, of outcast—as the film *Kes* so brilliantly portrayed. Because the underprivileged have never experienced freedom, or the sense of a self which has real autonomy over any portion of their lives, or the means of expressing their feelings, or creating something out of themselves, or of loving others as free and autonomous beings, because, in short, the underprivileged are often as deprived culturally and emotionally as they are materially, the ideals of Cooper's and Marcuse's revolutions are virtually meaningless to them.

Thus people who have grown up within the social roles of deprivation or underprivilege have not been given any opportunity to understand their 'oppression' in the same way as people who have chosen to emphasise or provoke the disapproval of society by embracing nonconformist behaviour as a 'solution to alienation'. A man cannot act in a way that seeks to resolve a tension between his sense of individuality and his perception of the expectations of others unless he is aware of such a tension and can conceptualise it, or at least relate it to some experiences or feelings. A man's notion of self in opposition to society's demands presupposes the ability to transcend his immediate situation, to see through the web of obligations and bonds which shape his behaviour, and perceive himself in some autonomous existence as an individual outside it. This requires particular kinds of perceptions and thought processes which have no special connection with intelligence or sensitivity. Goethe's first hero was highly intelligent and sensitive; yet the tragedy of Young Werther was that he was unable to allow the disintegration of his personality which his situation demanded. Rather than accept alienation, he sought integrity through a simple rural life and his love for a domesticated busy maiden; rather than accept the collapse of this sincere simplicity, he committed suicide, still holding to the ideal of an integrated self. Werther, with his single suit of clothes that he wore throughout his adult life, was denied, and denied himself, the means of expressing any identity other than the one his birth and upbringing had allotted him.

The characteristic modern middle-class disintegrated consciousness is a product of experiences which differ from those of working-class children. Bernstein's researches indicate how differently children use language to describe experience, and how middle-class children develop an 'elaborated code' which enables them to conceptualise their individuality and express their more subtle feelings.[11] Working-class children, disadvantaged from the start of the educational process, tend to be streamed into a system which prepares them like square pegs for the roles they will play as workers when they leave school. Such an education does very little, as Witkin has shown, to develop 'the intelligence of feeling', the power to express a personal point of view which is unique, and thus, by the educational process, to develop a sense of autonomy, creativity and individuality.[12] The discovery of the self, if it is to occur at all, must come by other means, and through other processes. Working-class identities and resistances to society's expectations are moulded in a social and cultural environment which is very different from the one that produces libertarian sensibilities.

In an extreme form, the contrast between a socialisation which gives rise to the sense of individuality, and the notion of personal freedom, and one that does not can be derived from the descriptions of the childhoods of two characters in the nineteenth-century novels we have already considered. On the one hand there is the illiterate, uncomprehending crossing-sweeper, Jo, in *Bleak House*.[13]

He goes to his crossing, and begins to lay it out for the day. The town awakes; the great teetotum is set up for its daily spin and whirl; all that unaccountable reading and writing, which has been suspended for a few hours, recommences. Jo, and the other lower animals, get on in the unintelligible mess as they can. It is market day. The blinded oxen, over-goaded, over-driven, never guided, run into wrong places and are beaten out; and plunge, red-eyed and foaming, at stone walls; and often sorely hurt the innocent, and often sorely hurt themselves. Very like Jo and his order; very, very like! [Dickens goes on to compare Jo with a sheepdog,] an educated, improved developed dog, who has been taught his duties, and knows how to discharge them. He and Jo listen to the music, probably with much the same amount of animal satisfaction; likewise, as to awakened association, aspiration or regret, melancholy or joyful reference to things beyond their senses, they are probably upon a par. But, otherwise, how far above the human listener is the brute!

By contrast, even at the age of eleven, Hardy's Jude Fawley had a notion of himself as something more than the orphan nephew of a village baker; the schoolmaster, Phillotson, had introduced him not simply to books, but to an identity of someone who 'was too clever to hide here any longer—a small sleepy place like this!'[14] Phillotson's departure to Christminster ('headquarters, so to speak') actually increased his identification with the man, his learning, and its academic origins. When he later sat dreaming, his aunt scoffed, 'Why didn't ye get the schoolmaster to take 'ee to Christminster wi' un, and make a scholar of 'ee?' To Jude this was no joke; he continued to apply Phillotson's standards to his own behaviour, feeding the crows he had been employed to scare, and wailing when chastised by the farmer that 'Mr Phillotson said I was to be kind to 'em.' In spite of his aunt's remonstrations, and her reminder that 'We've never had anything to do with folk in Christminster, nor folk in Christminster with we', Jude, even in his humiliation, recognised that there was an alternative within himself to the role of village scarecrow and scapegoat.[15]

If he could only prevent himself growing up! He did not want to be a man. Then, like the natural boy, he forgot his despondency, and sprang up. During the remainder of the morning he helped his aunt, and in the afternoon, when there was nothing more to be done, he went into the village. Here he asked a man whereabouts Christminster lay.

First gazing at it from afar, then studying Latin and Greek on his baker's round, Jude prepared himself for his escape from the expectations of his small community.

Another slightly later example of youthful awareness of alternatives to the expected role of a manual worker is provided in D. H. Lawrence's *Sons and Lovers*. Paul's brother, William, was very close to his mother.[16]

Then, when the lad was thirteen, she got him a job in the 'Co-op' office. He was a very-clever boy, frank, with rather rough features and real viking blue eyes.
'What dost want ter ma'e a stool-harsed Jack on 'un for?' said Morel.
'All he'll do is to wear his britches behind out, an' earn nowt.' ...
'He is *not* going in the pit,' said Mrs Morel, 'and there's an end of it.'

Later, Paul himself refused to collect his father's wages.[17]

'They're hateful, and common, and hateful, they are, and I'm not going any more. Mr Braithwaite drops his "h's", and Mr Winterbottom says "You was!" '

His feeling of humiliation by the men at the pit office encouraged his identification with his mother, and through her there developed his interest in writing, thinking and referring to books, and the love of the countryside and the garden. He and his brother shared her perceptions of the role of miner as dirty, degrading and unworthy of their potential.

Thus both Jude's and Paul's conception of themselves outside the roles their village communities expected of them depended on contact with others whose perceptions of the social organisation of the village was both different from and more complex than the perceptions of Aunt Drusilla or Mr Morel. The latter's uncritical acceptance of manual toil as both honourable and inevitable could be seen as the counterpart of Hegel's 'Heroism of Dumb Service', the integrated, simple concrete and specific perception of the self as embedded in an unchanging social fabric in a role from which there is no escape. The alternative disintegrated consciousness of the 'Heroism of Flattery' demands an ability to understand complex social relationships and to analyse interconnections between parts of a social system; Bernstein suggests this is impossible without an elaborated code of language, which most underprivileged children lack. Witkin has shown that in the creative arts, where this aspect of secondary education might be expected to be developed in literature and drama, the distinction between legitimate and non-legitimate forms of expression stops the process short of the full imaginative experience of the self in different relationships with others. Because the teacher remains outside the pupils' subjective experience of the relationships, he cannot help him to learn to feel them as part of himself, to say, like Paul and Jude, that what he feels is a resistance within his whole being to what society expects of him. Thus pupils can only express this resistance in actions which stem from the frustration of inadequate means of communication, which in turn are interpreted as non-legitimate by the staff, and suppressed.

In these ways, the education and socialisation of children from the lowest socio-economic class provides little basis for their understanding of their relationship with society as a whole, or their experience of themselves as individuals, with a measure of freedom and autonomy. Instead, they tend to be coerced and cajoled into being what society requires them to be; their behaviour is simply rewarded or punished in accordance with its suitability to the social role allotted to them. Like young animals, their playfulness, their mischievousness, their inquisitiveness, their experimentations are first tolerated, then increasingly repressed or forced into acceptable channels. The best that is expected of them is obedient performance, the Heroism of Dumb Service.

By the time they reach adolescence and early adult life, the frustrations of these expectations are becoming more pressing. The ways in which they are constricted and exploited by virtue of their position in the economic system, the non-availability to them of the means of a decent, healthy life, the absence of financial, material or communal resources for the construction of any alternatives for themselves, bear down upon them in instances too numerous and obvious for mention. They are offered minimal rewards for submissive participation in their exploitation. It is small wonder that they often react with behaviour which expresses rebellion against constraints without expressing a sense of the value of self or a meaningful concept of liberation—like crime, child neglect, family violence, vagrancy and drunkenness.

Hence, the implications for social policy which are derived from such libertanian analyses are largely irrelevant to the problems of inequality and injustice in our society. Because they presuppose socialisation into awareness of self, and the ability to express creative feelings, they have no clues to offer on how the nurture and education of the underprivileged can encourage these perceptions and capacities. Furthermore their observations on the 'social meanings' of such 'deviant' acts as drug use and homosexuality are not applicable, even by their own accounts, to the vast bulk of property offences and baby batterings, nor do their accounts of madness square with the experience of depressed wives or confused geriatrics. Hence the recommendations which apply to marijuana smoking—that we should encourage subcultures and avoid treating users as either criminal or sick—have no bearing on society's dealings with thieves, and the communal treatment of a few adolescent psychotics does not help resolve the plight of millions of elderly isolated widows. Libertarians bypass the great dilemmas of social policy in respect of the treatment of problem behaviour; they thus give tacit consent to the continuation of such standard treatments for crime and mental illness as imprisonment and traditional mental hospitalisation.

In so far as the libertarian approach offers a critique of the Welfare State, it is a very marginal one, concerned with certain aspects of the handling of the specialised problems of groups who have made a more or less conscious decision to provoke it into heavy repression or paternalism. The central problems of the Welfare State concern its attempts to define social rights and to compensate the deprived and underprivileged for their disadvantages. It has become increasingly clear since the early 1950s that these attempts are not effective in counteracting the economic forces which cause deprivation; forces which require the socialisation and regulation of these groups in order for them to perform roles in industrialised productive processes, and to provide a market for certain products. The post-war Welfare State has allowed a proportion of the working class some share of affluence and leisure, but it has not defined the free and equal citizenship of all members of our society. It has not provided a decent and secure life for all; it has not produced a cohesive society. In respect of freedom, it has not challenged the fundamental coercion and oppression which have characterised the relationships between the better-off and worse-off sectors of the community. This can be seen in the following official statements.

> If you are still unemployed at the end of four weeks, you can renew your claim for supplementary benefit, and you will then be specially interviewed. Unless there are good reasons why you cannot find suitable work, your allowance might be stopped at that time.[18]

> There has to be a certain amount of pressure on claimants to find work and stay in it and it is a matter of hard fact that this involves letting it be known that state money is not there for the asking for anyone who is able to work, but unwilling to do so while hotels, restaurants, cafes, shops and amusement centres are recruiting staff. The same thing applies in towns near farming areas where farmers need labourers for the harvest; where there are big building and public work enterprises; where there are factories recruiting unskilled staff for labouring or packing or other simple work, or where local authorities need staff for public utilities.[19]

> In the great majority of cases, even where the claimant does not consider herself to be cohabiting, the evidence necessary for a decision to be made is obtained by interviewing the claimant and, when appropriate, the man in question . . . It is only where the Commission's officers have good reason to believe that the claimant may be deliberately concealing or misrepresenting the facts about her relationship that the Department's special investigators are employed. These investigators have no right of entry into private premises except by invitation of the occupier. The initial purpose of their inquiries is to establish whether the claimant is or is not entitled to benefit.[20]

These quotations display a great deal of ambivalence, both about giving benefits and about allowing freedom. They demonstrate the extent to which we have failed to resolve the dilemmas which remained when nineteenth-century liberalism lost its credibility. Social obligation is no longer categorical; social roles are no longer God-given; the need for individual identity and self-expression are recognised in our understanding of the social order. Yet there are still expectations about the ways in which members of the 'lower classes' should live and work; and, while compensations for disadvantage are provided, their conditions are strictly defined in line with these expectations. Furthermore, while there is a desire to make compensatory benefits neutral, anonymous and impersonal (and hence ideally payable in cash), there is a nagging doubt that people's needs are personal and particular, and that financial provision may even be morally injurious.

This ambivalence is not confined to the services dealing primarily with income maintenance. It is seen also in the actions and attitudes of local authority social workers, who are increasingly concerned with interventions in ill-defined situations, aimed at preventing what are seen as undesirable outcomes. In spite of their continued subscription to the principle of client self-determination, social workers can be seen to be working to accomplish certain ends, which bear a close relationship to the expectations (in terms of work, family patterns, and so on) which are displayed in the Supplementary Benefits Commission's statements. Furthermore, social workers, too, use financial sticks and carrots to bring about the behaviour patterns they consider desirable. In his research into the use by Children's Departments of their powers under Section One of the Children and Young Persons Act, 1963, Handler found that cash payments, intended to be used only in emergencies to prevent the reception of children into care, were being employed as part of long-term plans which social workers made for families. But these plans were not shared with clients, because of the ambivalence and suspicion which accompanied financial provision.[21]

> When families faced eviction from council housing for failure to pay rent and the Children's Department entered into a rent guarantee agreement with the housing authority to stay eviction, it was department policy not to disclose the existence of this arrangement to the family, for fear that the family would think that the Department would remain available to pay the rent on future occasions.

In the case of other debts,[22]

> money could be used as a form of bribery to get the family to agree to the C.C.O.'s plan for self-help. In many instances, the department would be very forthright in insisting on specific behaviour changes before they would pay out money . . . When bribes failed, threats might be used to implement the plan. A C.C.O. who was handling a rent arrears case planned to have the family taken into court and threatened with eviction in order to shock them into 'seeing realities'.

What can be seen here at work are deep-rooted processes reflecting the fundamental dilemmas about freedom and welfare which have been with us since the first attempts at state provision for social needs. In this second part of my analysis I shall look back at the history of state intervention; and I shall suggest that the absence of a constructive, positive, social philosophy, offering a notion of true freedom and dignity for the lowest-status groups in the community, is the fundamental weakness of our present welfare institutions. The problem of freedom and the Welfare State stems from the fears which better-off citizens have about giving real liberty to those whom the social system denies the opportunity to develop a sense of uniqueness, of self, of autonomy, of worth, of existing beyond the work-role demanded of them by society. As Witkin puts it,[23]

> How strange and alarming is talk of freedom in the mouths of those who have never known it! Listen quietly to it, and you will hear a snarl to drain your life's blood. Talk of freedom stalks our urban industrial jungles . . . Talk of freedom is heady stuff. It is safest in the mouths of those who have known it.

9

The Origins of Social Engineering

In an earlier chapter it was suggested that, if the state was equally interested in the welfare of each of its citizens, it would intervene to prevent or make an end to the exploitation by one party of another (i.e. greater power or privilege of one over the other, or unequal obligations between the two), wherever it was convinced that such intervention would bring about a fairer distribution of influence and of obligations. It was also recognised that this aim was extremely difficult to fulfil.

In every age since the early nineteenth century there have been interventionists who, on various issues, by various means, and from various bases, ardently advocated state involvement with some such ends in view. These have always been opposed by non-interventionists who argued that such involvements inevitably brought about more harm than good. Before the 1830s virtually the only part in social relationships which the government played was through the Poor Law, which will be the subject of the next chapter. In this chapter I want to consider other major interventions which have been undertaken since that date, and the ideas upon which they have been based.

Because the philosophy and style of interventions have changed over the years, and because we have come to take certain forms of state activity for granted, it is not always easy to recognise the interventionists of former generations as such. The nineteenth century in general, and political economists in particular, are now usually associated with policies of *laissez-faire* and thus with non-interventionism. Yet utilitarians and radical liberals like Bentham, the Mills, Senior, Chadwick, Kay-Shuttleworth and Southwood Smith were all in various ways passionately concerned with increases in state intervention. However, their programmes for social policy involved two principles which placed strict limits on the involvement of the state in public and private relationships: first, that it was very seldom effective or necessary for the state to intervene in questions concerning private relationships between individuals (members of families, neighbours, landlord and tenant, etc.) which were far better settled by the parties themselves, who ultimately had recourse to common law; and second, that it was to the immense benefit of the whole population to let trade and industry proceed without the hindrance of state intervention in commercial affairs. Both these principles were based on a belief that the solutions to all social evils, private and public, lay in technical and scientific progress, which would increase prosperity; it followed that interventions were always in danger of slowing this progress, by postponing the solutions to problems. All these reformers also had implicit faith that relationships such as those between family members, landlord and tenant, employer and employee, were either 'natural' or else willingly undertaken to mutual advantage, and hence that the potential evils of interfering with them outweighed the possible good.

Of all the reformers mentioned above, perhaps the most interesting was Sir Edwin Chadwick, because, without being a truly original thinker, he was both a prolific and an outspoken advocate for a wide range of interventions, and involved in the actual creation and administration of several new government agencies. His origins as a Benthamite and his experience as an administrator, combined with his extraordinary energy and obstinate determination to carry all his ideas not only to their logical conclusions, but also into organisational practice, made him a formidable influence on his contemporaries, and his life's work has endured in such a way as to make a considerable impact on us today. During his long life (1800-90) he was described (by Mill) as 'one of the great contriving and organising minds of the age'[1] and (by Sir John Simon) as a man who 'beyond any man of his time, knew what large fresh additions of human misery were accruing day by day', and who fought to overcome them with 'sincere and disinterested zeal for the public service',[2] He was, in short, both the architect and the first major administrator of our modern social services.

Yet during his lifetime and virtually ever since he has been regarded as an enemy of the working class. He was immensely unpopular at the time of the implementation of the new Poor Law, and during the drafting of the first factory legislation, and his image among working people was derived from those two aspects of his career. When he was one of the Royal Commissioners on the State of Children in Factories, the operatives of Leeds signed a manifesto which contained the statement 'We are at a loss for words to express our disgust and indignation at having been threatened with a visit from an inquisitorial itinerant'.[3] The Chartists described him, over the new Poor Law, as one of the 'tools and mouthpieces of the Whigs'[4] and a 'worse than Russian satellite and adviser'.[5] They also justifiably linked his support for the creation of a centralised police with the enforcement of the Poor Law against working-class resistance, the two combining to produce 'the most frightful instrument of despotism—of *money despotism*—ever introduced into England'.[6] Chadwick was opposed to trade unions, and advocated the suppression of strikes by arresting pickets. His biographer, S. E. Finer, concludes:[7]

> We must conceive of Chadwick's State as one which he believed to be the essential precondition of economic progress, and which he was prepared to defend by force. For the working classes, his actions presented a very different aspect. They saw him, and they were quite right, the zealous engineer of the industrialists.

In the longer term, however, Chadwick can be recognised (mainly through his work in the field of public health) as the architect of measures and services that greatly improved the lives of urban working-class people; and paradoxically most of even his deservedly unpopular causes have given rise in one way or another to processes that are now regarded as contributing to ameliorations in the conditions under which working people live. Perhaps most significantly, the working class itself has changed, at least partly as a result of the success of Chadwick's measures, and has come to adopt a point of view on many subjects which is close to the one he held. For better or worse, it is doubtful whether he would have received such vigorous working-class opposition today as he did at the time.

Chadwick was a friend of John Stuart Mill, and shared Mill's opinions on economic questions. Like Mill, he adhered to the 'harmony school' of political economy, believing that employers' and workers' interests were complementary. He rejected Malthusian pessimism about an inevitable decline in standards of living as the population increased, arguing that wages would rise, so long as men were willing and able to work and be productive. 'For every mouth at Nature's feast, there was also a pair of hands'[8] he wrote in 1828. 'More efficient labour makes the return to the farmer's capital larger, and the consequent increase of the fund for the employment of labour enables and induces the capitalist to give better wages.'[9] However, Chadwick was unorthodox in that he emphasised that growth in the national product must be reflected in an increase in public, not just private, wealth. His thinking implied that, in maximising their gains, capitalists should also contribute as far as possible towards the public gain, and where their methods of production caused pollution, insanitary conditions, illness or damage, these should be subtracted from the total national product. It was the state's responsibility to intervene where a capitalist was refusing to recognise his obligation to maximise the public gain from his processes; he had no compunction about such interventions, because he considered that sinister interests caused a distortion which could not be regarded as free competition. Thus, in the case of the Poor Law, 'his activity was a ruthless and bureaucratic attempt to keep the ring clear for individual initiative wherever customs or vested interests stood in the way'.[10] In the field of public health, Chadwick was willing to expropriate inefficient water companies at low compensation to ensure an end to epidemics of cholera.

The logic of this calculus made him a fierce and passionate interventionist. 'More than anything, perhaps, the "preventive" aspect of legislation appealed to Chadwick.'[11] He agreed with Bentham that, 'The problem for the statesman is to define obligations and punishments in such a way that private interest shall be brought by artificial means to coincide with the public interest.'[12] In the process of achieving this, middle-class definitions of the interests of the individual were bound to be challenged, and Chadwick thus made enemies among his own class as well as among workers. For example, on the issue of child labour factories, his report recommended not only that government inspectors should (for the first time) invade private property to intervene between masters and their servants, but also that there should be compulsory industrial injury insurance, the contributions to be paid by the employer. In general, he recommended the use of civil servants and the police, acting in such a way as to make it difficult for individuals and groups to exploit their advantages against the public interest, thus 'invading the ancient sanctity of the Englishman's home', and using 'coercive power in order to bring private and public interests into natural conformity'.[13] Before he resigned from the Board of Health he wrote of the opposition his efforts there had encountered: '. . . (T)here are few men . . . so little loved and so intensely hated: and whose official position is so precarious.' Among a long list of individuals and interests opposed to him he listed the Privy Council, the College of Physicians, the water companies, the cemetery companies and numerous MPs.[14]

> We have moreover been obliged to excite a strong landlord interest against us, in unwholesome houses, which we could not but condemn and thus threaten those landlords, as they conceive, with expense. Two of the great Lords in the Cabinet are large owners of lands in this condition. . . . The town property belonging to the Prime Minister is much of it obnoxious to our censure.

The version of Chadwick represented by his contribution to the Poor Law Report of 1834 is thus by no means the full picture of him, or of his importance in the development of social policy. Even in that report, his evidence on 'collateral aids', the positive counterpart to his repressive measures, was never published. He was already concerned with the connections between bad housing, bad sanitation and high sickness and mortality rates, and saw them as an important cause of urban pauperism. He thought that expenditure on better housing might save money in the long run. He also considered that drunkenness might decrease if towns provided 'public parks and zoos, museums and theatres'.[15] He was interested in improving education for the poor, and gave evidence to the

Newcastle Commission in 1858 in favour of better facilities for poor children, including school meals and medical inspections. It was these positive proposals that contributed to the continued friendship between himself and Mill throughout the latter's life; yet in other ways Chadwick's interventionism was, by Mill's standards, both coercive and disrespectful of the liberty of the individual citizen. He always retained his interest in the police, and, writing on this subject before Peel's measures, he recommended that after imprisonment for short periods, felons should be under police surveillance for extended periods, their whereabouts checked, their access to specified places controlled, and associations with specified persons forbidden. A police force should be 'a well organised body of men acting on a system of precautions to prevent the necessity of punishments, to render infraction of the rights of property difficult.'[16] This was just one example among many of the 'artificial means' by which private interests could be *forced* to coincide with the public interest; prevention required far more regulation and control, far more direct influence by the government over individuals' behaviour, than nineteenth-century liberal consciousness desired, or considered it required. Whereas Mill moved away from his strict Benthamite upbringing to a more humanistic, optimistic liberalism which wanted to maximise the possibility of spontaneous virtue, Chadwick put Bentham's passionate and more pessimistic interventionism into practice.

The effects of the interventions which Chadwick initiated have been momentous. It is not merely that the forms of prevention and regulation for which he provided the blueprint have now become the standard instruments of government, the major tools of social and economic policy. What it is difficult now to comprehend is that the very notion of such interventions, and of their planned use to produce certain effects, did not exist before this time; that the processes of social engineering he started were thus the bases on which not only the Welfare State but also Keynesian economic measures are founded. We now take it for granted that governments make calculated interventions to affect the supply of housing, the numbers of hospital beds, the level of investment or the rate of unemployment. The notion of even gathering the information necessary for such plans, let alone the interventions themselves, was abhorrent to members of the working class and to manufacturers alike at the start of Chadwick's career. When the Royal Commission on the State of Children in Factories was set up, *Fraser's Magazine* stated[17]

These Commissioners have been appointed because of their supposed indifference to the questions of infant suffering, and their great capacity for political calculation, without any liability to any misgivings on the score of human kindness; and the dry question which they are to decide, is whether the merchant's gain does not more than compensate for the unparalleled wrongs and injuries due to the children.

Chadwick's questionnaire, which was administered in manufacturing districts, was attacked by *The Times* as 'a mass of impotent and stupid verbiage' and 'pomp and pretension combined with . . . vagueness and apparent insincerity of purposes'.[18] Charges of heartless calculation and dry commitment to theory followed him throughout his official career; he was denounced as an inquisitor as well as a persecutor of the poor.

The reason why his methods seemed so novel and so repugnant to his contemporaries was that the possibilities of social engineering, of the control of the vast mass of citizens' behaviour by a government which had the means of intervention at its disposal, had not yet borne in on early Victorian consciousness. The opposition Chadwick provoked from middle-class interests was mainly shortsighted and instinctive; the anti-Poor Law movement and the Chartists had a clearer notion of the implications of his measures. In fact, Chadwick was an environmentalist in more than the sense that he was conscious of the importance of the physical environment for health and welfare; he was also an environmentalist in the psychological sense. He saw that because people's behaviour was very much affected by external stimuli, there were very many means by which governments could have a direct and powerful influence on the day-to-day behaviour of all their subjects, and thus upon the whole social fabric. He recognised, in short, that in order to control and regulate, the government need not use direct coercion or the threat of punishment. It could use supervision and inspection; it could impose specific forms of taxation; or levy charges on actions it considered against the public interest; but above all it could foster measures it considered progressive or improving and thus directly or indirectly reward behaviour of which it approved. He himself favoured the simultaneous pursuit of all these measures to achieve better standards of public health.

A clue to the sudden relevance and practicability of these methods in the 1830s and 1840s is to be found in a paragraph of the 1834 Poor Law Report. The vast majority of that report is about the evils of the allowance system in rural areas; but one small section does talk about manufacturing industry. Whereas the argument about farm labourers emphasises the need for independence and diligence in such occupations, the paragraph on manufacturing notes:[19]

> The object of machinery is to diminish the want not only of physical but of moral and intellectual qualities on the part of the workman. In many cases it enables the master to confine him to a narrow routine of similar operations in which the least error or delay is capable of immediate detection. Judgment or intelligence are not required for processes which can be performed only in one mode, and which constant repetition has made mechanical. Honesty is not necessary where all property is under one roof, or in one enclosure, so that its abstraction could be very hazardous; and where it is, by its incomplete state, difficult of sale. Diligence is ensured by the presence of a

comparatively small number of over-lookers, and by the almost universal adoption of piece-work.

Chadwick applied many of the features of factory management to the government of cities. Since city life could provide, given a 'preventive police' and a less eligible Poor Law, an environment which could be much more consciously and carefully planned and controlled than the countryside, it offered far more scope for social engineering. The deplorable state of housing and sanitation was a challenge. Like a benevolent mill-owner, Chadwick set about improving conditions, providing amenities, making the environment more plesant and less hazardous. Like the mill-owner also, his motives were the maximisation of efficiency and productivity, the minimisation of costs. His biographer states that in 1840, when he was compiling his famous Sanitary Report,[20]

The prevention of disease was only another administrative gadget, a mechanical solution of an administrative problem. Where the evils were 'ascribable to physical causes', it was 'good economy' to 'prevent the evils', instead of indicting the parties for nuisance and paying the expense out of the Poor Rates.

Like a member of the elite in a Skinnerian Utopia, Chadwick was devising a carefully regulated environment in which his desired ends were automatically reinforced, and undesirable behaviour like idleness, sickness and crime were eliminated or diminished.

Such engineering required the administrative machinery for government interventions on a scale that had never been contemplated before this period. Chadwick was no democrat, and had scant respect for the parliamentary system. He advocated 'scientific' legislation, based on careful research and planning by permanent officials.[21]

The business of the civil service is the preparation of administrative improvements, is to examine consequences carefully, the ultimate and contingent as well as the immediate, the collateral as well as the direct. His business is to place before the Minister or through him to the Legislature, a sketch of the probable future more correct and complete than would have presented itself in the midst of present influences.

Before the 1830s, no such body of trained investigators and specialised experts existed in the government service. Chadwick's influence was in the direction not only of a larger bureaucracy, but also of a better trained and organised one. Open competition for entry to the Civil Service (introduced in 1870) was not, in itself, enough. He wanted cost efficiency analyses, time and motion studies, and the recruitment of experienced businessmen and managers to higher posts. He was also concerned with the evolution of bureaucratic structures, interdepartmental committees and the creation of an efficient chain of responsibility and control.

The creation of such a service changed the methods and functions of government, and made possible interventions that would previously have been beyond its scope. Before the 1830s, the business of both local and national government was mainly concerned with raising taxes, keeping the peace and maintaining the nation's defences. By the 1850s, Chadwick at least was recommending an extension of state enterprise which went beyond the powers of inspection, supervision and control he had already secured through the Factory Inspectorate, the Poor Law Board and the Board of Health. 'He wanted local authorities to go into business, and provide their own municipal waterworks and cemeteries.'[22] Where public works could not be put out to tender, for the most efficient firm to gain the contract, 'he urged that the capitals should be consolidated under one ownership and placed under the direct control of the State.'[23] He advocated the extension of public management of industry wherever waste and inefficiency could thus be prevented—for instance, in gas supplies. 'The earlier politico-economical doctrines as to competition must now receive considerable modifications ... To the question sometimes put to me—where would I stop the application of my principle—I am at present only prepared to answer "Where waste stops".'[24] He insisted that public enterprises like the Post Office, the drainage system and the prison administration were[25]

in promptitude and efficiency . . . so advanced as to be beyond a large proportion of joint stock-management and equal to professional or private establishments under individual direction. They sustain the conclusion that it is practicable to place the civil service *generally* in advance at every point of that private management which has been held up for imitation.

In all these opinions, Chadwick was well ahead of his contemporaries, and it was not for several decades that his advanced notions were considered as possible programmes for government action. From the 1870s onwards, positive interventions by local authorities (as in Chamberlain's Birmingham) indicated potential developments; yet the pace of change was very slow. Liberalism continued to be suspicious of interference with market forces, and aware of the dangers of corrupting the poor by doles. Under Gladstone, the Liberal Party remained true to its vision of a unified society, in which individual members of all classes participated as moral equals. Moral improvement could never be achieved by economic means. 'Collectivism, construction, socialism, were all anathema to Gladstone until the end of his life. His measures had aimed at the fulfilment of great moral ideas rather than the distribution of small material gains.'[26] At the end of his career, in 1891, under pressure from his radical wing, he endorsed the 'Newcastle Programme', which included a hotchpotch of state regulation of industry and welfare provision. But it was not until much later, after the landslide election victory of 1906, that the Liberals implemented a programme of social welfare reforms.

There has been a great deal of debate and disagreement between historians about the origins of these reforms by a government that was pledged to none of them (except progressive taxation) when it came to power. For the purposes of this chapter, their importance lay in the differences between their aims and Chadwick's principles of intervention, and their introduction of a new range of state institutions, dealing directly with citizens, and affecting their daily lives. To take first the example of health provision: the government was being urged (by the Minority group in the new Royal Commission on the Poor Laws) to adopt a much more thoroughgoing approach to the prevention of illness, through a reform of local government and its finances, and the break-up of the Poor Law. Instead, it chose a limited system of health insurance, which provided sickness benefits to some workers, and which proved to be a bonanza for the doctors, with their pink liquids and pills. Whereas Chadwick was concerned primarily with suppressing what he saw as the most conspicuous and destructive evils that gave rise to sickness and disability, Lloyd George dealt only with the consequences, and even then put almost half the cost of insurance on the worker. Instead of attempting a radical intervention which would influence economic processes, the reform aimed at compensating some of the victims of these processes by means of benefits.

Yet the Liberals were very unwilling to make such compensatory benefits available as rights. To take the example of unemployment benefit: the aim of the scheme was to provide temporary cover for workers in those trades that dealt with recessions by laying people off rather than by introducing short-time working.[27] The insurance principle was essential, both to finance the scheme without extra taxation, and to allow a differentiation between a group of workers who were treated as worthy of assistance, and another group, not covered by insurance, who were seen as justifying the harsh and punitive methods of the Poor Law, because of their improvidence and idleness. But even within the scheme, the cover was short term, and did not include those who lost employment through misconduct, while 'benefits were kept low to avoid encouraging unemployment'.[28] Thus, although the National Insurance Act of 1911 recognised a class of individuals, both unemployed and sick, whose misfortunes were not to be held to be their own responsibility, and whose assistance was to be provided outside the Poor Law, it gave the state limited responsibility for these victims, and even less for preventing the causes of their distress. An awareness of the wider economic processes giving rise to poverty and disease had not led to collectivist interventions in those processes.

Furthermore, the institutional expression of greater state involvement in social problems was in the direction of closer control over and supervision of the working class. Except for old-age pensions, which were non-contributory and distributed through the post office, the Liberal

measures   gave rise to national bureaucracies which regulated and
monitored workers' behaviour. Labour Exchanges were the first such
institutions, followed by the machinery of national insurance. The
government was anxious about the threat of disorder among the
unemployed, and feared a repetition of the riots of 1886 and 1887; these
measures tended to separate off the respectable redundant from the
habitually work-shy and the casual labourers. The new breed of civil
servants dealt almost entirely with working people at the face-to-face
level, supervising claims and establishing titles to benefits. Their
controlling functions did not escape the notice of writers at the time, who
saw that these institutions were no real substitute for radical changes in
the economic structure. 'To the poor, economic reform means a measure
of justice between the "haves" and the "have-nots"; but social reform
means "police" whether they are really required or not.'[29] Similarly,
Belloc described unemployment insurance as the imposition of a
regulating law on the worker, in exchange for benefits, which would give
rise to 'a servile state'.[30]

The economic and political climate of this period of Liberal
Government was one of increasingly overt conflict between Capital and
Labour. In the Taff Vale and Osborne Judgments, the House of Lords had
lent its support to the growth of a confident and aggressive mood amongst
employers, while the rise of the Labour Party and, later, a wave of militant
industrial action, indicated the resistance of the working class. The tactics
of the Liberal Government in the face of this conflict were opportunistic
and expedient. While steadily losing support in the country, and
eventually reduced (after two further general elections over Lloyd
George's budget) to minority rule, depending on Irish and Labour Party
votes, they introduced reforms which were sometimes ingenious
innovations, sometimes responses to pressures. The voice of Liberalism
would, according to Dangerfield, have been 'utterly lost in a world where
there were no dukes to hate and no poor to pity'.[31] Their measures were
directed against the rich, who were to be penalised for their monopolistic
excesses by progressive taxation; yet they 'were not designed to advance
the worker, but to propitiate him'. They aimed at diverting attention
from the more radical critique of the social order advanced by the
socialists; at using forms of state intervention consistent with
nineteenth-century individualism and its view of economic liberty. While
they had none of the Victorian optimism which accompanied a belief in
capitalism's ability to surmount all barriers to progress, they were none
the less unwilling to take the measures necessary to counteract its sinister
influences, or to use the state as an economic force in its own right.
Conscious of a slowing of economic growth, and of all the threats to
British supremacy, they were concerned with the defence of the kind of
society which produced Liberal majorities, 'where social ills would be
medicated but never cured; and where the ideal man would come more

and more to resemble an honest, tolerant, intolerable grocer.'[32] Their characteristic innovation was not so much the creation of an embryonic Welfare State, though their bureaucratic national agencies certainly laid the pattern for its institutional form. It was rather that, as a weak government caught between the rival offensives of Capital and Labour, they sought to defuse the conflict by creating the framework for a truce, a new set of institutions through which workers could be compensated for disadvantages rather than given any real improvement in their relative status or power. Whereas Chadwick saw his interventions as concerned with the unwanted byproducts of a largely benevolent industrial process, the Liberal Government was attempting to deal with structural problems of the economy (like falling wages and rising unemployment) by means of marginal welfare interventions.

The new institutions did create something of a buffer between the conflicting classes, and this buffer was sufficiently resilient with modifications and extensions to absorb the pressures of the inter-war years. Many of the conflicts between the employing class and the workers in this period were about welfare benefits—their terms, their levels, their duration. The existence of a less punitive way of dealing with unemployment than the Poor Law represented both a hope and an alternative focus for demands and protests. In his book *The Devil's Decade*, Claud Cockburn traces the political struggles of the 1930s over unemployment benefits and public assistance, and shows how administrative decisions were intertwined with political issues, and economic measures with class conflict and the regulation of the poor. The May Report of 1931 recommended a 20 per cent cut in the rates of unemployment benefit as one of the measures to balance the budget. The newly created Public Assistance Committees had begun to administer a harsher means test than had existed in the 1920s under the Poor Law Board of Guardians; now, as a result of the economy measures, 'transitional' unemployment benefits, too, became means-tested. The militant organisation of the unemployed, the National Unemployed Workers' Movement (whose slogan was 'Work at trade union rates or full maintenance'), attacked these measures by protest meetings and marches. In September 1932 prolonged rioting and clashes between police and demonstrators in Birkenhead followed the application of means tests to transitional benefits; many other Committees resisted implementing the test, and two were taken over by government commissioners. In April 1934, in the face of persistent NUWM pressure and growing public outcry, the standard rates of unemployment benefit were restored. But in the following year the newly created Unemployment Assistance Board which relieved the unreliable Public Assistance Committees of their responsibilities for the administration of means tests to the unemployed, introduced new scales which amounted to 'bold reductions right across the board'. The reaction to this was[33] immediate and sustained in every sector. The anthracite miners called a twenty-four hour protest strike. The South Wales Miners' Federation called an All-Wales conference and set up a council of action. In that area 300,000 people demonstrated. In Scotland and on Tyneside, as in South Wales, protesting women smashed the windows and sometimes stoned the doorways of the UAB offices. Protests came not only from innumerable individual borough councillors and county councillors but from whole county councils and local authorities speaking as elected bodies. Groups of doctors protested, religious organisations of all denominations protested. And many local Labour parties joined with the Communists in protest.

Within a matter of weeks the Government announced that any effective cuts in benefits would be restored.

It was thus over the provisions of the embryonic Welfare State that many of the bitterest political conflicts of the 1930s were fought, on issues which divided both the Labour Party and the trade union movement. Yet in a sense, the existence of these institutions as a battleground protected the Government from what might otherwise have been uglier conflicts. The Conservative ministers who effectively controlled the National Government used considerable skill in their alternation between attacks on the standards of living of the working class through cuts in benefit rates, and timely concessions when the power of the NUWM and its supporters threatened law and order (as in 1932 and 1935). Unemployment benefit and unemployment assistance represented the focus for a truce, an uneasy equilibrium which had been reached by 1935. Without these institutions, the class-based recommendations of the May Report, which saw the servicing of the National Debt as a higher priority than the provision of a subsistence standard of living to workers and the unemployed, might have served to drive larger numbers of people into communist or fascist activism. The achievement of the NUWM was to mobilise working-class opposition so effectively as to discredit and destroy the principle of 'less eligibility', and so to clear the ground for the creation of the post-war welfare institutions.

It was thus the experiences of the 1930s, as well as the isolation and deprivation of wartime, that led to the election of a new government, committed to the notion of a universal 'national minimum' standard of life, which the Welfare State should ensure. The post-war Labour Government set up state provision for a comprehensive health service, a planned supply of housing, universal secondary education, for family allowances and for social security for all whose earnings had ceased or were interrupted; it placed under state control the production and distribution of fuel and power; it was also committed to use economic interventions to maintain the level of employment.

Yet none of these provisions defined any new relationships either between individuals in society, or between the individual and society. The

Welfare State, according to its official fanfare, was to be the expression of 'the solidarity and unity of the nation, which in war have been its bulwark against aggression'.[34] This solidarity rested on hostility to a common enemy, and the unity which it produced had neither form nor purpose once the war was over. The national insurance scheme might provide for 'all citizens to stand together, without exclusions based on difference of status, function or wealth',[35] but the only fresh obligation to the state this entailed was the payment of contributions by those who had not previously done so; and as to obligations to each other, whether standing side by side or any other way, the addition involved by these measures was nil. The situation had hardly changed since the 1834 Poor Law Report defined the duties of rich and poor towards each other: the rich to make their required contribution to the common fund, without exploiting it to their advantage; the poor to live in such a way as to be 'the proper managers of their own concerns, that a man's wages ought to depend on his services, not on his wants, that the earnings of an ordinary labourer are naturally equal to the support of an ordinary family, that the welfare of that family naturally depends on his conduct, and he is bound to exercise any sort of prudence or economy'.[36] In short, industry, diligence and family responsibility, the traditional nineteenth-century virtues, were still the basis of social obligation.

What the state now proposed to do for its subjects, many a benevolent mill-owner had done for his employees. Provision for housing, health, education and social security neither created nor was created by 'solidarity' between employer and employees, nor between the employees themselves. What benevolent mill-owners did, they did for the sake of greater efficiency, higher productivity, and better industrial relations (i.e. the smooth running of the mill). The same strengths and weaknesses accompanied the provisions of the Welfare State. Protection against life's misfortunes and against poverty in old age, and the promotion of healthy and cheerful efficiency, are clearly a form of welfare. That this form of welfare gave rise to both insularity and conservatism had been proved in the 1930s in towns like Rishton in Lancashire, where well-cared-for workers stayed true to their Tory traditions, ignoring the militancy and co-operative solidarity of their more deprived fellow workers in Birkenhead and Bootle.

Concern for the kind of welfare characteristic of a paternalistic employer was increasingly evident in the Labour Party under the leadership of first Gaitskell and then Wilson. It was the Labour leadership that first used higher productivity as a political catchword; it was Labour that emphasised the technological revolution, greater efficiency and the 'redeployment of labour'. The Labour leadership has colluded in the tendency for political debate to imply that growth in the gross national product is more important than the quality of the society it sustains, than the priorities of that society, or the relationships between its members. The Labour leadership has used adjustments and additions to the benefits of the Welfare State, not to restructure our society, but to provide compensations or rewards to disadvantaged sectors of the population, the victims of industrial processes or social change.

The theoretical underpinnings of many of these attitudes and policies were revealed in Anthony Crosland's *The Future of Socialism* in 1956. Crosland argued that the politics of class conflict were no longer realistic in a situation where government had explicitly accepted[37]

> responsibility for full employment, the rate of growth, the balance of payments and the distribution of incomes. The main instrument for exercising this responsibility is fiscal policy . . . the government can exert any influence it likes on income-distribution, and can also determine within broad limits the division of total output between consumption, investment, exports and social expenditure.

As employer of 25 per cent of the workforce and a major source of investment expenditure, it could control productive decisions. Both state-owned and private-owned industries were similarly managed by salaried experts, and both should pursue the maximisation of investment through profit, which was the source of growth and dynamism, and 'determines both the strength and prestige of the firm, and the power and social status of its executives'.[38] He suggested that the essential characteristic of both types of modern industry was their large scale, which inevitably led to a concentration of decision-making powers in a few managerial hands, thus reducing the potential power of both workers and shareholders. He dismissed the notion of workers' control as outmoded and unrealistic in an age of technology and mass production; workers should take advantage of opportunities to earn good wages, and leave management to the experts, and politics to the politicians. Socialism should concentrate on giving priority to the socially unfortunate, and to the elimination of bad social conditions, and it should be concerned with the creation of social equality and a classless society. The former aim had already been more than partially achieved since 'traditional capitalism has been reformed and modified almost out of existence . . . Instead of glaring and conspicuous evils, squalor and injustice and distressed areas, we have to fuss about the balance of payments, and incentives, and higher productivity'.[39] The latter was largely a problem of re-education and changing attitudes; further equalisation of incomes through government interventions was no longer economically viable.

Such managerial politics have eventually created the general opinion among the electorate that government intervention is intended solely to reinforce, supplement or strengthen capitalist endeavour, to maximise productivity and profitability. Thus the public consensus and the mass media are outraged when Mr Wedgwood Benn advocates measures in relation to state financial involvement in industry which are little more than the application of the philosophy of Edwin Chadwick.

At the level of compensatory benefits what is different about modern Welfare State interventions from anything that Chadwick would have recommended is that the overtly punitive measures he considered essential were removed. Chadwick was convinced that the only way to achieve the diligence and industry necessary for an improving standard of living was to make the idle, imprudent and inefficient suffer: 'we do not believe that a country in which . . . every man, whatever be his conduct or character, [is] ensured a *comfortable* existence, can retain its prosperity or even its civilisation.'[40] The Welfare State appeared, with its unconditional 'national minimum' for all, to have challenged that notion. However, within a few years, that challenge had become muted. First provisions became more differentiated—the better-off received a different level of benefit or service than the worse-off. Then there was introduced a greater measure of discretion. Supplementary benefits were created to take over a much wider role than the residual National Assistance Board. Then, supplementary benefits in turn became more conditional, more aware of the dangers of abuse, more hedged about with disqualifications and special investigations. Finally, for a proportion of the poorest, a far greater element of supervision and control, as well as discretion, was introduced, with the use of social workers with powers of intervention at a personal level into the lives and families of claimants, demanding individualised behaviour changes as qualifications for benefits. Ultimately, it seems, social policy has edged its way back to Chadwick's point of view—but not overtly, not in principle. While still posing as the benevolent and rewarding paternalists of the immediate post-war period, governments have subtly reintroduced many of the controls and punishments of the Poor Law.

This would not have surprised Lloyd George. The man whose talent for improvisation produced the insurance principle on the basis of health and unemployment benefits, wrote soon afterwards that he considered it a temporary expedient, and that the Poor Law represented a far more comprehensive provision. It is to the traditions of that provision that I shall turn in the next chapter.

10
Two Concepts of Welfare

The interventions discussed in the last chapter took place against a background of an earlier form of state provision. Chadwick himself was as involved with the Poor Law as with the new services he initiated. All the interventions that have developed since the early nineteenth century have presupposed the existence of a system of poor relief which underpinned them. The Poor Law was, and in many ways still is, the fundamental basis upon which all other notions of 'welfare' provision are founded.

Yet the Poor Law was never a monolithic structure. A number of different, and often conflicting, aims and objectives, themes and counter-themes, principles and practices have characterised its history since the Elizabethan Acts of 1597-1601. The attempt, within the same limited system of provision, to create a framework to deal with the able-bodied unemployed, with unmarried mothers, with widows and orphans, with the sick, the mentally and physically handicapped, the insane, and the elderly, entailed inevitable contradictions. On the one hand, the prevention of idleness and fraud, the maintenance of law and order, and the enforcement of family responsibility; on the other hand, the provision of care, treatment, asylum and a last refuge: these functions were found to conflict and compete, both in the principles behind the legislation on poor relief, and in the practices of those who provided it. To give just one example: in the history of workhouses from the early seventeenth century to the early twentieth can be seen a perpetual struggle between central government and local administrators, the one seeking to establish institutions at once deterrent of idleness and conducive to habits of industry, the other, mainly for reasons of economy, concerned with the long-term provision of residential care for the chronically dependent.

But at an even deeper level than this kind of issue, there has existed a fundamental polarisation about the nature and purposes of poor relief, which has been fought out between two opposing philosophies throughout this history. Two rival concepts of welfare are even today being debated within and between political parties, the major social services and social work agencies. Both polarities were reflected in the system of poor relief that operated between 1601 and 1795; but since then the two have alternated in their supremacy.

Edwin Chadwick based his notion of the modern state and its role in bringing about an artificial harmony between private and public interests on a very strict and pure version of one of these notions of welfare. This was that each and every citizen must live his life in the expectation of providing for every necessity in it, both for himself and for all his dependants (in sickness and in health, in his full vigour and in his old age), out of his earnings from his employment. For the state to provide for any of these needs in such a way as to give rise to the expectation that they might be comfortably met without any care or exertion on his part would be to risk the corruption of the morals of *all* its citizens. On the one hand, for a man who received such comfortable provision, the temptation to rely completely upon it, to make no effort to be responsible for himself and his own, could turn him into a demanding dependant who expected everything to be done for him. On the other hand, a man who attempted to provide for himself would be penalised for doing so. Both his skill and diligence in employment and his prudent provision for his family would be devalued in relation to the other, for the other would be receiving a comfortable provision for doing nothing. Indeed, for the industrious and prudent man, his income, his savings and his property would all disqualify him from receiving the provision which the other acquired by idleness and improvidence; they would thus become a burden and a disadvantage, to be disposed of as quickly as possible in order to qualify for assistance.

The Poor Law Report of 1834, of which Chadwick was part-author, thus insisted that a sharp and explicitly punitive distinction be made between the independent labourer and the pauper. 'The first and most essential of all conditions [for relieving a man's destitution] . . . is that his situation on the whole shall not be made really or apparently so eligible as the situation of the independent labourer of the lowest class.'[1] Hence its recommendation that '. . . all relief whatever to able bodied persons other than in well-regulated workhouses . . . shall be declared unlawful.'[2] The conditions under which claimants should be relieved in such workhouses were[3]

to provide . . . *the necessaries of life*, but *nothing more*, to keep them closely to work, and in all respects under such restrictions, that though no man who was *really in want* would hesitate for a moment to comply with them, yet he would submit to them no longer than he could help; and would rather do his utmost *to find work* by which he could support himself than accept parish pay.

The offer of relief on the principle suggested by us would be a self-acting test of the claim of the applicant . . . By the means which we propose, the line between those who do and those who do not need relief is drawn, and drawn perfectly. If the claimant does not comply with the terms on which relief is given to the destitute, he gets nothing; and if he does comply, the compliance proves the truth of the claim—namely his destitution.

The notion of welfare which this account of poor relief presupposed was not of the individual welfare of claimants (relieving hardship, meeting need) but of the welfare of society as a whole. The report made it perfectly clear that it was concerned to create a healthy society, and that in order to achieve this, some individuals had to suffer. Indeed, it was only by the exemplary punishment of the few idle and improvident individuals who would require relief that the vast majority of the community could be enabled to be prosperous and virtuous. Once attempts were made to use state funds to alleviate distress, however unfortunately it might have come about, society as a whole was injured.[4]

even if it be in some rare cases a hardship [for a person of good character to enter the workhouse], it appears from the evidence that it is a hardship to which the good of society requires the applicant to submit. The express or implied ground of his application is, that he is in danger of perishing from want. Requesting to be rescued out of that danger out of the property of others, he must accept assistance on the terms, whatever they may be, which the welfare requires. The bane of all pauper legislation has been the legislating for extreme cases. Every exception, every violation of the general rule to meet a real case of unusual hardship, lets in a whole class of fraudulent cases by which that rule must in time be destroyed. Where cases of real hardship occur, the remedy must be applied by individual charity, a virtue for which no system of compulsory relief can be or ought to be a substitute.

The report was, of course, an explicit attack on the system of relief for the able-bodied which had developed in the years since 1795. This system embodied a completely different view of welfare, and an alternative model of society. This second concept of welfare suggested that poverty could be relieved in such a way as to prevent hardship, misery and resentment amongst the poor, and thus to prevent civic unrest and disorder. Instead of attempting to create a harmony of *interests* between all free citizens, as the 1834 Act did, it attempted to construct a harmonious society by recognising and providing differently for quite separate interests and needs in two sharply distinguished sectors of the community. In this way, the poor could be assisted; but not in the way one might consider assisting individuals from the other sector. All assistance should be conditional, and the conditions attached to it should reflect the necessity to supervise and regulate the poor, for the sake of ensuring their welfare. For this concept of welfare started from an assumption that a certain proportion of the population were incapable of managing their own affairs without assistance of one kind or another. The system of poor relief should always take account of their inadequacies and never provide for them in such a way as to give them more freedom and choice than they were capable of using beneficially. The state should expect to intervene frequently into the lives of the poor and their families, and once it gained admission it should exercise some form of control. Each need should be separately provided for as it arose: thus there should be provision for assistance with rent, food, clothing, fuel, and separate application should be made by individuals experiencing difficulties in managing any of these expenses. But all assistance should demand in return a pattern of behaviour in keeping with the definition of the role of the poor which this concept of welfare prescribed.

Whereas the first concept of welfare was about the welfare of the community as a whole, the second was thus about the welfare of the one particular sector, the poor; it defined, provided for and supervised the poor in such a way as to ensure that this version of their welfare was firmly implemented. It rested on the distinction between those citizens of whom it was reasonable to expect responsibility, diligence, prudence and independence, and those who required assistance. The latter's burdens were usually described in terms of paternalistic benevolence. Thus, for instance, William Pitt insisted in 1796 that there should be 'a proper line of distinction between those who are able to provide for themselves by their labour, and those who, having enriched the country with a number of children, have a claim upon its assistance for support.'[5]

In one sense, this approach was obviously more generous to the poor than the other. By relieving according to need rather than destitution, it allowed specific forms of assistance to people with some income and some property. In the same speech, Pitt argued that the exclusion of persons in employment from relief created a form of stigma, which should be removed; the system of public assistance should be liberal, flexible and free from elements of opprobrium and contempt. The Act of 1796 abolished the old workhouse test, and the provision that paupers should wear badges proclaiming their status:[6]

> Whereas the said provision . . . has been found to have been, and to be, inconvenient and oppressive, inasmuch as it often prevents an industrious poor person from receiving such occasional relief as is best suited to the peculiar case of such poor persons; and inasmuch as in certain cases it holds out conditions of relief, injurious to the comfort, and domestic situation, and happiness of such poor persons.

However, the conditions attached to the relief of labourers in employment made this system a doubtful boon. The Commissioners of

1834 found various methods in operation, the general purpose of which was to ensure that all labourers received a total income equal to their family's requirements (neither less nor more) made up partly out of wages for work, and partly out of public assistance. In some cases, the parish automatically made up the wages of those in regular employment, according to a scale related to the numbers of their children and the price of bread. In others, 'the parish . . . makes some general agreement with a farmer to sell him the labour of one or more paupers at a certain price, and pays the pauper, out of the parish funds, the difference between that price and the allowance which the scale . . . awards him.'[7] 'In many places the . . . system is affected by means of an auction . . . [At] Yardley, Hastings, all the unemployed men are put up to sale weekly and ten men [were] knocked down to one of the farmers for 5s.'[8]

In the Poor Law Report, the case against these and other practices was stated with overwhelming force. Its attack on them was in terms of the fundamentally selfish motives and corrupt methods of those who implemented them as a way to keep wages down 'even if they pay in rates what they would otherwise pay in wages, they prefer the payment of rates which recur at intervals, and payment of which may, from time to time, be put off, to the weekly ready-money expenditure of wages. High rates too are a ground for demanding an abatement from rent; high wages are not.'[9] The farmers 'prefer that the labourers should be slaves; they object to their having gardens, saying, The more they work for themselves, the less they will for us. They wish that every man should receive an allowance from the parish according to his family, and declare that high wages and free labour would overwhelm them!'[10] In manufacturing industry, some employers gained an unfair advantage over competitors by employing pauper labour at wages subsidised by the parish. 'Whole branches of manufacture may thus follow the course not of coal mines or of streams, but of pauperism; may flourish like funguses that spring from corruption, in consequence of the abuses which are ruining all the other interests of the places in which they are established.'[11] In concluding their remarks about the evil of the system, the authors of the report stated, 'We have endeavoured to account for it by the immediate gain which large classes have hoped to obtain, and in many cases have obtained from the maladministration, and from the constitution and character of the authorities by whom parochial relief is distributed and awarded.'[12]

Time and again, the report illustrated rural parishes in which the system of relief had distorted, corrupted and depraved the life of the community. The system of rate rebates for small, cheap properties caused a boom in speculative building of shoddy houses.[13] Rent guarantees were provided out of the poor rates to landlords, who, if not overseers themselves, were often relatives or friends.[14] Fuel debts were often met on a similar basis. The allowance system encouraged early marriages and large families.[15] The report built up a picture of shortsightedness, jobbery and corruption of almost millennial proportions, the apocalypse of which was the case of Cholesbury, an unfortunate parish in Buckinghamshire. Here the rates rose from £10 11s per year to £367 per year, whereupon[16]

> the landlords having given up their rents, the farmers their tenancies, and the clergyman his glebe and his tithes, . . . in October, 1832, the parish officers threw up their books. In Cholesbury, therefore, the expense of maintaining the poor has not merely swallowed up the whole value of the land; it requires even the assistance of two years of rates in aid from other parishes to enable the able-bodied, after the land has been given up to them, to support themselves.

In place of this chaos, the authors of the report constructed an alternative picture of a happy, functional community, with complementary social roles and reciprocal obligations, where virtue was recognised and rewarded at every level, where there existed a moral if not a material equality between citizens. If the Poor Law was to be the punitive instrument of this harmonious organism, the corollary was the freedom and dignity of even the humblest labourer. The only distinction of status which the law should recognise was that between the vast mass of independent citizens, and a 'small disreputable minority' of paupers, 'whose resentment was not to be feared, and whose favour was of no value; all other classes were anxious to diminish the number of applicants, and to reduce the expense of their maintenance.'[17]

However, the report provided a very dubious account of how the labourers it was so anxious to dispauperise were to attain the means of survival, let alone of self-fulfilment. While it provided some impressionistic evidence of higher wages and better treatment for workers in districts where the abuses of the allowance system and the labour rate had been discontinued, its promises rested ultimately on highly theoretical economics; on a theory of how with the abolition of subsidisation, 'first, the labourer becomes more steady and diligent; next, the more efficient labour makes the return to the farmer's capital larger, and the consequent increase of the fund for the employment of labour enables and induces the capitalist to give better wages.'[18] Furthermore, although it claimed to be equally concerned with the morals of every sector of the community, it actually described the behaviour of only two groups within it. In the first place, it talked of the administrators, the magistrates, the overseers and the members of vestries, about whose corruption it was fearlessly critical. But its second and main target was the working class, the actual or potential recipients of relief. It described this class as highly corruptible and vulnerable to demoralising influences in precisely those areas with which the corrupters were concerned—namely the provision of material and financial assistance. The caricature of a whole class of persons, intrinsically virtuous, independent, frugal, thrifty, industrious, much given to the care of its gardens and its few pigs or cows; yet on the other hand, once assisted in cash or kind, however sparingly, however occasionally, then immediately reduced to the most depraved and wretched bestiality—irresponsible, greedy, feckless, improvident in marriage, prolific yet neglectful in child-bearing and child-rearing, lawless, vicious, idle, fradulent; this ambivalent caricature has been passed down as one of the terrible legacies of the 1834 Poor Law.

Furthermore, the analysis it presented of a static village community was already considerably outdated before the report was written. In the last chapter we saw how the authors recognised in manufacturing industry an exception to their own maxims about the skill, diligence and dignity necessary for the independent labourer. Factory work was mechanical, unskilled, repetitive, and required only supervision and correction. Thus the dignity of the independent labourer could not be guaranteed by his wages. The stable rural hierarchy, the customary reciprocal definitions of the duties of each complementary social class, which the report attempted (with its references to Elizabethan statutes) nostalgically to re-create, was already condemned by the Industrial Revolution, by social and geographical mobility. Indeed, Chadwick for one, as a member of a manufacturing family, recognised full well that the adaptations of the Poor Law which he was criticising were in many respects one of the last organised efforts of the old rural elite to defend its privileges and advantages against the growing power of a new urban middle class, and that it was only the mounting crime rate and the outbreak of rioting and rebellion that had made this elite willing to dismantle this part of its machinery of rural protectionism. What the new law would create was precisely a free labour market, in which the rural poor, too numerous for the work available on newly capitalised farms, could move into the city, and swell the ranks of the industrial urban proletariat.

Hence it was the manufacturing sector of the economy, which the report hardly discussed, which provided the key to the future success or failure of the methods of poor relief which were proposed. Organised mass resistance to the new measures in the industrial North prevented their implementation for a time, and caused considerable modifications in administrative practice from the reports blueprint. But after the repeal of the other bastion of rural protectionism, the Corn Laws, the more prosperous and peaceful 1850s and 1860s allowed the working class to adapt its own institutions—trade unions, friendly societies, co-operatives and building societies—to provide for the misfortunes against which wages from employment were no guarantee, and to protect their members from the harshness of the Poor Law. But not all members of the working class were members of such organisations, and non-organised labour was the most vulnerable to unemployment in particular. As capitalist processes advanced, the percentage of the work force in regular employment did not increase,[19] and the fluctuations of the trade cycle became more marked. As working-class representation in central and local government grew, some kind of state protection against cyclical unemployment and chronic underemployment was demanded.

The measures taken by the Liberal Government of 1906-14 have been mentioned in the last chapter. These measures were in tune with the recommendations of a consensus of expert opinion. Both the Majority and Minority Reports of the Royal Commission on the Poor Laws (1905-9) gave considerable attention to the persistence of unemployment, short-time working and casual employment—the latter two conditions tending to reflect an attempt by industries to keep a reserve of labour equal to their maximum demand. Both reports made the organisation of the labour market by a national system of labour exchanges their principal recommendation, and both also endorsed the notion of insurance against unemployment. Yet neither of these measures was anywhere near adequate to deal with the situation in the 1930s, and Beveridge, writing during the Second World War, reached the Keynesian conclusion that 'the only way to ensure full employment in a free society was to create sufficient demand for the products of industry, so that the labour market should always be a seller's market rather than a buyer's',[20] thus counteracting the attempt by employers to keep a reserve pool of unemployed workers. Given that there were always more vacancies than men looking for jobs, Beveridge was confident that earnings would rise, provided always that 'responsible' trade union leadership exercised the restraint necessary to prevent a spiral of inflation. With skilled management by the state of aggregate demand, with planning of the direction of the demand, with organisation of the labour market, with a fair policy on pay and prices, and the co-operation of the trade unions to avoid industrial strife, the national income would rise steadily, and with it so would the real value of wages.

Yet by the mid-1960s, research was drawing attention to a problem which had been largely neglected since the Poor Law Amendment Act of 1834. With a very few exceptions, low wages had not been the object of social policy since that Act abolished their subsidisation out of the poor rates, and where low wages were combined with large numbers of children, the only compensation provided by the state was the small, weekly payment of a family allowance (at a level which had not altered since 1948 and which was the same for all citizens, rich and poor). The existence of an estimated one and a half million families whose earnings from employment provided a less than national assistance level of income,[21] and the mounting pressure of middle-class opinion outraged by this revelation caused government of both parties to reconsider the received wisdom of 1834 on this question. Eventually it was the Conservative Government that in 1970, following the lead of its Labour predecessor which had introduced selective rate and rent rebates, but taking the principle to its logical conclusion, revived the notion of wage subsidisation with the family income supplement. After nearly a century and a half of disfavour, the second concept of welfare had made its comeback.

The parallels between the philosophies and methods of the Tory legislators in 1796 and 1970 are extremely marked. Just as Pitt had argued that the exclusion of persons in employment from relief created an inflexibility which precluded the maximisation of selective assistance to the poor, so Sir Keith Joseph justified the family income supplement on the grounds that it would open the way for the whole poor sector to benefit from a range of specific benefits and subsidies. 'We hope to use it to provide a passport for the poorest to all the remissions available. It will give us contact with the poorest working class households about which far too little is known, and give us knowledge to ensure these families apply for rent and rate rebates.'[22] Thus the philosophy of the 1834 Report, which provided 'no motive for undue interference'[23] was replaced by a concept of welfare which demanded detailed knowledge about the income and expenditure of every poor family; which involved the state, item by item, in its separate needs for rent, rates, school meals, medical treatment, butter and beef. The poor who, for the previous century and a half, had been so scrupulously left unassisted, to budget on their earnings, on pain of instant corruption, suddenly found themselves in receipt of a grocer's list of their needs, and a bureaucratic test of their eligibility for assistance with each one of them.

Taken together with the creation of supplementary benefits in 1966, which raised considerably the amount of savings that had reduced or precluded qualification under the national assistance regulations, this increase in the use of selective benefits widened their scope to include people who would previously have been well outside the ambit of income maintenance provision; like the measure of 1796 it created a whole class of 'the poor' where previously there had existed only individuals on low incomes. Yet for the growing body of opinion within the legislature and the executive which favoured the second concept of welfare, even this did not go far enough. The provision of rebates, supplements, subsidies and coupons for each separate need did nothing to ensure that the poor applied these benefits in a manner appropriate to their welfare as a whole; it was still possible for them, within the scope of that part of their income not specifically earmarked for such needs, to mismanage to the extent of accumulating fuel debts or rent arrears, to get themselves evicted or to become destitute, quite apart from their well-known propensities towards family instability, delinquency and mental illness. What was required, therefore, was a combination of material assistance with supervision, a form of intervention at a much more personal level, concerned with the day-to-day details of the lives of the poor, one which would deal as much with the turmoil of their disruptive family relationships as with the chaos of their depleted finances. Such interventions could only be provided by social workers.

The most advanced expression of this notion of local authority provision was Section 12 of the Social Work (Scotland) Act, 1968, which stated, 'It shall be the duty of every local authority to promote social welfare by making available advice, guidance and assistance on such a scale as may be appropriate for their area.' This was a development of Section 1 of the Children and Young Persons Act, 1963, which provided for 'such advice, guidance and assistance as may promote the welfare of children by diminishing the need to receive children into or keep them in care.' In practice, both these provisions have increasingly meant that social services departments of local authorities encourage applications from and referrals of people with particular kinds of material problems—homelessness, rent arrears, fuel bills, debts or destitution—and then, in the name of 'keeping the family together', make limited payment, often on a loan basis, and usually accompanied by some form of supervision of the family's subsequent performance. This type of intervention epitomises the notion of the inadequacy of the poor: that their need is not so much a purely financial one as a mixture of poverty and incapacity; that their offspring can only be protected from the fecklessness of their parents by making relief of their needs conditional, specific and supervised. This form of social work is rapidly replacing the post-war, non-material kind (which was based on Beveridge's optimistic assumptions about the 'National Minimum').[24]

> Recent surveys have shown that although financial aid only accounts for a small proportion of the budgets of the social work department (about 1 percent) in some areas the vast majority of clients come to social work departments looking for financial aid rather than for more traditional work assistance. Thus it has been estimated that in Glasgow some 80% of all initial enquiries are in relation to financial assistance.

Almost 50 per cent of financial aid in Scotland is in the form of loans, and this method is also widely used in England, not so much because of the possibility of recovery, as for the opportunity of continued involvement by the social worker with the family.

The mechanics of such interventions follow very closely the precedents of the old Poor Law. Rent guarantees are of a form remarkably similar to the one quoted in the Report of 1834 in which W. Hughes, overseer, promised to pay the rent of a pauper to W. Hughes, landlord.[25] One local authority department guarantees the rent of a tenant in arrears to another local authority department to avoid eviction. Similarly, social services make agreements to pay the bed and breakfast or guest house charges of homeless families for indefinite periods. In Scotland, where fuel bills have become a specialised area of social work assistance, the Gas and Electricity Boards have reached a general arrangement with social work departments, in which the fuel authorities' commercial obligations and rights to protection against bad debts are recognised, and social work departments accept a primary role in providing lump sum payments to clear debts.[26] In effect, social workers are doing the work of housing authorities and public utilities, and often as a result of the policies of those organisations (for instance, the cessation of door-to-door rent collection, or the absence of slot meters). The difference is that social workers operate from a position of vague authority, often deriving from the threat that the children of the family might have to be received into care, yet with no clear-cut definition of their obligations to assist nor their powers to prosecute. Conversely, the client has no knowledge of his rights. This is particularly obvious in the case of urgent financial need, which arises when social security offices are shut, or are out of travelling range. Payments to destitute persons for food constitute the largest single item of expenditure of Section 1 payments in many English local authority areas; yet social work clients have no clear right to such payments, nor are there any appeal procedures if they are refused. This use of Section 1 is simply an administrative convenience, by arrangement with the Supplementary Benefits Commission, which has no satisfactory emergency service to fulfil its obligations to meet urgent need out of office hours.

The practical implications of these policies will be discussed in a later chapter. What concerns us now is the sort of notion of the rights and liberties of the poor which they entail. The concept of welfare on which they are founded is that there is an irresponsible and unreliable sector of the population which can only be prevented from placing itself and its offspring in situations of distress and hardship by frequent interventions which entail supervision and control. This concept of welfare places a very high value on intervention, and the supervision of people who are 'at risk'; it assumes that the benevolent and parental vigilance of authority can forestall a whole range of misfortunes, so long as it has the powers to control almost every situation that may arise. Intervention is provided by making the 'at risk' population dependent upon that authority for a variety of concessions, benefits, subsidies and grants. Of course, this implies that every family whose income is below a certain sum is 'at risk'—that poverty necessarily entails a form of irresponsibility which requires intervention by social workers. The problem of this frequent repetitive and paternalistic intervention is that it tends to create frustration, which in turn creates a form of impulsive resistance which can easily be perceived as irresponsibility, and thus brings about a self-fulfilling prophecy. The best and saddest example of this cyclical process was the practice of preventive supervision of 'at risk' patients in mental hospitals, where those considered to be in danger of attempting suicide were constantly attended and kept safe from potential self-destruction. When preventive supervision was discontinued, the suicide rate fell by half.[27]

It is slightly ironical that it is within the Conservative Party, where the philosophy of specialised selective benefits was most extensively developed, that its implications are now being most vigorously questioned. It is even more ironical that the spokesman of the section of the party that is now most outspoken in its questioning should be Sir Keith Joseph, who as Secretary of State for Health and Social Security from 1970 to 1974 was responsible for the implementation of that philosophy. Just as Sir Keith Joseph has reverted to an older Tory orthodoxy in monetary policy, so, at a time of economic crisis, he has steered his party towards that gold standard of Tory social policy, the 1834 Poor Law. Like the authors of the famous Poor Law Report, he has woven together an ingenious defence of the virtues of private enterprise (endangered by the corruption of excessive and misguided state intervention) with a prescription for the morality of the poor (endangered by the same).

In the speech in which he first showed his new face (September 1974) he simultaneously attacked expansionist monetary policy and attempts to forestall unemployment.[28]

> The effect of over-reacting to temporary recessions has been to push up inflation to ever higher levels, not to help the unemployed, but to increase their numbers . . . If policies are to be judged by the criterion of the greatest good of the greatest number, then excessive expansion of the money supply has been found wholly wanting, in practice and theory alike.

For the first time since the war, a major political spokesman had repudiated Beveridge, and asserted that some people might have to pay the price of unemployment for the good of the majority.

His second and more publicised speech went much further than this. Although attention centred on his remarks about the birth rate among the lowest socio-economic classes, his theme was the much wider one of the morals of the poor in a permissive Welfare State. He accused socialists and other left-wing influences of spreading corruption.

> It is just because their message is that self-discipline is out of date and that the poor cannot be expected to help themselves, that they want the State to do more . . . But the only real lasting help we can give to the poor is helping them to help themselves; to do the opposite, to create more dependence, is to destroy them morally, while throwing an unfair burden on society.

After drawing attention to the rising birth rate in classes 4 and 5, and particularly in illegitimate births, he suggested that there were 'whole groups and classes of people' who required 'remoralisation'. His whole attack was on the 'false freedom' of the socialist 'New Utopia'; he reasserted the 'old virtues', such as 'stress on self-discipline and on standards'.[29] In short, the man most responsible for the reinstatement of the second concept of welfare had announced that he was converted back to the first, and to a version of it more abrasive and contentious than any proclaimed in the previous thirty years.

The outcry that followed this speech obscured many of the most interesting facets of this historic conversion. In spite of the existence of enormously expensive social services, of whole new professions of 'helpers', of complex research programmes and university departments, a highly intelligent former Minister chose to express himself about the basis of the Welfare State, and not by coincidence, in precisely the same moralistic and punitive tone and language that was used in the nineteenth century. Ultimately, the debate about welfare is still being carried on, in politics and in the social services, between two simplistic concepts, both of which make massive assumptions about the nature of people who earn low incomes, or who depend on state assistance. The new Sir Keith Joseph now assumes that these people are as potentially corruptible by any form of assistance as he formerly considered them to be needful of it.[30]

> Parents are being divested of their duty to provide for their family economically, of their responsibility for education, health, upbringing, morality, advice and guidance, of saving for old age, for housing When you take responsibility away from people, you make them irresponsible. Hand in hand with this, you break down traditional morals.

Once again, the caricature is presented of the honest industrious labourer, tilling his allotment and saving for his retirement, rudely corrupted by the blandishments of state schools, the National Health, a council house and an old-age pension, and reduced, at a stroke, to a depraved brute, without a word of advice or guidance to offer to his offspring. 'Can we wonder if the uneducated are seduced into approving a system which aims its allurements at all the weakest parts of our nature—which offers marriage to the young, security to the anxious, ease to the lazy, and impunity to the profligate?'[31] 'Are we to be destroyed by ideas, mischievous, wrong-headed, debilitating, yet seductive because they promise so much?'[32] The first of these questions was posed by the authors of the Poor Law Report of 1834; the second by Sir Keith Joseph in 1974. Basically, they convey exactly the same view of the working class.

Yet the view that they challenged was no more realistic; indeed, the second concept of welfare assumed the constitutional inferiority of the poor. In his former guise, Sir Keith Joseph used to quote the Director of Social Services in one industrial area who said, 'We have 20,000 households in this city. Nearly all our problems—delinquency, truancy, deprivation, poverty and the rest—come from about 800 of them. And I think that most of the families have been known to us for five generations.'[33] It was on statements like this that he had founded his theory of the 'cycle of deprivation'—'parents who were themselves deprived in one or more ways in childhood, become in turn the parents of another generation of deprived children.'[34] Above all, this theory was an attempt to account for multiple social disadvantages in terms of family patterns. 'It is where there is a combination of bad factors—problems associated with poverty, poor housing and large family size, for example—that children are most at risk.'[35] 'The most vulnerable—those at the bottom of the economic and social scales—are those most likely to be affected.'[36] The implication was that these factors combined to produce a certain type of personality—impulsive, immature, hedonistic, lacking foresight, demanding, childlike—which was incapable of meeting the needs of the next generation, and consequently reproduced offspring in its own image. Only interventions that dealt directly with these family patterns could translate material provision into effective assistance; without this personal supervision, such benefits would be squandered—an explanation of why 'in spite of long periods of full employment and relative prosperity and the improvement in community services since the Second World War, deprivation and problems of maladjustment so conspicuously persist.'[37]

Such a concept of welfare thus contained a caricature of the working class which was every bit as gross as that of the 1834 Report. It is the persistence of these two stereotypes, rather than of deprivation, which must be counted the greatest mystery. On the one hand, the image of the worker as corrupted by official assistance has survived several generations in which old-age pensions, state education, the Health Service and council housing have been provided; social problems continue to be interpreted as arising from these provisions as provisions, rather than from the ways in which they are distributed, rationed or withheld. On the other hand, research evidence on the non-correlation between poverty and other social problems is persistently ignored. No generation was more materially deprived than that of the 1930s; yet in that era nearly all forms of social deviance had a lower incidence in poor areas than in rich areas, and the crime rate was low.[38] Even in the 1960s, the highest rates of deprived children were found in affluent areas, not poor ones.[39] Yet these stereotypes have survived, in spite of the successes of the post-war welfare institutions, and the notion of a National Minimum for all citizens which they promoted. Today it is these two far older concepts of welfare which struggle for supremacy as the underlying philosophies of the Welfare State.

Neither of these two notions of welfare considers that it is beneficial to provide people with a decent standard of living as a right. The first concept insists that no country in which 'every man, whatever be his conduct or his character, [is] ensured a *comfortable* subsistence, can retain its prosperity, or even its civilization'[40] and accordingly avoids state provision, except on punitive terms. The second concept extends as a condition of assistance, an ever wider blanket of preventive supervision over one sector of the population, to protect it from the consequences of its own inadequacies. Neither concept sees state services as potentially strengthening for citizens; neither sees provision as a means to liberty and independence. Neither believes that by providing an adequate income, decent housing, a health service and free education for *all*, by treating all as free and equal citizens, the state can help create a better society. These basic reservations about the value of state intervention by those who frame our social policies are reflected in the functions and methods of all our present-day social services.

The conditions placed upon the provision of welfare by both of these models ensure that the institutions of welfare are also means of controlling the behaviour of whole classes of citizens, seen as potentially deviant. In both models, the distinctions between assistance for the needy and control of the deviant are unclear, and the same institutions often pursue both ends. In the next chapter I shall discuss how other traditional methods of social control have come to be merged with welfare provisions, and with what results.

11

Punishment, Treatment and Control

In an earlier chapter it was suggested that social control is as universal as social nonconformity. We all have expectations of others' behaviour towards us, and consequently we are involved in influencing the behaviour of others in all our social roles, as well as being influenced by them. The important question about social control, therefore, is not whether it is necessary (since it is unavoidable) but how it can best be achieved. We need to consider the different results of various methods of social control.

In this chapter I shall try to show how both the philosophy and the methods of the state's institutions for controlling deviant behaviour have changed since the nineteenth century. In particular, I shall suggest that as the social sciences provided a more complex analysis of the influences on behaviour, punishment began to be seen as a less adequate means of control, and was increasingly replaced by limited reward. Finally, I shall indicate how the provision of welfare has come to be very closely linked with other measures of social control, and how social work has begun to occupy a key role in relation to both the welfare and the controlling function of state intervention.

In the nineteenth century, the method of social control most favoured by writers about social policy was law backed by punishment; yet the way in which these authors understood the effects of punishments prescribed by the state was complex. The state's power to punish was seen as not merely coercive; it led also to a self-interested involvement of citizens in the performance of their social roles, and it served to clarify and reinforce the values which all members of society were expected to share. Whereas modern liberal consciousness sees punishment as an evil which may occasionally, unfortunately, be necessary for the coercion of the most antisocial elements in the community, the nineteenth-century view of punishment (which originated in the notions of the state expounded by seventeenth- and eighteenth-century contract theorists[1]) was derived from the utilitarians. Since the state's primary responsibility was to guarantee the security of its subjects, its duty was to create laws which simultaneously protected both their individual interests and the general public good. Any breach of such laws thus threatened the security of all, and needed to be met by punishment in order to prevent further antisocial behaviour. Bentham wrote, 'The general object which all laws have in common is to augment the total happiness of the community, in other words to exclude mischief.' The effect of punishment was deterrent.[2]

> General prevention ought to be the chief end of punishment, as it is its real justification. If we could consider an offence which has been committed as an isolated fact, the like of which would never recur, punishment would be useless . . . Punishment is elevated to the first rank of benefits when it is regarded not as an act of wrath or vengeance against guilty or unfortunate individual . . . but as an indispensable sacrifice to the common safety.

As we have seen, Chadwick put Bentham's theories into practice over a far wider range of social problems than those covered by the criminal law. His biographer has pointed out the very close parallel between the famous 'less-eligibility principle' and Bentham's rule for the administration of his 'Panopticon' prison. Bentham had written: 'The ordinary condition of a convict saving the regard due to life, health and bodily ease ought not to be made more eligible than that of the poorest class of subjects living in a state of innocence and liberty.'[3] Chadwick wrote: 'The condition of the recipient [of poor relief] should not on the whole be more eligible than that of any labourer living on the fruits of his own industry.'[4] The regime of the workhouse was clearly a punishment in utilitarian terms; poverty which required relief was treated exactly as a crime.

The justification for this view advanced by the Poor Law Report was exactly that which Bentham used for the punishment of law-breakers; that the claimant 'must accept assistance on the terms, whatever they may be, that the common welfare requires'.[5] However, there was a difficulty in this view which even the report acknowledged. Poverty was not a criminal offence, and even requests for relief could stem from circumstances beyond the individual's control. The implication was that the greatest happiness of the greatest number required that on occasions the innocent should suffer punishment 'to which the good of society requires . . . [them] to submit'.[6] Thus in order to ensure industrious habits among labourers and the free play of economic self-interest, an unknown proportion of the population was to be treated with intentional severity, regardless of their individual merits. This was a breach of the principle established by the contract theorists, and forcibly expressed by Hobbes. 'All punishments of innocent subjects, be they great or little, are against the law of nature. For punishment is only for transgression of the law and therefore there can be no good to the Commonwealth by punishing the Innocent.'[7]

The utilitarians were able to escape the implications of this important inconsistency in their arguments because there was another, older justification for the punishment of individuals which was unrelated to questions of deterrence and the public good. The Christian tradition described punishment mainly as a consequence of moral failure: God punishes sinners for breaking His laws, not to deter others or to consolidate His rule, but to annul the individual's guilt. Similarly, the individual who offended against society's moral laws deserved punishment, as retribution and as reassertion of his responsibility for his actions. This view of punishment had survived as the moral and religious counterpart to the deterrent notion of criminal law, and it was reflected in the social philosophy of writers like Bosanquet and T. H. Green. It was also an important basis of the Victorian social workers' ethos.

The field of social policy was a territory over which both legal and moral authority held sway, and the Poor Law Report was able to disguise the quasi-legal punishments which it prescribed as forms of moral retribution. Its argument was that the state should not provide a comfortable form of relief of need, for fear that this provision would corrupt a large number of citizens—'*demoralise*' them, in its own words. Thus uncomfortable provision was necessary, not to enforce a specially created punishment, but to ensure that the natural consequences of idleness, fecklessness, vagrancy, etc., were not artificially removed by thoughtless assistance. The state should not undertake to repeal . . . the ordinary laws of nature'[8] but to ensure instead that 'the penalty which, after all, must be paid by someone for idleness and improvidence' should fall on the 'guilty person or on his family'.[9] The effect of the old Poor Law had been 'to repeal *pro tanto* the law by which each man and his family enjoy the benefit of his own prudence and virtue. In abolishing punishment, we equally abolish reward.'[10] Similarly, the Charity Organisation Society, which embodied in its principles the thinking of the early social workers, had among its functions 'the repression of mendicity and imposture'.[11] It turned away two-thirds of applicants for assistance, mainly on the grounds that to help them would be to undermine their sense of personal and family responsibility. 'To give material relief, food or money, to everyone who asked for it on the sole conditions of their being what is commonly called deserving and in want, even after the most careful verification of these conditions, would inevitably do more harm than good.'[12] Such refusals, even if they led to the admission of a family into the workhouse, were seen as less likely to destroy their morals than would careless aid.

The retributive theory of punishment was that it was a sort of negative right; that a responsible citizen should expect to be punished for offences against the law (and for moral failures) by his fellow citizens. The acceptance of punishment was part of asserting a claim to hold other rights as a citizen. He was seen, in being punished, as expiating and making reparation for his offence, and thus restoring his reputation and status in society. Being sufficiently responsible to answer for his conduct, punishment confirmed his citizenship. This apparently very theoretical and unrealistic argument is by no means without its adherents today. In the debate over the reform of the juvenile courts in the 1960s, the probation service took up a very similar position, defending the child's right to be punished for his offence, and thus recognised as a responsible person, rather than treated as maladjusted and in need of care, protection or control. Similarly, in relation to adults, H. B. Acton has argued, 'In being punished instead of being treated or cured, an offender is being regarded as a responsible person. He will not like imprisonment, but he may think it less humiliating than being sent to hospital to have something done to his brain or his testicles.'[13]

The blending of utilitarian notions of deterrence and Christian notions of retribution produced a theory of social control which admirably fitted mid-Victorian liberalism; punishment both promoted the common welfare and emphasised individual responsibility. But the same evidence which by the end of the century cast doubt on the individual's capacity to avoid unemployment, poverty or homelessness in an industrialised society also undermined the retributive elements in social policy provisions. The Charity Organisation Society's leaders who served as members of the Royal Commission on the Poor Laws from 1905 to 1909 started with a desire to reassert the principles of 1834 and ended by recommending labour exchanges, pensions and unemployment and sickness insurance. The Liberal reforms of this period were based on the view that the state's role was not to enforce a moral equality by inflicting penalties on those who failed, but rather to provide individual citizens with protection against the worst effects of material inequality, or compensations for material injustice. The state took it upon itself to organise, train and dispense limited benefits to its least fortunate citizens rather than to punish them.

These changes in the social philosophy of liberalism were perfectly reflected in the penal system. Whereas in medieval times the retributive view had mainly given rise to corporal punishments, the utilitarian deterrent approach found its best expression in imprisonment. Prison building reached its peak in the middle of the nineteenth century—in the six years after 1842, fifty-four new prisons were built, providing 11,000 separate cells.[14] A centralised, paramilitary prison service was created out of a chaos of locally administered gaols, and a uniform regime, based on segregation, silence and containment, was imposed.[15]

Up to 1895 the 'manifest' task of the prison system was deterrence. In reality, at an 'extant' level, the task was control . . . The policy of separation (keeping the prisoners segregated from each other in their cells) is the best example of a method which contributed to both punishment and control.

But in that year, a Departmental Committee presided over by Herbert Gladstone stated that 'We start from the principle that prison treatment should have as its primary and its concurrent objects deterrence, and reformation.'[16] The report argued that instead of seeking to impose upon the prisoner conditions worse than any he would experience as a free man, prison should attempt to make him more fitted to an honest life when he was released; instead of trying to make him abstain from crime through fear, it should try to train him for a better way of living. This could be done by amongst other things allowing prisoners to work in groups ('in association'), provided there was careful supervision and proper classification. But once this was allowed, the coercive control of the separate and silence systems had to be replaced by control based on a system of rewards for good behaviour. 'And so there was set in motion the process of control which has been used in the English prison system since 1898—the promise of privilege.'[17] Remission, association, flexibility of sentence, home leave and parole were all rewards which could be used to maintain order. Just as the Liberal Governments of 1906-14 used benefits to construct a new superstructure for social policy to replace the least reputable and most visible aspects of the Poor Law, so within the prison service, control by reward largely replaced control by coercion, without ever removing the punitive and coercive basis of the penal system.

The consequences of some features of the new prison regime are worth mentioning in view of this close parallel. As prison conditions were improved, sentences grew longer. Preventive detention, a new method for dealing with recidivists, introduced in 1908, which allowed an extra sentence of five to ten years for recidivism in addition to that for the actual offence, simultaneously introduced extended imprisonment and a new concept of 'conditions of detention less onerous in some respects than those of ordinary penal servitude'.[18] An early Commissioners' Report saw the dangers of association under such conditions offset by 'the extensive privileges which preventive detention prisoners enjoy. There is so much to lose!'[19] Similarly, the borstal system for offenders between sixteen and twenty-one was introduced in the same year; but whereas, before the Prevention of Crime Act of that year, early experiments in training for young prisoners had been attempted with short fixed sentences, the borstal sentence was for a period of one to three years, the time of release depending on good conduct. 'The borstal institution then, as now, depended for its stability entirely on a system of rewards.'[20] The notion that prison could operate on the basis of retraining and reformation of character, on the willing participation of prisoners in a process of treatment for their antisocial behaviour, reached its zenith between the wars. Ultimately, however, it rested on the threat of coercion, and was only achieved (where it was achieved) at a price of longer sentences and a greater risk of 'institutionalisation'. Furthermore, as J. E. Thomas argues,[21]

> as restrictions are removed, those which remain become more
> intolerable . . . eventually it becomes apparent that reformation,
> which means something more than the issue of extra letters, logically
> demands the removal of all restrictions. At last the community of
> inmates is left with only one major restriction, the wall, which is the
> most intolerable of all.

Punishment presupposes loss of freedom; training and treatment do not. Thus claims about prison as reformation ultimately face the question of why compulsion is necessary. Where a system of rewards is really a means of control disguised as training or treatment, this contradiction is likely to be frequently exposed. The same contradicition is inherent in other aspects of the Welfare State.

An important aspect of the debate about punishment and treatment which has continued since the Second World War has been the definition of the role of psychiatry in social control. The first part of this debate was ostensibly to decide which kinds of behaviour denoted mental illness, and which moral failure, in order to determine which merited treatment and which punishment. Much confusion derived from the difficulty of defining mental illness. Thus for instance Lady Wootton considered statements such as those by Dr Bernard Glueck, the Supervising Psychiatrist at Sing Sing Prison, that[22]

> the question of responsibility (for criminal behaviour) would not
> have to be raised, if the concept of management of the anti-social
> individual were changed from that of punishment as the main
> instrument of control, to a concept of the anti-social individual as a
> sick person, in need of treatment rather than punishment.

She examined the implication of the second part of this statement that criminality was a form of mental illness, but found no satisfactory scientific criteria for mental health or illness by which questions about criminal responsibility could be answered; all such attempted definitions were clearly infected by concealed value judgments and cultural norms. She concluded:[23]

> If mental health and ill-health cannot be defined in objective
> scientific terms that are free of subjective moral judgments, it follows
> that we have no reliable criterion by which to distinguish the sick
> from the healthy mind. The road is then wide open for those who
> wish to classify all forms of anti-social, or at least criminal, behaviour
> as symptoms of mental disorder.

However, unlike many of her contemporaries, Lady Wootton, herself a magistrate, was not alarmed to discover that 'today we have very little idea as to who is sick and who is sinful'.[24] Instead, she saw this as an encouraging sign that the question of responsibility might be allowed to wither away; what mattered was not questions of medicine or morality, but simply the problem of devising means of removing or inhibiting the inclination to delinquency, for the good of all concerned, including the delinquent. This would involve 'a shift of emphasis in the treatment of offenders away from considerations of guilt and towards choice of whatever course of action appeared most likely to be effective as a cure in this particular case.'[25] Such a pragmatic approach did not necessarily carry the implications either that crime was a disease or that it was morally wrong, and the 'treatments' it received could appropriately be anywhere along a continuum from pills to punishments. The sentencer's skill lay in fitting the offender to the appropriate remedy.

There were a number of reasons why social policy tended to take Lady Wootton's line. In the first place, there was a sharp increase in the crime rate after the Second World War, and in spite of fluctuations the long-term trend since then has continued to be upward. Whereas throughout the years between the wars, the daily average male population of prisons and borstals never totalled more than 12,180, and in many years it was under 10,000, by 1950 it stood at over 20,000, by 1965 it reached nearly 30,000, and recently it has been over 40,000. Overcrowding in prisons has been an issue since 1948, and alternatives to imprisonment have become an increasingly urgent priority in recent years, as prison building has failed to keep pace with the rising prison population. Psychiatric treatment of offenders as a condition of probation was included in the 1948 Criminal Justice Act; the 1959 Mental Health Act went much further in creating a category of persons called psychopaths having 'a persistent disorder or disability of mind ... which results in abnormally aggressive or seriously irresponsible conduct ... and requires or is susceptible to medical treatment', and providing in Section 60 that a person convicted by a court of an offence punishable with imprisonment, and suffering from a psychopathic disorder 'of a nature or degree which warrants the detention of the patient in a hospital for medical treatment', shall, if the court considers it the most suitable way of dealing with him, be detained in hospital, or placed under the guardianship of a local authority. However, psychiatric treatment for criminals forms only a very small part of a range of new methods, broadly classifiable as treatments, which have been made available to courts as alternatives to prison sentences. Hostels, training centres and community service were the positive counterparts of parole, suspended and deferred sentences; all were aimed at avoiding 'unnecessary' imprisonment for those who might respond to other methods. Yet, in spite of these alternatives, there has been no question of the substitution of treatment, still less psychiatric treatment, for punishment; prisons are fuller than ever before, and prison regimes are no more influenced by psychiatric notions now than they were fifteen years ago. Indeed, since the Blake and Mitchell escapes and the Mountbatten Report, there has been a re-emphasis on security and confinement. Thus alternative sentences are part of a range in which punishment, and specifically imprisonment, is still the basic element.

Just how important this basis still is to social policy makers has been well illustrated in the attempts to reform the law in relation to juvenile offenders since the early 1960s. Radical proposals, first made by Lord Longford's Study Group in 1964, for 'changes in our judicial procedure which will take children of school age out of the range of the criminal courts and the penal system and treat their problems in a family setting',[26] have been so successfully resisted that more than ten years and two White Papers later, despite the moderate reforms of the 1969 Children and Young Persons Act (most of whose important innovations have never been implemented), the actual changes accomplished have been very marginal. In so far as a lower proportion of juvenile offenders now have to appear in court, this has been achieved mainly through an increase in police cautioning rather than family casework by social workers.[27] But although total numbers of juvenile court appearances declined immediately after the Act, they have now risen again to above the old level in many areas; furthermore the uses for under-seventeens of detention centres, borstals and remands in prison have all increased since the Act.[28] Although many writers have claimed that these phenomena are the results of a misguided attempt to treat the depraved as no different from the deprived, it seems clear that the whole history of the Act equally reflects the unwillingness of legislators, magistrates and administrators to dispense with punitive methods of dealing with young offenders. As Jean Packman puts it:[29]

> In effect, two contradictory notions of juvenile delinquency were in collision; . . . the four English reports in particular mirror the to and fro of the debate and the Acts encapsulate the compromises reached and the sometimes futile attempts to reconcile the irreconcilable.

Yet to a great extent the conflicts between the notions of crime as moral failure and crime as mental illness or maladjustment have been a phoney war; social policy's agenda has been more to extend the notion of 'treatment' to include such 'structured environments' as approved schools, locked wards and prisons than seriously to challenge the punitive basis of legal sanctions in the name of mental health or good adjustment. For instance, the facts that what were once called reformatories for juvenile delinquents are now called community homes, that they are administered by social services departments rather than under the control of the Home Office, and that their inmates are there on care orders rather than sentences, all have some important implications, but do not reflect fundamental alterations in our understanding of crime and its consequences. Rather, they reflect our tendency to make less rigid distinctions between delinquency and other forms of deviance; between deviance and deprivation; between liberty and loss of liberty; between punishment and treatment. We now have a concept of crime as being just one amongst many 'social problems' which demand solutions involving some or all of several elements—social work, psychiatry, residential provision and secure containment. The fact that all these elements are usually referred to (sometimes euphemistically) as 'treatments' should not lead us to suppose that they all necessarily have any direct connection with medicine, psychiatry or science.

Indeed, the second part of the debate about mental illness and personal responsibility stems from a quite different anxiety—that psychiatry is encroaching not upon the territory of the criminal law, but upon the liberty of the ordinary (middle-class) citizen. While the first part of the debate concerned such relatively academic and neutral topics as the relative merits of flogging and electric shocks for criminals, almost all of whom were working class, the second part comes much nearer home. The incidence of mental illness requiring hospital admission since 1959 has not only been much higher than that of detected crime, but also much more evenly distributed between the social classes. Most of this increase has been in voluntary admissions, which was precisely the intention of the 1959 Act; yet what was seen as a progressive move towards the removal of the stigma surrounding mental illness has come to be regarded with suspicion. Doubts centre around a number of interrelated questions. To what extent is mental 'illness' comparable with physical illness? Are its symptoms the signs of a disease attacking the patient, or are they reflections of experiences and feeling which, though confusing and chaotic, are not essentially different from his other mental and emotional processes? Should treatment consist of the immediate suppression of symptoms by physical methods like ECT and drugs, to enable a quick discharge from hospital and reduce the risks of institutionalisation, or should it offer succour, nurture and asylum from the outside world to the patient as a distressed person? Should compulsory treatments for the removal of symptoms be imposed upon patients in the name of their welfare, or should the law be more concerned to protect the liberty of citizens, and allow detention in hospital only for behaviour that directly endangers the patient or others?

The first of these questions was not taken very seriously at the time when the 1959 Act was being prepared. The Royal Commission which reported in 1959 simply assumed the notion of mental illness, presumably on the grounds that understanding certain forms of behaviour as denoting sickness led to more humanitarian attitudes and treatments. The Act itself defined 'mental disorder' in terms, among other things, of 'mental illness', but made no attempt to define mental illness. Powers of compulsory detention without a court order were given, for various lengths of time, either 'in the interests of the patients' health or safety or for the protection of other persons'. Since then philosophers, psychiatrists and others have pointed out that in many crucial respects mental illness cannot be seen as analogous to physical illness, and that attempts to deal with it as if it were a strictly comparable phenomenon lead to dangerous confusions. This is particularly so in questions about compulsory treatment. Anthony Flew quotes a psychiatrist describing cases of 'very ill people'.[30]

> One may detain and treat, if necessary surgically, an unconscious patient in hospital, assuming that he would have consented to treatment if he had been conscious. The great innovation in England and Wales came in 1959 with the Mental Health Act, when psychiatrists were allowed to treat people incapable of consent without judicial permission . . . The duty of society towards a handicapped member is to treat him as a minor or as someone who cannot take responsibility for his own treatment.

Flew points out that many people compulsorily detained and treated are not so much incapable of giving consent as unwilling to give it, and that unless the analogy with physical illness can be properly substantiated (rather than misleadingly implied by reference to unconsciousness) there are grave risks that psychiatrists will treat various forms of quite conscious and deliberate nonconformity as if they were insanity.[31] The American psychiatrist, Dr Thomas Szasz, goes much further than this and argues that there is no such thing as mental illness, and that the whole medical basis for treating both the neurotic and the insane as sick rests on a willingness by psychiatrists to accept as ill some people who are pretending to be so.[32]

The second question has also been treated philosophically as well as scientifically. Starting from the analytic viewpoint of existentialist philosophy, R. D. Laing has suggested that the seemingly cryptic statements of allegedly psychotic people are not only meaningful to themselves but also comprehensible to others, given a willingness to understand their social situations.[33] The essential point in Laing's argument for the purposes of this question is his insistence that the 'symptoms' which have been taken to denote disease are in fact ways of living an impossible life, of responding to conflicting demands, or surviving in the face of overwhelming pressures. Thus 'breakdowns' are not the collapse of healthy mental functioning, but rather the disintegration of false self which has been cultivated as a defence against others' demands. Laing and his colleagues have provided many examples of the intelligibility of apparently meaningless words and actions in terms of the patient's family or social circumstances, and of patients' increasingly sane responses to genuine efforts to understand their communications in these terms. It is doctors, he argues, whose behaviour is meaningless, when they treat their patients either as malfunctioning machines, or as victims of disabling illnesses.

This point of view leads directly to the third question, for if 'symptoms' are reflections of thoughts and feelings that are no different in kind from those of sane people, or if they are signs of an attempt to find a better expression of the 'true' self, it follows that physical treatments like drugs and ECT which are designed to suppress these symptoms are a form of violence against the person. Since these 'symptoms' usually arise from tense and destructive family situations, people who suffer them are particularly prone to pressures from other family members to accept such treatments, and if they refuse, the family can consent to their compulsory detention. This is the position, argued by David Cooper in *Psychiatry and Anti-Psychiatry* and elsewhere,[34] and it is the basis of the treatment provided by existentialist psychiatrists in their 'houses', where madness is not treated as illness, but as a process of potential rebirth. A description by a patient and her doctor of a five-year stay in one of these houses is presented in *Mary Barnes: Two Accounts of a Journey Through Madness*, in which Mary's regression to the earliest stages of infancy—incontinence, inability to feed herself, angry violence and mischievous play—was followed by the very slow reconstruction of a persona very different from the brittle nurse and teacher she had been before.[35] Mary Barnes had been treated in a conventional mental hospital before this process, and her brother, diagnosed as schizophrenic, had been an in-patient for many years. Existentialists would argue that the contrast between Mary now—spontaneous and independent—and her brother, who still lives in semi-institutional surroundings, reflects the different effects of medical methods and of empathy and nurture. Other non-existentialist critics of present-day psychiatry have condemned drugs and ECT for more pragmatic reasons. Andrew Malleson points out that they have not affected either the incidence or recovery rates of hospitalisable mental illness; that whereas 13.6 million working days were lost through mental illness in 1950, the figure in 1970 was 20.25 million; that drugs are addictive and are easily used for overdoses (an overwhelming proportion of the increase in suicide and attempted suicide since 1950 has been caused by barbiturates obtained by prescription); and that the assimilation of conditions like alcoholism into the category of mental illness has not improved rates of 'cure' compared with other methods.[36] He argues that, like many nineteenth-century medical treatments, modern psychiatric methods tend to be increasingly necessary to patients without in the long run improving their functioning; this helps to explain very high readmission rates to mental hospitals. He concludes that the treatment of behavioural problems as illness simply reduces the patient's sense of responsibility for himself, and increases his dependence on medical protection from ultimately unavoidable human feelings and problems.

The fourth question, however, is the difficult one of how to deal with people who are by common consent mad but who do not wish to receive medical attention. The notion of Laing and his colleagues would presumably be that the existence of sufficiently warm and accepting environments into which such people could retreat would, except in extreme circumstances, obviate the necessity for compulsory detention and treatment. However, such propositions are quite unverifiable, and the impression one gets from descriptions of Laingian 'houses' is that their appeal would be confined to people of intellectual or artistic tastes and bohemian aspirations, whereas the highest incidence of behaviour diagnosed psychotic is among the lowest socio-economic class—the group most prone to compulsory admissions. Second, very few opportunities for such treatment exist at present. Even Mary Barnes, who was desperate for help, was told by Laing to stay sane for two years until he got hold of the necessary accommodation—a feat she only narrowly achieved. Her brother has still so far been unable or unwilling to embark on the same process, in spite of her efforts to help him.

There is still a real question, therefore, of how the law on compulsory detention might be altered to give more respect to the liberty and dignity of citizens. Szasz, on the basis of American experience, argues that personal responsibility is being undermined, and people are being dehumanised, as a result of their antisocial behaviour being attributed to mythical illnesses. Using psychiatric classification to mitigate crimes often involves longer detention in mental hospitals, and the loss of identity and autonomy. 'What such "patients" need is not a doctor or psychotherapist, but a policeman or jailer.'[37] Flew less radically proposes that behaviour should only be treated as illness if it can be shown to be such; otherwise the law should protect from interference and punish for infraction. The proposals are both backward-looking, in that they employ traditional liberal methods both to enforce personal responsibility and to protect individual liberty. Only the genuinely sick should be treated with supportive care; wrongdoing should be punished; obligations should be upheld; independence should be encouraged. Apart from continued difficulties about the definition of illness, these proposals presuppose a return to the combination of deterrence and retribution in Victorian punishment.

This debate about the role of psychiatry only touches upon two problems of social policy which are wider and deeper than its terms allow. The first is the problem of encouraging or enforcing social obligations. What Szasz calls 'malingering' is only one way in which people may from time to time seek to escape their responsibilities by means of statutory provisions. Many such phenomena have nothing whatever to do with illness, but rest on appeals to other social conditions or problems. 'Voluntary unemployment' is one example from the field of social security; desertion by wives of husbands is another. It is possible to make oneself homeless in order to obtain housing. Finally, there are many men in prison by choice, because they find life there preferable to that available in the outside world. Whether Flew likes it or not, his example of the murderer who gave himself up immediately after shooting his fiancée, and insisted on being executed, is another case of using statutory responsibility to avoid an obligation (in this case to let live, to live and to die). While all these actions might in some circumstances be described as moral failures, they might equally in others be described as rebellions or as protests against impossible or unjust expectations, or against inadequate provisions. The use of mental hospitals and out-patient clinics for these purposes is simply the mode of evading or challenging obligations most favoured by the middle classes; it should therefore not be considered in isolation.

The second problem is whether notions of deterrence and retribution can or should be integrated with treatment. Treatment is clearly an attempt to influence behaviour, and thus a form of control; but equally clearly it is not necessarily a punishment. However, whatever they may say at conferences, psychiatrists do overtly or covertly use the threat of compulsory detention to ensure voluntary admission, and of locked wards to procure co-operation in treatment methods. Psychiatry's critics are thus right to suggest that there are elements in its practices which if not specifically used as punishments for refractory behaviour are at least used as threats to induce conformity with hospital standards. This is why it is tempting to suggest that either health (Szasz) or mental health (Flew) could be rid of these elements of deterrence and retribution, and could concentrate on 'pure' treatment, if punitive methods of control, including all or most detention, could be for breaches of the law, and could be carried out in prisons. However, this would necessarily assume that there existed opportunities and provisions to allow people to be both sane and law-abiding. The notion that people can thus be freed from the interferences with their liberty and dignity constituted by psychiatric encroachments assumes the possibility of a satisfying and independent life in the absence of these encroachments; or else it assumes that those whose lives are so frustrating or whose obligations so onerous that they are driven insane can be deterred from harming others by the threat of imprisonment. In the latter case, it is hard to see how this is much of an improvement on the present situation. It is always tempting to suppose that if provisions are made extremely unacceptable or unpleasant, then people will somehow find ways to live their lives satisfactorily without them. In the nineteenth century, punitive conditions for the relief of poverty did not give rise to prosperity for all, and large numbers of people with every kind of social disadvantage were punished by the conditions of the workhouses and the prisons as a result. In the same way there is every reason to suspect that the threat of imprisonment would not deter a great many deprived and disadvantaged people from going mad, and in the course of their insanity breaking the law, if only to obtain some sort of asylum.

Furthermore, there is reason to doubt whether even 'pure' physical medicine is as free from elements of social control as Flew suggests. His argument is that our test of whether or not a condition is a disease should be whether it is perceived by the sufferer to be inconvenient, unpleasant or painful, or potentially so; and whether he wishes to be rid of it. But quite a number of patients with physical illnesses resist recognising their early symptoms, resist doctors' advice about how to avoid their development into more serious conditions, and resist treatments prescribed for them. Even when the illness is recognised as serious or potentially fatal, co-operation with treatment is not automatic. In Solzhenitsyn's *Cancer Ward*, Kostoglotov knows that he has cancer, but postpones coming to hospital until he is close to death. Eventually he co-operates with treatment, but when he discovers that his therapy is destroying his sexual powers he refuses further co-operation. Doctors who are well aware of such attitudes and resistances among their patients develop methods for dealing with these, such as threatening people in the early stages of illness with hospitalisation, and withholding details about the side-effects of treatments from patients with more serious conditions. Such methods are clearly ways of influencing patients' responses other than by obtaining their full consent to treatment. Thus it seems unlikely that the measures suggested by Szasz and Flew would be sufficient to purify medicine of the elements in treatment they deplore.

Finally the notion of confining deterrence to a small, highly stigmatised sector of the criminal law in order to free treatment from its taint rests on the theory that all provision for individual needs is potentially corrupting because it can undermine independence and responsibility. Thus the principles of 1834 stood on a basis of 'general deterrence' represented by the less eligibility of the workhouse and the prison, and on the non-availability of any other state provision for individual needs. This is now far from being the case. Rather there are a collection of loosely linked provisions, and mental hospitals form a part of one particular chain, which includes out-patient clinics and local authority hostels. Most of these chains contain elements of provision, prevention, protection, supervision, control and punishment. For instance, social security includes benefits by right, benefits by discretion, surveillance by special investigators, semi-punitive residential provision in re-establishment centres, and the punitive cuts and disqualifications of the wage stop, cohabitation rule, etc. Services to families with children from social services departments alone include playgroups, foster-care, financial assistance, supervision, prosecution for neglect, and a range of residential provision, from temporary accommodation to ex-approved schools for delinquents. Even the penal system now includes a wide variation between open borstals and maximum-security prisons. Thus it is simply not within the power of psychiatrists alone to 'remoralise' the population by treating only those who are ill according to strict medical criteria and leaving the rest to strenuous liberty or rigorous punishment. Other services operate in such a way that difficult behaviour with no possible medical classification could variously qualify a person for a financial grant, many years of intensive supervision, a place in a hostel or vocational training.

Indeed, it is arguable that the main onus for determining the boundaries between treatment and punishment, prevention and prosecution, for enforcing responsibility or providing assistance, now lies with social workers much more than with psychiatrists. Even in the field of mental health they have a significant role in decisions about hospital admissions; but this is a tiny proportion of their overall responsibilities in comparison with their obligations in the processes of deciding who should be taken to court for juvenile delinquency and who should be prosecuted for cruelty to or neglect of their children, and which of those who should not, should be given financial assis- tance, or family casework, or both. As I argued in chapter 10, the philosophy that underpins most of these interventions has very little to do with mental health. It is that there is a proportion of the population, distinguishable mainly by their economic and social status, which requires frequent interventions both to make available strictly limited and conditional assistance, and to provide supervision and control. In cases where these interventions are concerned with mental illness, with delinquency or with parental failures, they are at least limited by certain statutory definitions—though the Acts of 1959, 1963 and 1969 all gave broader and vaguer terms for preventive interventions and indeterminate supervisions. But in cases of many material needs, of homelessness, of destitution and of debt, the interventions they permit are extremely ill-defined, and the clients' rights unspecified. Thus a whole class of the population is considered to constitute a social problem just by its existence, and the kind of range of provisions available for dealing with various forms of deviance is held in readiness for members of this group to deal with nothing more nor less than its neediness.

There has recently been developing a remarkable congruence

between the powers and responsibilities of social workers and others dealing with seemingly different forms of behaviour which share the label of 'social problem'. The common features of these powers are: limited material assistance; faith in the efficacy of control through supervision; the use of short-term removals from the home environment as a means of enforcing this form of control; a blurring of the distinction between liberty and compulsory detention; and the integration of residential and fieldwork provisions. As one example exhibiting most of these features, the development of the probation service in the last ten years shows provisions for criminals falling in line with those for other problem categories. The powers of the original probation service gave it little in common with either local authority social work or the prison system. Probation officers were to 'advise, assist and befriend' those given conditional liberty, in lieu of sentence, for offences. There was an element of retribution in the officers' power to require the offender to report regularly, and he was also expected to be industrious as well as honest; but the offender had to consent to the order, and his rights and obligations under it were clearly specified. Probation was without much question a species of liberty rather than a species of imprisonment; the two were about as sharply differentiated as they could be, while still both being orders of the court. But in the 1960s there developed a number of responsibilities for probation officers which were not so clearly separated from the penal system—notably parole, with its powers of recall during the remainder of the sentence. Now, with prisons overcrowded, the Younger Committee has proposed that probation officers should be responsible for the supervision and control of young offenders on two kinds of orders, neither requiring the offender's consent, and both giving the officer stronger powers to enforce more conditions. Suggested conditions included the specification of forbidden associates and places of resort, the stipulation of place of residence, of training or educational courses. But most controversially, one of the proposed orders contains powers for a seventy-two-hour detention, without judicial process, where there is suspicion of *intention* to commit an offence. By tradition, probation has not seen itself as specifically concerned with preventing offences in this almost physical sense, or with controlling the offender—'advise, assist and befriend' did not imply control. It is true that these measures are being developed with the intention of providing a much fuller range of provisions, short of imprisonment, which can enable more serious or persistent offenders to remain in the community, and that these provisions have not been developed either by the probation service or voluntary bodies. However, many members of the service have been concerned at the arbitrary powers to intervene in details of offenders' lives, to impose serious restrictions which would be quite unacceptable to anyone who aspired to liberty. If these proposals are accepted, probation officers will become simultaneously agents of the penal system ('screws on wheels') and possessed of powers of detention rather similar to those of social workers under the Mental Health Act.

There are important questions about these new methods of social control, in which social workers are so much involved. Is their considerable and expanding use justified, or are controls being imposed unnecessarily on people who could be given much more freedom? Are they effective in bringing about the desired results, or are they sometimes counterproductive—do parents sometimes neglect their children or delinquents re-offend just to fight or spite their supervisors? Do the provisions they entail give people opportunities to lead a satisfactory life they would not otherwise enjoy, or are they restrictive and frustrating? Do they provide a specialised supplement to benefits enjoyed by other citizens, or are they an inferior provision for people excluded from the services available to the majority? These are the questions that will be considered in the next chapter.

12
Citizenship and Social Work

In Chapter 7, I discussed the dilemmas of interventions in others' lives, and considered the philosophical bases of social work. I want now to analyse the interrelations between these problems and the issues of social policy that have been discussed—that is to say, the difficulties of interventions by agents of the state in the day-to-day personal and family lives of citizens. I shall suggest that, in spite of social work's historical antagonism to state provision, the profession has become enmeshed in a form of intervention required by the paternalistic tradition of welfare, and a preventive approach to deviance, and that this has significantly curtailed the freedom and citizenship of its clients.

Early social workers identified themselves as being in opposition to state intervention. In the tradition of the 1834 Poor Law, they were vividly aware of the dangers of giving 'help' that did more harm than good. They believed that the kind of social problems represented by child neglect, by alcoholism, by prostitution and other forms of degradation among the poor, were the result of selfish and thoughtless interventions by members of other classes. Indiscriminate giving, either by the state or by charities, destroyed the fragile identities of families struggling to maintain their freedom and dignity, and to fulfil their social obligations. 'Not alms but a friend'[1] was Octavia Hill's prescription for cultural poverty; only warm, personal relationships, conducted in a spirit of moral equality, could overcome the dehumanising efforts of industrialisation, the urban environment and the segregation of the social classes.

Right up to the end of the Second World War, the social work profession was very much outside the orbit of state provisions. Apart from the probation service, which had grown very slowly over the previous forty years, and the few American-trained workers in the Child Guidance Clinics, the dominant British social work tradition was of family casework in voluntary agencies—the tradition of the Charity

Organisation Society. Even after 1948 this tradition remained identifiable and separate (both in method and in ethos) from that of the new local authority departments. Family caseworkers were not at first seen as valuable assets to be incorporated into state services, nor was their segregation in voluntary agencies seen as damaging evidence of incompatibility between the state and social work. One reason for this was that the new services—Children's Departments, Welfare and Mental Health—were introduced not so much to implement new programmes as to mitigate the bad features of the pre-war Poor Law institutions. Just as probation had not attempted to take offenders away from the courts, but rather to humanise and individualise the court system, offering an alternative to imprisonment for a few, so local authority social work tried to inform the old provisions with a new spirit. The *personal* element in dealings with children in public care was to be the new child care officers' task. The Curtis Committee (1946) pointed out that[2]

> no office staff dealing with them as case-papers can do the work we
> want done—work which is in part administrative, but also in large
> part field work involving many personal contacts and the solution of
> problems by direct methods, in particular the method of interview
> rather than official correspondence.

For Curtis, the most important task of the new child care service was the provision of suitable foster homes, in preference to the old, large Poor Law institutions,[3] and the very specific nature of social work's new task was reflected in the widely adopted designation 'boarding-out officers'.[4] Such work could be seen as an application of the principle of individualisation of care, rather than as a form of state provision which undermined family responsibility. The social worker's role was to ensure that alternatives to family life were as humane and non-institutional as possible.

Second, the whole of the delicate and controversial business of income maintenance was taken out of the hands of local authorities, and thus of social workers, and given to central government departments. Thus local authority work raised none of the thornier issues over which the early social workers had been hostile to public services. Not being in any way involved in the provision of financial aid, they were in little danger of threatening the independence of the poor. It seems unlikely that many of the first local authority social workers thought deeply about their role in the Welfare State or social policy. It was quite possible for their departments to see themselves as safety nets, providing a more compassionate form of care for the very few who could not survive with the assistance of the major social services.

Less than twenty years later, neither of these conflict-reducing conditions still applies. Instead of a safety net below the major services, local authority social work has become a first line of defence against particular manifestations of intractable social problems which the major services have failed to overcome, in income maintenance, housing, health and education. It has become an alternative to these services, a special provision, giving a wide range of assistance to the poorest and most deprived sector of the population. It has become a method of social policy intervention, a means of provision. In this chapter I shall trace how social work has come to occupy this role, and how it affects relationships between social workers and their clients.

The key to the involvement of social work in the policies of paternalistic welfare provision is the principle of prevention. Retrospectively it can be recognised that the tentative steps the Children's Departments, in particular, took in the direction of preventive work with families in the 1950s provided administrators who were struggling with the failures of the major services with an opportunity to thrust social work into a new role. In imitation of the work of the Family Service Units, some departments appointed specialist workers to concentrate on multi-problem families where there was a high risk of several children coming into care through eviction, or the breakdown of family relationships, or the mental health of one of the parents.[5] Jean Packman says that 'by the mid 1950s, most children's departments were actively engaged in preventing admission of children to care and in working towards the rehabilitation of those in care with their families.'[6] It was this work which set in motion two separate trends. The first was the demand by social workers for powers to give financial and material aid to prevent family breakdown, and avoid the type of catastrophes that might lead to children coming into care. This pressure led to the inclusion in the 'preventive' clause of the Children and Young Persons Act, 1963 (Section 1), of the power to give assistance, as part of a programme of family casework. The second was the move towards a unified local authority agency, to deal with the problems of families as families, to avoid fragmented concentration on arbitrarily defined 'problems', and to minimise overlapping, buck-passing and interdepartmental rivalries. The struggle for a unified agency came to be closely associated with the attempt to reform the juvenile courts system, and to replace court appearances by referrals of delinquents' families to social workers for investigation and supervision. In a very attenuated form, these reforms were incorporated in the Children and Young Persons Act, 1969, which gave some powers for voluntary preventive work as an alternative to a summons; but in the meanwhile, following the Seebohm Report, the new unified department had been created, not as a family casework agency, but as a social services department.

The title was significant; by the end of the 1960s there was already pressure on social workers to provide a new range of services rather than to just give human and personal comfort to those in distress. The reorganisation of local authority social work was thus largely undertaken in the spirit of efficient co-ordination of resources; administrators sought structures which enabled the identification of quantifiable needs and the delivery of measurable services, according to predictable patterns of supply and demand. Social work, as a vague and unquantifiable commodity, became simply the means of service delivery—but an important means. The clients of the new agency were identifiable by their neediness and by their inability to survive without special assistance. Social work was the way of translating provisions into visible changes in their life styles. Paternalistic social policy recognised this as the ideal form of intervention for families with 'multiple disadvantages' and 'social problems'.

Social workers' willingness to do preventive work, their anxiety to take earlier referrals of clients' problems, to forestall by intervention rather than to wait for disaster, has encouraged other agencies to identify large numbers of 'welfare cases', and to send them to social services departments for all their needs. They see 'welfare cases' as specially needy people who cannot make proper use of ordinary provision. They come to recognise the signs and signals which mark out a welfare case in their office, their consulting room or classroom. Obvious multiple neediness becomes synonymous with requiring social work intervention. As a result, people referred to social services departments very often do not get the benefit of what are supposed to be universal services. The existence of a local authority department, which has come to specialise by target group—the most needy—rather than by specific problem, actually deprives many of those referred to it of what they should be getting from the major services, and gives them an alternative and in many ways an inferior service in its place. To take the example of social security: the closing of small local supplementary benefits offices, the running down of visiting services and the increasing inability of the enlarged service to deal with urgent and exceptional need have all resulted in a tendency to redirect very deprived claimants towards social services departments, even if their needs are purely financial.[7] The BASW Poverty Group's research found that in the London boroughs, about half of all payments under Section 1 of the 1963 Act were to people who were on supplementary benefits, and almost all such payments were for items like food, rent, bed and breakfast, furniture, fuel and clothing, for which they could have claimed from the Supplementary Benefits Commission. This assumption of responsibility by social workers entailed a loss of rights for clients. There is no right of appeal, either against refusal of a payment by a social worker, or against the amount paid (and many payments are very small). Social workers give many more payments by voucher or in kind than social security officers; they also give more secondhand clothes and furniture. Scottish social workers make almost half their payments in the form of loans.[8] Above all, the client does not have the protection of publicly known rules, and may be required to submit to subsequent supervision for an unspecified period. This is the price which is paid for provisions which do not add to the assistance available, but rather replace other benefits which are already unsatisfactory enough. The result is that people designated 'welfare cases' lose rights; in becoming clients, they lose part of their citizenship.

The notion of providing for all the needs of the most deprived members of the community out of a restricted, rate-based budget was presumed to have been discredited when the National Assistance Act abolished the Public Assistance Committees. Yet there are still academic commentators who argue that its rehabilitation in social services departments has not gone far enough; that the Poor Law, which took so long to break up, should be reassembled. Professor Lafitte suggests that welfare is 'indivisible'; that[9]

> the expertise required in cash welfare is not specific to a health, an education, a housing or a treasurer's department. It is social. It is concerned with poverty, with relative deprivation, with minimum living standards and other aspects of social policy; and the experts in these matters are, or should be, in the social services department . . . As things are in many places, a family helped by the social services department may simultaneously, or within a short time, receive or deserve to receive attention from the treasurer's department (rate relief), housing department (rent allowance) and the education department (clothing grant, remission of school dinner charge)—not to mention several services outside local government. Would it not make sense to transfer administrator responsibility for some or all of these other local government relief functions to the social services department?

But the 'welfare' Professor Lafitte wishes to bestow in its indivisibility upon the poor is hardly the sort of welfare the rest of the population would wish to enjoy. The mark of a welfare service which dealt exclusively with the means-testing and supervised provision for *every* need for the poorest sector of the population would be (as with Public Assistance) its stigma. The rest of the population would tend to measure its welfare in terms of the distance by which it could steer clear of such an agency. Social services departments may presumably be allowed to cultivate some forms of expertise other than those required to ration benefits to the poor; and if we must have means tests in our services (as paternalist politicians insist that we should), then we should surely not concentrate them all in such a way as to segregate our poorest citizens, out of sight, into a Poor Law destitution authority where the rest of us are never forced to set foot.

In practice, the trend towards this kind of segregation has already created enormous problems in social services departments. The transfer of responsibilities for material benefits has meant an inflow of referrals which is overwhelming. Some services have had to be rationed (like telephones for the elderly and disabled, aids and adaptations, home helps and meals on wheels), so that there are waiting lists in many areas which run into years and get longer and longer. Other services, which social workers should be adequately skilled to provide well (like mental hospital aftercare), are widely neglected. In some areas even statutory cases, such as children in care, remain unallocated. Social workers wanted to do everything, to prevent everything, and have ended up not being able to do anything properly. As has happened so often in the past, services for the poor have become poor services.

These difficulties have been increased by the willingness of administrators in social services departments to take on the inappropriate tasks which other agencies thrust upon them. In talking to ex-students whom I have trained, I have been amazed to hear of the referrals they have been expected to follow up as social workers. It is as if social services middle managements go around other agencies offering to take over any of their work which is trivial, fiddly or troublesome. Social workers are expected to vet applications for free bus passes, or to award disabled drivers' car badges. Alternatively, managers insist that they visit every single referral, however nonsensical. I have heard of social workers being expected to follow up complaints about flags not being hung straight, or dogs hunting in packs, or chip papers in an old lady's garden. More dangerously, they send social workers to tackle emergency situations in which their skills are totally unhelpful, like assisting families in danger of flooding by a giant burst water tank. Just because a family is poor, it does not mean that it needs a social worker rather than a plumber; yet time and again 'welfare cases' are given 'assistance' which is useless or even harmful. Social services managements often try to avoid criticism by giving a fifth-rate service to every single referral, rather than rigorously selecting situations in which a social worker really can help.

The paternalistic trend in social policy has also been linked with the use of social work as a means of dealing with deviant behaviour. In 1948 social workers were virtually only involved in the investigation and supervision of deviance in enquiries for the court, or as a result of court orders. The preventive principle now encompasses the prevention of court appearances. When this notion was first presented in the debates leading up to the 1969 Children and Young Persons Act, it was argued that it would be an extension of the protection given to children from the lifelong stigma of criminal convictions, thus it would enhance their civil rights. Now it often seems a more subtle and intrusive form of social control. Social workers have at their disposal a range of provisions to treat the client, but the decision-making processes within social services departments by which clients are allocated between these facilities are far from clear, and clients' rights are less well defined than in court situations. Furthermore the blurring between assistance, supervision and punishment has even crept into the names by which court orders are known—'Intermediate Treatment' being highly descriptive of a facility which, though in itself not punitive, is somewhere in a no man's land between help and punishment.

There is a danger that social workers are simply serving to disguise or legitimate methods of dealing with deviance which are disrespectful of clients' rights. One example seems to illustrate this danger. In a Westcountry county, a scheme of 'school patrols' was set up, under which a policeman and a social worker toured a town in a police car, stopping children to enquire whether they had a valid reason for being absent from school. For civil rights reasons, this procedure would seem very objectionable; truancy is not a criminal offence, so the legality of police involvement is open to question. The presence of the social worker would seem to have been covering this lapse with a cloak of respectability. In practice, it was found that very few children did not have valid reasons; but when the reasons given by most of those stopped were checked with the school (by walkie-talkie), it was discovered that, through poor internal communication, the headteacher was seldom aware that a junior teacher had excused the child, or sent him on an errand. As a result, much unnecessary distress was caused to children. One social worker told me that, during the course of the day he did his 'school patrol', they stopped two adolescent girls, both of whom had been sent home at the onset of their periods. In the whole day they found only one truant. However, when the social worker challenged the whole notion of the patrol in his department, it was justified by his superiors on the paternalistic ground that it might uncover unmet need. A child found wandering might say that he had no shoes to go to school in, and could fill in an application for a clothing grant in the police car! When the dubiousness of this kind of justification was pressed by social workers, the patrols were discontinued.

Paternalism and prevention may have been the justification for increased social work interventions in deviance, but the results hardly bear witness to social work's effectiveness in preventing the outcomes to be avoided, or assisting people to avoid them. More admissions to mental hospitals are voluntary than before the 1959 Act, but there are many more admissions now than before it. A lower *proportion* of juvenile offenders who are apprehended reach court, but the absolute number who get to court is as high or higher in many areas. The number of juveniles in borstals, junior detention centres, prisons and remand centres has risen.[10] The Younger Report imposes more controlling conditions on some of those supervised by probation officers, but will this mean that fewer will be imprisoned, or simply that more will be supervised, and more controllingly? The trend seems to be not towards a liberalisation of the controls on deviance, but towards the identification of a larger group of people who need to be closely watched, and the appointment of a larger number of social workers to watch them. New powers for social workers reflect a social philosophy which defines a certain proportion of the population as burdens or threats, so irresponsible as to be regarded as morally inferior, and therefore not to be trusted with the liberties that full citizens enjoy. Being kept at large in the community, being prevented from going to court, or entering an institution, comes itself to involve such constraints and frustrations as to be something considerably short of a life of freedom.

In order to look in detail at the way in which these policies are worked out in the actual relationships between social workers and their clients, I shall take the particularly difficult example of child abuse. There is, because of the publicity attached to a few tragic cases, a big increase in reported child abuse, and social workers have to investigate every allegation. Inevitably, because of the stereotypes which operate in the public mind, a considerable proportion of allegations concern people perceived as 'welfare cases', who are deprived or unusual in some visible way. So when the social worker goes to investigate a complaint, she often finds a family which is not significantly different, at first sight, from other families who refer themselves, or are referred by other agencies, for some form of material assistance. There is therefore a strong temptation for the social worker to fudge the issue of child abuse; never to state the precise purpose of the visit, or the nature of the complaint. Very often referral agents increase the temptation by being deliberately vague, simply offloading their anxieties on to the social worker, rather than making a specific allegation. It then becomes very much easier for the social worker to use the visit as a vague investigation of the family's 'welfare', to see if any service is required. More dangerously, if problems about child care do emerge, the temptation is to treat these as if they were requests for one of the range of provisions from the welfare pantry—day care, playgroups, holidays, or priority on the housing list. But if the social worker really does begin to feel anxiety that the children are at risk, this process can insidiously be carried a stage further, still without clarification of what is going on. The family can become a case, to be visited in a vague supervisory way, to check up, for the social worker to cover herself. The danger here is that, rather than helping, the social worker can instead become part of the client's nightmare. The situation is never defined; the reason for supervision is never spelt out, the problem is never brought out into the open. I feel that these are the circumstances that lead to Skinner and

Castle's research finding that among the seventy-eight battered children in their study there was a much higher rebattering rate among families known to a protective agency than among those who received no supervision. As they say, 'the findings suggest that multiplicity of workers and over-frequent observation can increase family stress, and a type of supervision of a family which is limited to anxious watchfulness without specific treatment goals is not in the child's interest.'[11]

In the tragic cases which have been so much publicised, the clients were not new referrals who had not been investigated quickly enough, but cases known to several departments (but the direct responsibility of social services) for considerable periods. The problems of the poor and the badly housed, of one-parent families and parents with too many children, are real enough, in both material and emotional terms, but anxious and unfocused visiting does not convey to a confused and guilty mother an acceptance of her as a person; a desire to know and share her feelings; a real wish to understand the best and the worst about her—her dreams, her hopes, her disappointments, her despair. It conveys instead the implicit message that she is classified as a welfare case—the sort of person who is in difficulties, and who must be given supervision, support and assistance. The reasons for the continued social work presence, or the aim of it, are never clarified to the client. Instead, there is an insidious, often long-term collusion between the weakest and most defensive aspects of the client's personality, and the most anxious and spook-ridden areas of the worker's professional responses. The worker picks up the client's fears at gut level, but rationalises these—the client is temporarily overburdened, needs help or a break. The response therefore, after rationalisation, is protective, maternal, benevolent, but inadequate. It treats basic despair as if it were a bad day, a loss of form. The client is alternately frustrated by unrealistic reassurance and by protective anxiety. She is neither helped to share her real feelings, nor trusted to rely on her own resources. It takes a special kind of courage for social workers to help clients face the worst aspects of their situations, and of their feelings about them, to share with them the testing of their own ability to find their own solutions to their problems. At first, clients tend to go along with the seductive offer of a parental sort of support, a buffer against reality. But sooner or later they start to rebel against the dishonesties and deceptions of such a relationship, and to test out the social worker, and the genuineness of her response. Tragically, they often act out their rebellious anger with social workers on their children. They push the social worker further and further towards the brink, daring her to say what cannot be said, to bring out into the open the real reason why she continues to visit.

Very often, this sort of destructive parent–child transaction between worker and client is set in motion because the worker is trying to suspend judgment on the client. Because the client has 'multiple social problems', she should be helped, not judged. This is a muddled application of social work's non-judgmental principle. In an investigation of child abuse, one important part of what is at issue is a factual question about what has happened. Has the child been neglected or injured, or has it not? This is a question of fact, and the client has a right to receive a clear decision on the facts. She has, in effect, been accused of something, and she should be told whether she is considered guilty or not guilty. If the client denies the allegation, but the worker continues to have doubts, the client should know this. Every citizen accused of breaking the law is entitled to this much, whether the matter goes to court or not. To deny a client such a judgment on the facts is to give her an implicitly adverse judgment or her as a person—that she cannot face the truth, or be held responsible for the wrong she has done. In a factual investigation, 'non-judgmentalism' becomes exactly its opposite, becomes instead a form of judgmental classification of the person. What the client gets is the implicit decision that she, as a welfare case, requires certain forms of social work intervention. But she has not received any information on which she can act, or any decision she can challenge. Only if the social worker gives a clear decision, first on the facts, and then on what follows from the facts, can the client act meaningfully or effectively. The decision that she did abuse or neglect her child is not irrevocable; even the judicial removal of her child into care can be challenged on appeal, or she can take some steps to improve her position, to try to get it back. But the decision to classify her as a welfare case may well be irrevocable; once embarked upon, the steps in a career as a social services client are very difficult to retrace.

Policy-makers and administrators have committed the state to a massive protective yet infantilising provision for the needy; social workers translate this into actual relationships in which provision becomes a form of denial of citizenship, and of adult identity. Very often, they are motivated partly by their awareness of social injustice. Radical social workers have advocated an abandonment of the attempts to establish personal relationships with clients in favour of a policy of giving 'quick material aid',[12] while others have simply felt that they should suspend judgment, make allowances and try to mitigate the effects of inequality and deprivation as best they can. The results have been disastrous for social workers and clients alike: the usurpation of rights to 'universal' benefits and services; the wholesale giving of second-hand goods and second-rate sympathy; and above all, a loss of shared standards and human communication in contacts between social workers and their clients. In my experience, clients who refer themselves to social services departments increasingly complain that social workers take a defensive stance; offer standard, official answers, are seldom open with them; give quick, ready-made solutions; want to appear concerned and caring, but also to retain their secure neutrality. Social workers increasingly complain of clients who use social services provisions unscrupulously, who expect to hand over all their problems to 'the Welfare' to solve for them, give misleading accounts of their misfortunes, and expect miraculous solutions. What both are complaining about are the official stereotypes of the welfare game. Since there are no rules (in the sense of rights, entitlements, appeals procedures, etc.) in contacts between social workers and clients, the only appropriate standards which can be applied are those of fairness, honesty and openness. Social workers, as officials dealing in welfare, but without clear definitions of their powers or their clients' rights, have to attempt to establish a common language with them, some kind of framework in which their problems can be meaningfully discussed. The paternalistic welfare framework casts clients as immature, irresponsible and needy, in a material sort of crisis, but also a personal kind of mess, in imminent danger of some catastrophe—about to break up, or break down; never angry, always threatening; never confused, always mental; never upset, always suicidal. The social worker is cast as parental, watchful, essentially a dispenser of expertise, resources, therapy or services; a different kind of being, on a higher plane. This paternalistic scenario has to be recognised and overcome before client and social worker can meet as adults and fellow citizens.

To achieve this, the social worker has to work out his personal solutions to two kinds of problems. On the one hand he has to work out how to communicate with the products of social injustice and inequality without condescending pity or compensatory partiality. If the client is no more than the victim of social and economic forces, the manifestation of structural conflicts and defects in our society, then the role of social worker is invalid. Unless the client is an adult human being, who is free to choose between alternatives, and whose choices have the same moral implications as those of other citizens, social work is nothing more than cold-blooded social engineering. Equally, if clients' difficulties stem exclusively from their position in an unjust state, how can social workers reconcile themselves with the notion of working for the state? The only solutions consistent with the principles on which social work is based depend on the notion that there is, in spite of present inequalities, a way for social workers to be fair and open and honest with clients as representatives of the state, and that there is an ideal of fellow citizenship towards which worker and client can strive together. Only in this way can the social worker's official position and his personal integrity combine, so that his relationship with his client becomes a form of communication of a coherent social philosophy. Official social work by definition expresses a relationship between state and citizen. By an adult, equal relationship which truly respects the client's freedom and dignity, as on a par with his own, the social worker expresses an alternative to the view of the client as a welfare case.

Such a process cannot escape the second kind of problem to which social workers have to find solutions. To offer oneself as a fellow human being to people in various kinds of distress is to be a particularly vulnerable sort of sitting duck. There will always be defensive, devious and disturbed clients who will use this opportunity to turn the social worker inside out, to churn up his inner organs and delight in the very nasty mess they create. I have tried to describe elsewhere[13] my own experience as a social worker of this kind of process, and to state my own belief that this is an occupational risk of social work, and that social workers should recognise and work with it rather than defend themselves against it. If we are sincere in our offers of ourselves to people, we will be at risk, and there will be desperate and unscrupulous people who will draw us into situations and feelings which will be uncomfortable or much worse; which will lead us to question our motivations, our principles, the whole bases of our existence. We have to be willing to experience tensions and contradictions, to behave oddly or badly, and willing for our clients to recognise this; and then we have to find the strength to recover, with them, and in finding our own way back, to help them find theirs.

A rejection of paternalistic concepts of welfare in social work therefore entails some attempt to distinguish between different kinds of responsibilities. The essence of helping people in a personal way with their personal problems should be that the social worker takes the same kind of responsibility as he would in dealing with an adult friend or member of his family; that his standards are personal standards, expressions of himself. At the opposite end of the scale are referrals where the attempt to deflect the client to a social worker is a violation of his rights as a citizen. Here the social worker should feel it his responsibility to defend the client's rights as if his own were in danger. But an active approach to welfare rights in housing and social security, for instance, should not become yet another professional skill whereby the social worker deskills the client, and aggrandises his own empire. The social worker should fight alongside the client for his rights, rather than negotiating behind his back or over his head; he should not become so technically proficient as to be yet another expert the client needs to survive in a complex, mystifying world. But there is a third category of responsibility, in which the social worker has to make some provision, or perform some assessment for a provision, because his department has been made unequivocally responsible for that provision. Here he can really only try to be honest about the extent and the limitations of what is available. Too often, politicians have tried to make political capital out of social services provisions; social workers have to be prepared to publicise the inadequacies and shortcomings of their own departments.

The paternalistic concept of welfare underestimates the value of freedom and the dangers of harming people by trying to help them. It makes simplistic assumptions about the ways in which people are able to benefit from assistance, advice and supervision. It ignores the extent to which people's lives are fragile constructions, which hang together by threads of pride, obstinacy, secret hopes and small pleasures.

Blundering, well-meaning interventions or anxious attempts to give guidance or exert control can cause havoc or tilt a delicate balance in the wrong direction. All human relationships have great potential for damage and hurt, and helping relationships are particularly difficult. The offer of help to another human being through a relationship (if it is to be done well) assumes a security, a sensitivity and a commitment which few social workers could hope to achieve with any consistency. It may often be much safer and of more assistance to define the statutory context of the worker's powers and duties, and to let the client choose how much to invest emotionally, rather than to attempt to impose a personal relationship in situations where its value is questionable. It may be better not to imply that the social worker is a helper, concerned and caring, when we know that he has such power to do harm; but rather to let the client discover these things for himself, if they are there to discover. Prevention of disasters by social work intervention is at best a fairly unverifiable business; we can seldom produce hard-and-fast evidence of its occurrence. Statistics from most fields of deviance suggest that attempts to identify situations that are likely to lead to outcomes that are to be avoided are unreliable, and interventions are often counterproductive. For instance, the District of Columbia Youth Council project on juvenile delinquency, which applied therapeutic interventions to at-risk schoolchildren, produced a higher rate of delinquents than in the control group.[14] Yet little has been learnt from such findings. Governments place increasing faith in the mass application of a welfare model based on social work to people whose major identifying feature is their vulnerability to well-meaning interference.

Freedom is a very precious commodity, particularly to the deprived and underprivileged. Social workers should approach such people with a good deal of humility and diffidence. The fact that they come armed with clothing grants and bus tickets only makes them a more suspect boon. It is bad enough to be assaulted by a benevolent therapist; it is probably worse to be taken over by a machine dispensing discretionary benefits and advice on how to make them last—a kind of modern Mrs Pardiggle. The ability to give help without unnecessarily or destructively reducing freedom should be one of the most cherished skills in social work. We could still benefit from lessons in 'perfect respectfulness', and we should remember that Victorian social workers showed no embarrassment in referring to their clients as friends, and as fellow citizens.

Part 3
A Welfare Society

13
Family—Support or Suppression?

In the second part of this book, I suggested that welfare institutions have at different times pursued notions of state interventions which reflected two concepts of welfare. The nineteenth-century model allowed social engineering to create a more favourable environment, but forbade assistance to individuals, except on punitive terms. The earlier and later model was paternalistic in its attempt to create protective provision for a dependent sector of the population. Both models conceived welfare institutions as controls upon the behaviour of a potentially deviant and dissident working class. Recently, the second model has merged welfare provision with other measures of social control, and has used social work as an important means of bringing both to bear on individual citizens.

In these final three chapters, I want to consider the preconditions for a true welfare state; I want to examine whether any institutional expression of the state's concern for the welfare of its citizens can avoid the pitfalls of the two models I have identified. In particular, I want to discuss the question of whether welfare provision can be reconciled with the free and equal citizenship of recipients of state assistance. The nineteenth-century liberal view of freedom suggests that this is by definition impossible, since assistance is only given to those who have failed to meet their obligations to provide for themselves; therefore they must necessarily suffer constraints and disadvantages. The libertarian view of freedom is equally discouraging, for it argues that welfare institutions are necessarily agencies of state control, and must impose obligations in line with the dominant economic and social order. Both these views reflect the characteristic notions of the relationships between freedom, provision and social obligation of their respective philosophies. But, as I argued in the first part of the book, alternative views of these relationships can emerge if we are willing to re-examine the nature of our obligations towards others, and of the forces which influence our patterns of social behaviour. Accordingly, I wish now to embark upon an analysis of what seem to me to be the crucial issues in any attempt by the state to bring about an improvement in social relations between its citizens.

The social obligations I shall discuss in this chapter concern the responsibilities of the individual towards his family. Social policy has always tried to enhance rather than to diminish the sense of family responsibility. It has been anxious that provision should not weaken the ties of obligations between family members; it seeks either to avoid 'unnecessary' provision, or to provide in such a way as to encourage or enforce responsibility.

What is the nature of the individual's obligation towards his family? Traditionally, it has much to do with adult and able-bodied members of families providing something for dependent and non-able-bodied members, which is best provided by them rather than by somebody else. But there is plenty of room for dispute about everyone of these terms. Who is adult—is the power and responsibility of adulthood to be confined to parents, or does it include offspring at a certain age, and if so, at what age? Who is able-bodied—for instance, is being a woman, or a wife, to be regarded as a species of non-able-bodiedness, and thus of dependence? What sort of provision, if any, can parents make better for their offspring than any others could? Are elderly members of families to be seen as adult, and hence responsible, or as dependent, or as neither? What is the definition of a family, and should such things exist at all?

All these questions about definitions of family obligations have been interwoven with questions about state provision, for the state's terms of assistance and control express its interest in the family. Thus, for instance, in the economic crisis of 1930 grandparents were for the first time included among those whose means could be assessed in determining the assistance to be given to a claimant of poor relief: and in 1935 the new rates of benefit applied by the Unemployment Assistance Board increased the proportion of his children's earnings which was to be assessed as available for the support of an unemployed father—a measure intended to increase the sense of responsibility of offspring for parents which in fact led to many young unmarried adults leaving their parental homes.[1] Recently, the Finer Committee, reporting on proposed alterations in provision for one-parent families, stated:[2]

We have had to investigate and form conclusions about many matters which are the subject of moral, religious and social controversy, to explore the interaction between law, social security and social administration, and the no man's land between their managing institutions; and to concern ourselves with human relationships at personal, sexual and familial levels.

The Committee's report found that changes in the divorce laws and in the pattern of employment of women had important implications for state assistance to one-parent families. 'In approaching the financial question . . . we were the beneficiaries of changes which both enabled and obliged us to take up a posture which was entirely different from any that was possible in the past.'[3] The implication is that state provision is intended to reflect and reinforce a definition of family *mores* and responsibilities.

Let us first consider the question of the obligation on parents to provide something for their children, and of how its nature could be stipulated in present-day terms. One possible statement of this obligation is Parsons and Bales's—'the socialisation of children so that they can truly become members of the society into which they have been born'.[4] In the second half of this chapter I shall discuss libertarian objections to this kind of statement; in the meanwhile, I want to consider the extent to which this definition of parents' primary responsibility for children is reflected in the provisions of the Welfare State.

At first sight it would appear that most state services reinforce this sort of definition in the way in which they complement and supplement the socialisation functions of the family without ever challenging parents' primary responsibility. The health service, state education and child welfare services all represent specialist tasks which presuppose that parents exercise overall guidance and control of children in moulding them into good citizens. Family allowances, child tax allowances and the dependants' allowances in national insurance benefits all reflect the spirit of a state concerned to enable responsible parenthood, while the law relating to juvenile delinquency and child neglect reinforces the same notion.

Yet there are other rules governing state provision which suggest that the primary responsibility of parents is not for socialisation of children but for financial support of them. For instance, the supplementary benefit regulations provide that 'liable relatives' must be sought out and assessed for their ability to pay to support their offspring. The purpose of liable relative investigations is not to attempt to make parents be personally responsible for their children's upbringing. In fact, as the Finer Committee reports, deserted wives are often pressurised into obtaining judicial *separations* from their defaulting husbands, in order that a court order may be obtained for the husbands to pay maintenance for children. Since the amount a wife receives in supplementary benefit 'is likely to exceed the amount of the maintenance order, this procedure is often not of the slightest direct or immediate benefit to her'[5] (or to the children), but is simply a way of saving the state money. The father's primary responsibility, therefore, would appear to be to prevent his children from being a burden upon the state, not to ensure their satisfactory upbringing.

Alternatively, where a parent is forced to approach a social services department for financial assistance, the terms on which this is given suggest that this form of financial dependence on the state gives social workers the right to exercise some control over the way in which parental responsibility is being exercised. Handler, reporting on his research into the way in which Section 1 of the Children and Young Persons Act, 1963, was being used in 1968, says:[6]

> The Children's Departments' position was that because practically all 'down and out' families have 'relationship problems', the caseworkers must try to get these families to accept help (with such problems) . . . They explained and justified this use of money as a means to gain confidence and facilitate rehabilitative casework.

This attitude suggests that application for this form of assistance constitutes such a confession of failure in the primary task of parenthood that it gives rise to a right for the state to assume part of the overall management of the socialisation of the children of the family. Since the application for financial assistance admits to failure in no responsibility other than that of preventing children being a burden upon the state, what is implied is that this is the primary responsibility of poor parents. Social work assitance does not complement the parental role, by taking on a specialised task; it supervises and attempts to modify the performance of the parental role. In this case, it does so in response to a request for financial help, not for help with family relationships. £2,426,000 was dispensed in assistance on these terms in England and Wales in 1973-4.[7]

It is instructive to note that, at the other end of the social scale, parents who can afford to do so are able to have their children nursed, minded, played with and educated by others throughout the years of their childhood, and so long as those they employ are competent, they will be regarded as excellent parents. Even if, as in Henry James's story, *The Turn of the Screw*, they inadvertently entrust some of these responsibilities to an alarmingly unsuitable servant, with fatal results, they will be considered to be guilty of bad judgment rather than criminal negligence. Presumably this implies that, in showing themselves able to provide for their children financially, they have discharged their primary responsibility. The duty to give satisfactory *personal* guidance thus becomes secondary. Whereas requests for financial assistance give the state an ill-defined right to intervene in family affairs, the financially independent are protected from such interventions unless their offspring break the criminal law.

This primary obligation on parents, and particularly fathers, to minimise expense to the state by supporting their families—which amounts to an obligation to provide for their own out of income from work—exerts a dominant influence on other forms of state provision. The Finer Committee itself, attempting to construct a state income for one-parent families which would give them security and reduce stigma, recognised the constraints of this principle but did nothing to try to overcome them. It insisted that its 'Guaranteed Maintenance Allowance' was to be payable to those families which, by virtue of the dependence of the children and the sole responsibility for the upbringing of a single parent, were handicapped from the point of view of providing income from employment. 'G.M.A. is intended to help the parent who is bringing up children single-handed, and facing all the financial and social difficulties of doing so.'[8] But the corollary of this is that the terms under which the GMA is provided must never conflict with the principle of the obligation for financial independence of able-bodied intact families; thus GMA must never treat lone parents in a way that would appear to give them advantages such families do not enjoy. 'A cohabitation rule in GMA would therefore be unavoidable.'[9] The report accepts the Supplementary Benefits Commission's argument:[10]

A man who is entitled to Supplementary Benefit living with a woman not his wife is entitled to benefit for her, and for their children, when he is sick or unemployed; it would be manifestly unreasonable if, while he is in work, his partner could claim supplementary benefit . . . in her own right . . . [This would be] to treat the women who have the support of a partner both as if they had not such support and better than if they were married. It would not be right, and we believe that public opinion would not accept, that the unmarried 'wife' should be able to claim benefit denied to a married woman because her husband was in full-time work . . . to leave the choice to pay or not to pay to the man, and to make no effort to get him to maintain [his cohabitee and her children] . . . would be inconsistent with the Act and *repugnant to the general view of family responsibility.*

In order not to clash with this philosophy, Finer's Guaranteed Maintenance Allowance becomes little more than an upgraded supplementary allowance (plus the proposed tax credits, which would otherwise attach to contributory but not supplementary benefits) with rather more generous conditions for disregarded income.

The report never asks or answers the question why a guaranteed income should not be provided by the state for all families containing dependent children. Why should not the state ensure a decent financial provision to enable every child to have adequate support, and every parent the security in which to bring them up? If the primary duty of parents is the socialisation of children, and if this task is crucial to their future citizenship, then why should not state provision guarantee that during the limited period of their children's dependence, parents can concentrate on this task and on doing it well? Instead of limiting guaranteed payments to one-parent families in order to be fair to two-parent families, why not give a guaranteed income to all families with children?

Let us suppose for a moment that each adult, or each of a pair of adults, with responsibility for the care of children, received an income for themselves and for the children from the state sufficient to give them a decent standard of life; let us suppose also that this income was so related to the tax system that all the family's additional income from earnings or capital was taxed at a standard rate; that the sole condition for qualifying for this provision was that of having day-to-day care of a child or children. If a man left his wife, he would lose any entitlement to the guaranteed income if she had care of the children. If she lived with another man, she would have no *claim* on his income either; their financial arrangements would be their own business, not that of the state.

One obvious objection to this scheme would be that the state could not afford it. I shall discuss this objection in more detail in the next and the final chapter. At this point it is worth mentioning, however, that this is partly a question about priorities *within* our system of income maintenance, as well as about priorities between expenditure on income maintenance and other expenditure, like defence. In our social security system, we do not make adult wage earners in any way responsible for their elderly parents, except by reducing supplementary allowances to pensioners living in their offspring's home. We treat the provision of an adequate income to the elderly as a state rather than a family obligation. This is not so in other countries, where an income for families with children is more a state obligation, and an income for the retired is less one. In France, for instance, a much higher priority is given to income support for families with children. There are a large number of fairly generous benefits for parents; but pensions are very restrictively provided, and non-contributory benefits for the elderly are at a low level. Furthermore, adult wage earners are assessed for their responsibility to maintain elderly parents who apply for assistance, even if they are living in a different part of the country.

Another way of stating this objection is that if this provision were made, as of right to every parent, then few adults would work as much as economic prosperity (let alone economic growth) required, and that many would not work at all; this would place an impossible burden of taxation on those in full-time work. This objection raises the issue of motivations and incentives for work (which will be further discussed in the next chapter) and also the allegation that the availability of an adequate income for parents would encourage large families and an extended period of childbearing, and would lead to less rather than more responsible parenthood.

These objections rest on the claim that particular forms of provision, or the lack of them, sustain particular patterns of family life and working habits. They apply, not to the population as a whole, but to one class within it. Few people would suppose that flourishing barristers or medical consultants or chartered accountants would be content to live on their guaranteed incomes, with their opportunities for high earnings, high status, social and political influence and job satisfaction. There would be unlikely to be an avalanche of stockbrokers and solicitors sacking their *au-pair* girls and staying home to look after the children; the parks and playgrounds would hardly be crowded with merchant bankers and business managers playing football and pushing prams. The provision of a basic income for families would be an irrelevance for the wealthy, and for those with high earning power, except in so far as it increased taxation. Those whose incentives to work would be most affected would be those with dull, unsatisfying jobs and low earning power. They would be motivated to work much less; and they would certainly have little incentive to use up all their potential leisure and family hours to earn overtime, since much of the present motivation to do so arises from the fact that their wages from a normal day's work are barely adequate for a decent standard of life, or quite inadequate.

In the case of such people, social policy considers that it is necessary to place conditions upon any assistance to them which require them to show that they are at least attempting to support their families from their earnings; and that unconditional or unsupervised provision would have such a depraving and corrupting effect that, in the absence of the requirement to do an honest day's work, they would almost certainly turn to drink, abuse their spouses, maltreat their children and indulge in a round of promiscuity and crime. These views are implicit, for instance, in both versions of Sir Keith Joseph's social philosophy. In his first phase, when he outlined the theory of the 'cycle of deprivation', he was suggesting that a proportion of the population required, not only a concentration of the greatest amount of assistance, provided selectively and item-by-item for a range of specific needs, but also, and often in conjunction with such assistance, a concentration of social work intervention designed to break into potentially destructive family processes, which would otherwise produce another generation of deprived children. In his second phase, heralded by his speech on the population, he suggested that provision which implied that the poor did not have to help themselves destroyed them morally as well as throwing an unfair burden on society, and that thoughtless provision had created whole groups and classes who needed 'remoralisation', and who were adding (often illegitimately and always onerously) to the population at an alarming rate. Both positions suggest that unconditional provision gives rise to an excessively high birth rate among the poor, and to lowering standards of parental care and responsibility.

Both views therefore link virtue with work, with a man providing for his family from earnings; and depravity with idleness and dependence. Both assume that the primary responsibility of men as husbands and fathers is to give financial support to wives and children. A family's moral status is directly related to the father's work record and earning power. Failure to work and provide is seen as the greatest moral lapse, and necessarily leads to many others. The ethos social policy thus imposes upon the working class is not simply one of virtue through toil, but of the man's role as provider. The corollary of this is that the woman should be the homemaker, the housewife, with responsibility for bringing up the children. If the husband's obligation is to earn enough to prevent his family being a burden upon the state, the wife's is to bear and raise children, and look after the home.

Clearly it is not only social policy that reinforces this pattern of family life. Although about half the adult female population under retirement age work outside their homes, their average weekly wages are only about half the average wages of men in similar occupations.[11] The pattern of female employment in industry together with the fact that three-quarters of the eighteen-year-old girls in our society receive no training or higher education at all,[12] creates a situation where a family's income is maximised by the man's working full time plus overtime, with the woman's wage as a supplement. This gives rise to a stereotype of man's work as outside the home, and of woman's primary responsibility within it. Her role as houseworker and childminder is taken for granted, while her 'help' with the earning of income is on a par with her husband's 'help' in the home.

It is among working-class families that this stereotypical division of responsibilities is most marked. In *The Sociology of Housework*, Oakley reports that of her sample 'half the working-class husbands are low on their participation in both housework *and* child-care'.[13] She found that the middle-class husbands in her survey had high or medium participation in housework but 85 per cent of working-class husbands gave little help with the work in the home. The typical reason given by working-class husbands for not helping with the housework was that they already did a day's work, and that this was the woman's job.[14] She assessed three-quarters of the working-class families as having segregated marital role relationships, and 90 per cent of the middle-class families as having joint marital roles.[15]

It would be wrong to suppose that any new form of state provision could on its own radically alter a pattern of family life; but a change in social policy is one of the steps which would be necessary before people could be free to choose between alternatives. If the man no longer necessarily had the primary responsibility to provide for the family out of income from his work, then simultaneously, the woman would not necessarily have the primary obligation to look after the children and do the housework in her husband's absence. At present social policy is one link in the chain which binds working people to a particular form of family life. All the evidence suggests that at present the expectation upon women to be primarily houseworkers plays an important part in their education and socialisation, and leads to a limitation of their abilities and aspirations to participate in the other important issues and activities of wider society. Research has indicated that even though girls enter secondary schools more advanced than boys in intellectual, physical and psychological development, and stay at school as long as boys, they leave with fewer formal qualifications.[16] Even in coeducational schools, girls are excluded from a large range of subjects in school curricula which help boys to embark on better careers. Only a third of A-level students are girls, and only a quarter of university students.[17] All this suggests that women are having their political, creative and industrial energies stifled and repressed from a very early age. Oakley found that among working-class housewives, their concept of themselves was inextricably tied up with their domestic duties. 75 per cent of working-class wives mentioned their housewife role in the first two of ten statements about themselves, compared with 25 per cent of middle-class wives, and only 15 per cent made no mention of their housewife role, compared with 60 per cent in the middle-class group. Several working-class wives were only able to make a few statements, all about their domestic responsibilites. Oakley suggests, following Bernstein's analysis of language codes and social class, that[18]

> While all women are socialised for domesticity in much the same way—by identifying with their mothers (and/or other adult women) as housewives, internalizing the conviction that they must be housewives in their turn—for the working-class woman the linguistic process of role learning is such that 'I' becomes part of the role. To put it somewhat differently, conceptual differentiation of self from role is inhibited by the mode of language used which mediates the process of role learning.

Perhaps it is not so much the mode of language as the absence of alternative experiences of the self in other roles that determines this process. The consequence, in any case, is that working-class women, while they disliked housework tasks as much as did their middle-class counterparts, and while they got less satisfaction from the child care aspects of their responsibilities, nonetheless were more 'domesticated' in the sense that they more accepted their housewife role.[19]

I do not wish to imply that marriages with joint roles are 'better' than marriages with segregated roles, but simply to point out that middle-class families at present have some opportunity to share domestic tasks, and do so to some extent, while working-class families do not. But Oakley found that even among the mainly middle-class

182 A Welfare Society

families with joint roles, 'marriages characterised by jointness in leisure activities and decision-making are not necessarily those where husbands help a lot with housework and child-care'.[20] In other words, the attitude to marriage as an equal partnership and as companionate did not always lead to husbands actually *doing* many housework or child care tasks. Presumably this has largely to do with the fact that all the husbands in her sample had full-time jobs, and all the wives had young children. It seems that until work is restructured to allow much more part-time employment for men as well as women, the traditional division of responsibilities is likely to continue, and men are unlikely to play more than a subsidiary role in the home.

However, a guaranteed income for all families would be an important step towards the breaking of traditional work patterns. With some of their responsibilities for providing income removed, working-class men in particular would be motivated to work less outside the home; however, women would be more motivated to get outside employment if their domestic responsibilities were correspondingly lessened. A two-parent family could choose between living entirely on their guaranteed income, sharing the domestic and child care tasks; or either of them could work full time or part time. Given this choice, and an equalisation of employment opportunities and wages, it seems likely that more couples would choose a pattern in which both worked part time. This might result in more employment for women, which would partly compensate for the reduction in incentives to work for men. However, there would clearly be other important implications of such a scheme which will be discussed in the next and the final chapter.

One important aim of a guaranteed income to families would be to provide a better opportunity for parents to see their primary responsibility in terms of socialisation of their children, while at the same time redefining the terms of the good citizenship for which they are being prepared. Instead of presenting citizenship in terms of manly toil and maximisation of earnings for men, and domesticity for women, as it implicitly does at present, social policy would allow alternative patterns of living and give working-class people a freedom of choice they do not have now. Social policy can never determine the quality of family life in any direct way; whether people's life together is joyful or miserable, a source of vitality and energy or a deadening, depressing thing cannot be dictated by state assistance or denial. In the past, income maintenance policies in particular have, in attempting to influence family life, made it cramped and restricted, limited its scope, denied opportunities and narrowed choices. A guaranteed income would at least promote freedom and allow a variety of styles of life for the sector of the population social policy has previously sought only to restrain.

However, there are some critics of the Welfare State who would argue that state support for the family in any form necessarily expresses a collusion between the two most powerful forces restricting the freedom of individual citizens. According to this view, state provision for parents to socialise children for their roles as citizens is no more and no less than the old alliance by which the family in its structure, its controls, its inequalities of power, its values and its conventions moulds children according to the dictates of the state. Libertarians argue that the individual should not be socialised, by the family or any other institution, into behaviour that conforms with society's expectations. He should be allowed to develop according to his own true nature, to experience and know himself, and to choose his own best ways of being himself. The family is the microcosm in which the child first feels the dominance of others more powerful than himself, and learns to behave in ways that reflect their pressures rather than his feelings—so losing what Nietzsche described as 'the wholesome healthy selfishness that wells from a powerful soul',[21] ceasing to be 'self-realising', becoming false and affected. It thus becomes part of the libertarian programme for disbanding the hierarchical, authoritarian state to abolish the hierarchical authoritarian family, and to destroy the machinery by which the state employs the family to do its dirty work.

Among the several themes in libertarian writers' critique of the family, one which recurs most regularly is their deprecation of its preparation of individuals for their sexual roles. Of the writers already considered in earlier chapters, Marcuse, Laing and Cooper all give considerable attention to the way in which the family's prescriptions limit the expression of sexuality, and channel libido into work, aggression, competition, possessiveness and commercial consumerism. For the purposes of this chapter, I want to concentrate on the specifically feminist version of these criticisms, and particularly on Germaine Greer's book *The Female Eunuch* which gives eloquent expression to it.

Greer shows very vividly how gender stereotypes are used to maintain a system of relationships in which women are always passive, submissive and subordinate. She argues that this derives from an understanding of male and female sexuality in which the man is always the active, dominant and aggressive partner; thus the key to woman's liberation is the repudiation of this stereotype of her sexual role. She sees this as the necessary first step for women before they can assert their resourcefulness, application, initiative, ambition—all the qualities denied to them in their traditional role.[22]

It is often falsely assumed, even by feminists, that sexuality is the enemy of the female who really wants to develop these aspects of her personality . . . In fact the chief instrument in the deflation and perversion of female energy is the denial of female sexuality for the substitution of feminity or sexlessness. For, no matter which theory of the energy of personality we accept, it is inseparable from sexuality.

This leads Greer to analyse political liberation largely in terms of sexual liberation, and to insist that women's subordination is essentially an expression of the psychological and social castration in their relationships with men.[23]

> we cannot argue that all will be well when the socialists have succeeded in abolishing private property and restoring public ownership of the means of production. We cannot wait that long. Women's liberation, if it abolishes the patriarchal family, will abolish a necessary substructure of the authoritarian state, and once that withers away Marx will have come true willy-nilly, so let's get on with it.

However, ultimately it is the traditional domestic and child rearing obligations of women rather than their sexual roles which Greer is forced to challenge in order to argue her case, and the issues these raise are really quite separate. She virtually takes for granted that a sexually active and intellectually alive woman will refuse to take responsibility for the dirty work of looking after a home or any children she might bear. Yet the actual tasks of housework and child care do not disappear because emancipated women refuse to do them. Her own solution to the personal dilemma this would give her, if she had a child, is typically honest and direct, but also very revealing. Having noted approvingly the excellent child care traditions of the extended families of peasants in Calabria, she[24]

> hit upon the plan to buy, with the help of some friends with similar problems, a farmhouse in Italy where we could stay when circumstances permitted, and where our children would be born. Their fathers and other people would also visit the house as often as they could, to rest and enjoy the children and even work a bit. Perhaps some of us might live there for quite long periods, as long as we wanted to. The house and garden would be worked by a local family who lived in the house.

Such an arrangement clearly puts the day-to-day responsibility for both house and children on the peasants, and particularly the peasant woman. Thus Greer can only deal with a situation in which she otherwise 'could not accept any responsibility for the consequences'[25] (i.e. the child) at the expense of another, less sophisticated, emancipated and privileged woman. Similarly, arguing that a woman should not be afraid to leave her husband and children, she says, 'In many cases, the husband is consoled by being allowed to retain the children and can afford to treat them better with less anxiety than a woman could. He is more likely to be able to pay a housekeeper or a nanny than a woman is.'[26]

The other side of her argument against a notion of domestic responsibility is that children suffer from the claustrophobic restrictions of family life. Here she restates many of Laing and Cooper's criticisms of the modern nuclear family, with particular emphasis on the tendency of women with empty lives to foster an unhealthy mutual dependence between their children and themselves. Above all she deplores what is seen as the self-sacrificing element in motherhood and the reciprocal obligation on children to be grateful. She is surely right to suggest that having children should be seen not as a duty, but as a privilege, to be undertaken in a spirit of joy and not of sacrifice. It would be far better if fewer women had any children, and if those who loved children had more; parents who resent their children because they only need them to fulfil conventional expectations of family life should never be parents at all. But to say that there is no obligation on adults to have children is not to say that having children does not impose obligations, or that children benefit from an upbringing in which their parents feel no responsibility for them. If there was no pain and no hard work in bearing and rearing children then there would be little danger that mothers would resent them or regard themselves as martyrs. The defining characteristic of good parents is not that they enjoy every minute of being parents, nor that they only do for their children what they get pleasure from doing, but that they do what they do (including the painful and boring bits) in a spirit of love. This form of altruism is both self-denying (in the sense that it does involve a curtailment of other more pleasurable interests and activities) and self-fulfilling, in that it is often stimulating and creative, and employs human faculties which are not fully used in any other task.

The love that good parents need to show their children is of a different kind from the love adults feel for each other. Greer's analysis of possessiveness and exclusiveness in sexual relationships exposes the insecurity, resentment and disgust that underlies conventional definitions of marital responsibility. Sexual equality and sexual freedom are necessary prerequisites for an honest, trusting, self-realising relationship between adults; but they are not in themselves sufficient conditions for the provision of a good emotional climate for the upbringing of children. Couples (or single parents) need something more in order to provide their children with an emotional basis for growth into adulthood. Conventional family obligations are the unsatisfactory expression of an attempt to compromise between the requirements of a loving adult relationship and the needs of children. An important part of the reason why these conventional definitions are unsatisfactory is their failure to distinguish between what is needed for a good adult partnership and the qualities of good parenthood, to spell out quite clearly that not all loving couples make good parents (and vice versa). For Greer and others to suggest that better parenting will necessarily follow from better sexual relationships is simply compounding a traditional error. The decision to bring a child into the world is a quite different kind of decision from the decision to enter into a loving adult relationship, and only those who can afford to employ nannies, housekeepers or peasants to look after their children can evade the responsibility to re-create their adult relationships in a form which allows the expression of parental love and care at the birth of a child.

Communal living arrangements between groups of adults only help resolve the tension between sexual and parental roles if they allow adults to concentrate parental tasks, either in terms of time (by taking turns to do particular tasks for several children) or in terms of specialisation, with different adults taking on specific tasks. It is significant that in R. D. Laing's community at Kingsley Hall, where Mary Barnes went 'to learn to live again', her resocialisation from babyhood was accomplished by a group of adults and other 'children', but the principal responsibility for her growth to a new adulthood, and much of her day-to-day physical care, were undertaken by Dr Joseph Berke. In their books, Laing and Cooper give little attention to the nurture of young children, except to say that parents tend to abuse their power and deny their children autonomy; yet from Mary Barnes's and Joseph Berke's accounts it is clear that his responsible parental love was the major factor in her recovery. While there may well be examples of groups of adults sharing responsibility for this nurturing process (in much the same way as extended families did and still do in many societies), the important point is that it is shared rather than abolished, and that a group of friends have to re-create the sense of identity, endurance and common purpose, which characterised the extended family, in order to achieve this.

The same tendency to suppose that the presence of an unnecessarily restrictive definition of obligation implies the absence of a human need is evident in what Greer says about state provision for families. She argues that the state's promises of 'social security' exploit the fantasy (particularly common among women) that one's life can be made secure and proof against uncertainty, hazard and the loss of love. The Welfare State thus becomes a tool of repression, 'militating against . . desires for job control and any interest in direct action'.[27] Liberation demands that people should abandon this fantasy of security against disaster in favour of the kind of personal security which allows them to consider insecurity as freedom. But while such arguments may apply well to sexual relationships, they are quite misleading in the matter of an income for survival. For the sick, the elderly, the disabled and the handicapped, state provision does not provide security at all, but it does provide the means of survival. An adequate income is not security but a necessity, and any notion of personal freedom presupposes an absence of the kind of gnawing anxiety which besets people who have no reasonable grounds to believe that they will be possessed of sufficient income to survive ordinary misfortunes.

Greer's objection to state provision for families is that it reinforces precisely those destructive tendencies that family life sets in motion—the abdication from the energetic and lively pursuit of personal fulfilment in the name of safety, comfort and ease, and the acceptance of unsatisfying work and debased status in exchange for regular financial support. I would argue that it is not state provision or even the family itself which gives rise to these tendencies, but the collusion between patterns of employment, the *form* of state provision and the norms of modern family life. All three prescribe that men should work mainly to maximise the family's income for consumption, that women should seek security in financial dependence on a man, and should cultivate domestic virtues in exchange, and that children should in turn be prepared for these roles and with these priorities. State support for the family has consisted in making benefits payable to men, as heads of families, conditional upon their being able to give evidence of at least having attempted to support their dependents; and on making women claim the support either of their husband or of the man with whom they are living. My proposal of a guaranteed income would support the family in an entirely different way. It would give an income, as of right, to each *individual* adult with care of children, thus favouring neither single parents nor couples. It would not force men to work to provide, or women to claim to depend. It would allow the maximum choice—of work patterns, of child care patterns, of styles of living. It would not disadvantage individuals who chose to bring up their children in communes of adults, or couples who joined together to make a joint household. In short, it would not support a traditional pattern of family life, but would provide an income for people who wanted to bring up children to do so in conditions of freedom.

However, this solution to the problem of state provision and family responsibility should not be taken as the defining characteristic of a true Welfare State. It would surely be a mistake of a very serious kind to make state provision in such a form that it centred around providing an income for domesticity alone, or a system that recognised as the only virtue to be encouraged the care of dependent members of the community. I have argued that libertarians, while rightly criticising the state's part in creating a myth of security in a certain pattern of family life, have underestimated the difficulties of combining personal liberty with provision for the needs of the young, the sick and the old. I do not mean to imply that a good society would be one in which *every* citizen gave highest priority to these tasks. Such a state would be insufferably dull and insipid; it would be uncreative, unstimulating and unchanging in its dreary worthiness. Libertarian writers do well to remind us how much our daily cowardices, self-deceptions, passivities, acceptances of the intolerable, idlenesses and omissions are connected with our half-hearted obeisances towards conventional family obligations, and how seldom the needs of the vulnerable really justify the empty sham of such an existence. A true Welfare State should never seem to uphold or encourage the false security of domestic retreatism; rather it should enable the good and joyful parenthood of adults with a real desire to bring up children. Meanwhile, and for as long as conventional morality insists on the false values of uniformity and conservatism, people like Germaine Greer who defy fate and time by refusing to opt for security, and by seeking nothing short of the ideal in all their adult relationships, represent heroic examples in a humdrum world.

However, it is not only in the question of responsibilities towards the dependent that the libertarian critique of social obligations oversimplifies and confuses a number of issues. Several similar problems arise in relation to the obligation to work, which is the subject of the next chapter.

14

Work: an Essential Characteristic of Man?

The problem of freedom is linked with that of work in any society; but in a society where individual identity is no longer closely associated with a work role there is a special problem. As with women, so with workers; if freedom to express individual identity is associated with escape from tedious, exhausting and debasing toil, and from the social role associated with doing it, how then is the work to be done? If a true identity is sought through attitudes and activities which presuppose an absence of work obligations, then those who have to work are not truly free. Yet if work needs to be done, some or all must choose to do it, or be forced to do it.

Is work the natural expression of man's powers—of his struggle to overcome nature's constraints and to create his own world? Or is it unnatural toil, a form of servitude imposed on men by hostile environments, from which they strive to escape? Does the notion of a community or a society entail work—cooperation in common projects to promote the general good—or does a true concept of the general good entail the gradual disappearance of work as we have known it? Which of man's needs are best supplied by his own labour? Should teaching, consoling, healing and caring be seen as work? Is work done directly in the service of one's own or others' needs different in kind from organised work with no immediate social value? These are vast questions, involving enormous complexities; yet the ultimate problems about a Welfare State demand some sort of answers to them. I have argued throughout the second half of this book that our present Welfare State presupposes not only the necessity of work in its current form, but also the necessity of forcing the working classes to work—of prescribing penalties without which it is assumed they would be idle. The Welfare State is one of the means by which we in our society get our work done.

In this chapter I want to analyse whether these and the other means our society now uses of getting workers—and particularly manual workers—to work are necessary, or in the interests of the common good, and whether other ways of getting work done could be found, more consistent with freedom for every citizen.

The first major means our society employs is the socialisation of children for work roles, mainly by education. The routine and discipline of school are in themselves often seen as a preparation for work; apart from teaching necessary skills, school instils habits of industry. In primary school, learning and play are not rigidly distinguished; but in secondary schools, learning becomes a form of work which is made distinct from other activities. Even those subjects—like the creative arts—which encourage limited self-expression are seen as in some way different from school work proper, which is intended to equip pupils for their roles in employment. Those who reach the sixth form can exercise a little more personal choice in methods of study, and can escape some of the rigidity of this process, which therefore applies most strongly to those who leave school at sixteen. It seems that in the early years of their secondary education, and even under comprehensive regimes designed to promote educational equality, children are classified into potential employment categories, and that the least academically promising at this stage are virtually deskilled as a preparation for unskilled work roles. Barry Hines's novel, on which the film *Kes* was based,[1] and his television play *Speech Day*, illustrated this process.

Ivan Illich has suggested that the purpose of a compulsory school system in a society like ours is to force all to compete in the same race for the rewards of higher education, which are so complex and expensive to provide that only the very few can qualify to receive them. The rest, however, will necessarily be seen as inferior.[2]

> Age-specific, compulsory education on an unending ladder for life-long privileges cannot increase equality, but must favour those who start earlier, or who are healthier, or who are better equipped outside the classroom. Inevitably, it organises society into many layers of failure, with each layer inhabited by dropouts schooled to believe that those who have consumed more education deserve more privilege because they are more valuable assets to society as a whole.

Illich's argument that the expansion of education has not benefited the underprivileged is supported by illiteracy statistics in this country.[3] He suggests that a status hierarchy based on education deprives the 'undereducated' of any esteem and respect, and ultimately undermines even their value to themselves. 'In New York, people with less than twelve years of schooling are treated like cripples; they tend to be unemployable, and are controlled by social workers who decide for them how to live.'[4]

The aspect of this process that modern liberal consciousness seems to find most disturbing is that the classification of individuals into employment categories is not by intelligence and ability. Study after study has revealed that children from 'ordinary' manual working-class backgrounds tend to fare worse as the educational process continues, and to fail to find their way into higher education, while children from materially deprived backgrounds are much more disadvantaged from the start.[5] These findings suggest two things: that, in the competition for higher educational privileges, a working-class family and neighbourhood environment is a handicap; but also that the family life and culture of members of the working class are positive influences in the direction of working-class occupations. The notion of groups of people whose work roles are determined at least partly by their place in a culture of manual work rather than by their individual intelligences and aptitudes disturbs the modern liberal mind, but it is still presumably an important contributory factor in the willingness of part of our population to do manual work. If manual work roles were the sole prerogative of those who had higher aspirations, but who had failed, there would be fewer who willingly undertook them. The fact of low educational aspirations among working-class children suggests that the processes Illich describes as having been imposed by compulsory education have not been as successful as might be supposed.

None the less, in imposing a work-like discipline on much secondary education, schools do little to give a positive value to manual work or to the social roles of those who perform it. Yet they face a dilemma: they cannot really offer potential workers education either. The values which education promotes are often in direct conflict with the traditional values of working-class culture. For instance, the geographical mobility which is an essential element in social mobility conflicts with a sense of locality and of community. But, above all, education encourages each individual to discover and realise his full potential as an individual, whereas working-class culture emphasises group loyalty and solidarity. It is in the nature of our society that schools should only offer the fulfilment of individual potential to those outside manual working roles; for manual work processes are perceived as requiring only a particular species of technical skills. Any school system, including a comprehensive one, therefore selects a minority of individual students for education, in this sense. For the rest, schools do not directly challenge working-class values, but rather reach an accommodation with them for the period of the child's schooling.

This does not imply that mobility is confined to those selected for higher education, or that the identities of working-class children are determined by their culture or their education. On the contrary, occupational roles are apparently less and less influential upon individual identities and life styles in every social class. The conditions of employment and of housing which contributed to the creation of a working-class culture have largely disappeared. What E. P. Thompson calls the 'making of the English working class', the evolution of its traditional attitudes, institutions and modes of communication, occurred through the regimes and circumstances of factories and towns in the early stages of the Industrial Revolution. What is characteristic of alternative life styles which break with traditional working-class patterns (whether they are those of rebellious youth or of materialistic middle age) is their perception of individuality in terms of an escape from work, and from work roles. The worker's lack of educational aspiration does not mean that he wants to be tied to a social role and an identity defined by his employment; and, if he remains loyal in many ways to class values, he does not define his individual identity in terms of them. Work is simply what the worker exchanges for his wages, which enable him to buy what he needs for his 'real' life; the work he happens to do does not dictate his other social characteristics. He identifies with his fellow workers as fellow wage earners, people who like him have to do manual work for their income, rather than as others who share a common way of life.

The second major means by which our society gets its work done, the organisation of industry and commerce, largely reinforces the educational process. Nowadays it is fairly rare to find attempts to promote the value of manual work as a good thing in its own right. The structure of industry makes little effort to give the processes of production themselves any pleasant or favourable connotations. Work is made more attractive by improving its context (better working environments, more facilities for workers) rather than its content, but mainly by improving the rewards for it. Where possible, employers link the higher wages (which are seen as the major factor inducing work) directly with the performance of the task, and so make higher outputs produce higher rewards. The system of work and wages in modern industry can be seen as a very successful type of conditioning, where actions which are for the worker strenuous yet meaningless become associated with a desired outcome, and thus are regularly if unenthusiastically performed. The value of work for the worker is measured partly by how bearable he finds the tasks, but mainly by the size of his wage packet, and it is seen as the means of providing an income for consumption and for the valued aspects of his life. This attitude is reflected as much in modern working-class industrial institutions (like the trade unions) and in the recent political philosophy of the Labour Party as in the ethos of industrialists. It is also reflected in the Welfare State's institutions. The obligation to work is perceived as roughly on a par with the obligation to pay taxes. The individual's contribution is meaningless on its own. It is not the expression of his particular individual contribution to society's productive effort. It is significant only as part of a mighty aggregate.

His work, his taxes, his national insurance contributions are all anonymous elements in the national tithe on the meaningful and pleasurable aspects of life, dues that each individual must pay for membership in a prosperous society. Going to work to provide an income to support one's life style is evidence of an acceptable level of participation in society's productive effort, just as paying taxes and contributions is an acceptable form of participation in the Welfare State.

It is to the anonymous, automatic, conditioned nature of these work processes that libertarians draw attention, insisting that industrial conditioning spills over into every other aspect of the worker's life. Marcuse suggests that the worker who imagines that he is enjoying the benefits of higher wages and more leisure, of a more prosperous and permissive society, is in fact in the grip of an unconscious process whereby his fundamental instinctual drives have been modified, and what has been produced is a distorted 'second nature', in conflict with his true potential. Even his personal relationships are dominated by motives of possession, consumption, competition and aggression. Yet given the very great significance which libertarians attach to the organisation of work and its rewards, as being the determining factor in other social relationships, they have very little to say about the future organisation of work in a better society. They concentrate instead upon personal liberation, upon the overthrow by individuals or groups of the effects of these processes on them. But just as women's liberation is more concerned with exposing the exploitation and dishonesty of conventional definitions of sexual roles and marital obligations than with alternative and better means of bringing up children, so writers on liberation from the capitalist work ethic give little attention to a new and better organisation of work. We need, among other things, to consider whether we should be moving towards a reduction of work obligations, or a change in the nature of work, before we can even determine in which direction the road to greater freedom lies. For would not any attempt to alter the domination of machines over men in processes of production increase the amount of work needed to maintain our standard of living?

One solution to this dilemma is to suggest that it is not technical and automated processes of production *per se* which destroy freedom, but rather the way they are organised under capitalism. According to this view, large-scale production of articles requiring complex construction and a division of labour into specialised, technical tasks could be accomplished under some other principle of organisation, producing according to other priorities. Thus the scale and methods of production would still be determined by machines, for their size and complexity would dictate the tasks that men performed in relation to them. It would be the nature, quantity and distribution of output that would change, not the productive processes themselves; they would continue to develop in the direction of full automation, towards being independent of human operation. Work would thus eventually wither away. The inefficiencies and contradictions of advanced capitalism, the fact that beyond a certain point industrial expansion has created more meaningless work rather than saved labour, are all explained by the pursuit of capitalist goals, and not by the nature of industrial processes themselves.

However, what this solution does not explain is what will motivate people to work until the fully automated society is accomplished. If it is accepted that work is really the prerogative of machines rather than men, and that the ultimate aim is to free men from work obligations, then it is clearly contrary to men's true natures to work, and only some artificial motivation will induce them to do so. This is presumably the basis of the libertarian critique of present work motivations—that capitalism has created a gigantic paraphernalia of conditioning devices which motivate people to work and consume according to its priorities. But if this were removed, then what would replace it? Men could not be forced to work, by threat of starvation, for that would be a return to the barbarism of early capitalism. They could not be bribed by wages either, for that is the present system which is under criticism. It must therefore be assumed that their motives would be liberated enlightenment—the perception of the necessity for all to work, even though each person's contribution to the state's work effort was itself meaningless. If we assume that work is unsatisfactory and contrary to nature, that tasks are performed only in the service of machines, then workers' motives must be altruistic. They must work because they share a common definition of society's objectives, because they wish to contribute to meeting the needs of their fellow citizens. Their work will not only be alien to them, but also intrinsically unrewarding, both in its nature and in its outcome, for their own needs would presumably be met irrespective of their work performance if it were a non-competitive economy. This solution therefore demands a very high degree of altruistic identification with fellow members of society, and a shared consensus about social priorities quite unlike any present-day Western society.

The second horn of the dilemma is to suggest instead that work is not contrary to man's nature, but that its present organisation denies the possibility of men's fulfilling themselves through work. According to this solution, it is not simply that capitalist priorities distort production and distribution, but also that the scale and methods of modern production are anti-human, and destroy the possibility of satisfaction and self-expression through work. Thus Illich, for instance, argues that new productive processes have (because of the pursuit of industrial expansion and economic growth for their own sakes) been developed past the point where they give maximum benefit to all, and are used to exploit both workers and consumers. Highly technical, large-scale production of goods and services requires mechanical bureaucratic control, and 'increasing manipulation of man becomes necessary to overcome the resistance of his vital equilibrium to the dynamic of growing industries'.[6] Illich suggests that political control of the growth and direction of production should aim at creating a society in which each member had 'the most ample and free access to the tools of the community'.[7] By 'tool', Illich means not only technology, but also education, medicine, transport and so on; and he argues that all these should be limited to a scale consistent with 'conviviality', which is defined by contrast with industrial productivity and conditioned responses.[8]

> People feel joy, as opposed to mere pleasure, to the extent that their activities are creative; while the growth of tools beyond a certain point increases regimentation, dependence, exploitation and impotence . . . Convivial tools are those which give each person who uses them the greatest opportunity to enrich the environment with his or her vision.

If people maximised their autonomy by insisting on controlling their own work, then processes of production would follow human methods and pursue human ends. In this way Illich hopes that work would be restored to its status as one of the natural attributes of man, one of the means by which he expresses himself, in co-operation with others.

The difficulty of this suggestion is that it implies that all productive units should be small scale and all productive processes relatively simple. If it is the service of machines and of technical priorities which turns natural work into unnatural toil, then the organisation of work processes should always ensure that the machine does not dominate the man, or the process reduce the individual to the anonymous status of a cog in the large engine of production. This would seem to entail, not simply the reduction of our standard of living, but a drastic reduction. If production was to be the communal, workshop or cottage-industry affair that this relationship between man and technology would entail, there would be very little scope for the construction or maintenance of goods and services of the complexity that our present level of development requires.

Illich is anxious to avoid this conclusion, and insists that he does not require *all* work to be convivial.[9]

> What is fundamental to a convivial society is not the total absence of manipulative institutions and addictive goods and services, but the balance between those tools which create the specific demands they are specialised to satisfy and those complementary, enabling tools which foster self-realisation.

Once again, however, this argument runs into difficulties over motivation to work. If Illich is suggesting that convivial modes of production will be motivated by spontaneous feelings of creativity, by a positive desire to produce, what will motivate those who produce telephones or lorries, or who keep the electricity supplies operating or mine coal? If they are to work for wages, and for the rewards that wages can buy, in the form of consumer goods and services, then their consciousness will be altered by both work and consumption. The basis of their motivation to work will be industrial conditioning, as before, and the logic of its processes will demand the increases of production and consumption, and the technical advances which Illich abhors. Alternatively, they will refuse to work in non-convivial conditions, and will insist on a scale and methods of production inconsistent with the complexity of what they are required to produce. This in turn would mean that some measure of coercion could be required to get people to do work which would neither be sufficiently intrinsically satisfying nor sufficiently financially rewarding to attract workers.

A similar problem exists in the actual conditions of present-day work. There are, at opposite ends of the scale, tasks that are performed according to very different motivations and under very different conditions. For instance, in creative activities like the theatre, and in certain special situations like some therapeutic communities, small teams of individuals work very closely together in circumstances which require considerable sacrifices of their leisure time, and curtailment of other activities, for very small rewards. Here the motivation is supplied mainly by shared perceptions of the intrinsic value of the work. At the opposite end of the scale, some industrial processes which are dirty, unsatisfying and laborious to perform are carried out for equally small rewards, but with extreme reluctance, by people who are only working because their economic survival compels them to do so. The fact that the first group is willing to work as it does provides us with relatively few clues as to how the second group's working life might be made more satisfying except by paying them higher wages. Society has dirty work to be done; in so far as it requires men rather than machines, what other reward can motivate them to do it?

This leads us to the third major means by which our society gets its work done, the organisation of the provisions of the Welfare State. Benefits are controlled in such a way that there should be no temptation for workers to depend on them as a more desirable way of obtaining a subsistence than work. The relationship between wages and benefits, between working and claiming, is a question of comparative status as much as a calculation of money levels. Work is (apart from education) the main arena in which individuals compete for privilege, status and wealth. Some individuals compete less successfully than others, and their lower status and power position is reflected in lower wages. Still others are so unsuccessful that they cannot get work at all, or cannot earn enough to live at an acceptable standard. State benefits provide compensation for those unfit to work or who cannot get jobs, and supplements for those with low earning power. But the two sources of income denote differences in status. The levels of money incomes paid as salaries and wages measure individuals' success in competition, but state benefits measure only degrees of failure, with means tested and discretionary benefits representing the ultimate failure. Thus the first way in which benefits are used to induce work is by the fact that they are used to denote a lower status than that of worker. Workers would not work in a competitive society, it is assumed, unless their status as workers was adequately differentiated from that of non-workers. The differential between workers and claimants is thus the one underpinning all the other pay and status differentials between groups of workers.

The other means by which benefits are regulated so as to induce work lies in the various disqualifications, cuts, checks and discretionary powers available to the authorities. Refusal or removal of benefit are the ultimate weapons. Some benefits have time limits—unemployment benefit a year, earnings-related supplements six months, for instance. In supplementary benefits, time limits are sometimes shorter (the four-week rule is occasionally replaced by simple refusal of benefits); while their range of discretionary cuts and additions provide more flexible means of reducing or increasing benefits to reward or penalise behaviour. In their evidence to the Fisher Committee on the abuse of social security benefits, the Supplementary Benefits Commission stated that 'there has to be a certain amount of pressure on claimants to find work and stay in it',[10] and went on to describe how they need the benefit system to ensure that seasonal, casual and low-paid employments were not kept short of staff. The assumption, therefore, is that only some form of coercion or punishment will make unskilled people work in occupations in which the wage levels are little above, or in some cases below, benefit levels, and where work tasks or work conditions are particularly unpleasant.

In the last chapter I argued in favour of a guaranteed income as a right to all families with dependent children. There is a strong case to be made for a similar income to be paid to each individual adult, the only qualification being that he is a citizen. While this income might be increased for people who were handicapped or disabled or to old to work, it would otherwise abolish the distinction between employed and unemployed people, between workers and claimants. Instead of regulating benefits in such a way as to enforce employment in organised work, to keep industry supplied with workers, and to reinforce industrial conditioning, the Welfare State could provide a basic income which all forms of work would increase, subject to taxation. The state would thus be encouraging all forms of work, but enforcing none.

At first sight, this proposal would seem to raise the problem of motivation for work in an even more extreme form than any of the others. If an adequate income for a decent standard of living were provided for all, who would bother to work? Surely not nearly enough productive work would be done to sustain the standard of living? Would not goods and services soon cease to be available, and the revenue from taxes required to pay these state incomes immediately dwindle? In short, would not the country go bankrupt? But these fears rest on assumptions about the present nature of work and motivations to perform it, and about the relationship between wages and benefits. The first is that people need to get *all* their income as a direct result of the work they do in order to be willing to do it—that like laboratory rats or pigeons they have to be rewarded immediately for the performance of their tasks, and have to see their reward as depending entirely on that performance, or they will not do it. The second is that people require a competitive work situation, in which there is a hierarchy of status, which is measured in terms of money rewards, and that without adequate differentiation in wages, they will not work hard enough to sustain the national product necessary for a high standard of living. Third, it assumes that any benefits provided by the state must necessarily denote an inferior status for the recipient, because they are not rewards for any work performed; that benefits encourage idleness; and that particularly if any person chooses to live entirely on such benefits, the spectacle of his doing so will undermine the motivations to work of others.

It is not impossible to imagine a state in which none of these assumptions applied. If every citizen got part of his income from benefits, there would still be an incentive for all to work. The direct rewards of work in the form of salaries and wages would be much less than under the present system, because taxation on earnings would be very much higher, but all work would be rewarded. This is not the case at present. Low wage earners are in a position where they lose benefits by working at all, and lose more benefits the harder they work. They get more for doing nothing that they do for working, and as the work they can get is often unpleasant, there is very little incentive to work, other than coercion by the authorities. If the money incomes from work of *all* citizens were more equal because of higher taxation, competition would certainly be less of a motive for work, but resentment based on the distinction between a group whose income comes from wages, and a group whose income comes from benefits, would also be reduced. Since all citizens would receive state benefits (rather in the same form as family allowances), all would be on an equal basis; all would have some incentive to work, and be under an equal obligation to do so; but all could choose how much work to do, so opportunities for coercion and exploitation by both the state and employers could be greatly diminished.

However, I would recognise that at present we are not in a position where such a system could be immediately successful. It is instructive to consider which factors present the greatest obstacles to such a plan, and what changes would be needed before it had any chance of succeeding. Of the elements considered in this chapter, the conditioning provided by all three—school, organised work and state benefits—would be against the success of a guaranteed-income system. I shall consider each of these briefly in turn.

What education would need to achieve to enable a guaranteed-income society to operate would be to equip children to work in conditions of freedom. At present since work is not, for most of the population, a free choice, it does no such thing. Secondary school work is more imposed and external to the child than primary school learning. In spite of the so-called 'permissiveness' of modern secondary school education, its ethos is still the preparation of children for work roles via a work pattern which is both a discipline and a selection procedure. The preparation provided by the actual content of the work is largely phoney; for children who leave school at sixteen, most of it is irrelevant, and the rest could be learnt much more quickly and efficiently in other ways. It equips them only for work which is in turn imposed and external, and which they will do without personal involvement or self-development. For the rest, who will be selected for further education which allows more freedom and choice, it represents a series of hurdles to be surmounted, to provide proof of their fitness to proceed.

To be education for freedom, schooling would need to provide opportunities for children to learn directly, as individuals and as groups, to make choices, to understand the consequences of their choices, to experience their interdependence, to discover their effects on each others' lives. Instead of being required to concentrate on acquiring a series of technical skills, they could spend at least part of the time learning from direct experience (for instance, in role-playing exercises) about human interaction and relationships. At present our society is so guiltily aware of how it imposes an exploitative discipline of manual work on a proportion of its population that it requires of schools that they deny this proportion of its pupils the discovery of themselves as free agents, that instead of teaching them to be, they teach them only to do. Politicians then announce that the poorest and least successful of such people require 'remoralisation'. The real moral education of our citizens should occur in schools where, instead of being classified, segregated and trained for work roles, they could learn to value and respect each other as people, and each others' skills, including skills in manual work.

As far as the organisation of work is concerned, at present it relies almost completely upon the rewards of wages, and their cunningly differentiated distribution (which creates the incentives of a status hierarchy), to disguise the exploitation and waste of human potential involved in its processes. Without these two sources of power over their employees, employers would have to look to the content of work, and the human factors in productive methods, in order to get people to do it for them. New workers' co-operatives which have taken over bankrupt firms have succeeded in retaining a workforce, all of whom earn the same modest wage (from the manager to the cleaners). This lends some encouragement to the view that the present organisation of work is not the only viable one, and that if it would be unrealistically optimistic to suppose that people will work for altruistic motives, it may be reasonable to suppose that work, and even modern industrial work, may be reinstated as one of the attributes of man, and consistent with his notion of a full and free existence.

As part of this process, there may be something to be applied from the small groups or teams, whose members are relatively undifferentiated by role or status, which operate in some middle-class occupations. In such groups, members are accepted as individuals, bringing particular abilities and skills, rather than as performing specialised tasks by virtue of their work role. In this way, work could build on what education might begin, by giving workers the opportunity to divide up tasks in their own way, to use each others' abilities more economically, and give each other value and respect. The hardest or most tedious tasks could be more equitably shared, rather than made the responsibility of the least competitive or least fit. Work could then, instead of being what a man does as the duty attached to his station in life, become part of his relationships with others. It would not involve a return to a society in which individual identity was defined in terms of work role, for modern man would demand the freedom to move from project to project, and would invest more in his private than his working relationships. But it might mean that he would feel personally involved in his work, and responsible for it in a way which is rare at present; and that people saw each other in terms of the contribution they could make together to a work project, rather than as competitors for the rewards of work—the right to leisure and freedom from work. In this way it might incorporate something of the libertarian ideal of inclusive participation, while still allowing an area of personal privacy in leisure hours, which most people see as the major boon of modern industrial processes.

Finally, the people at the moment perhaps least able to make constructive use of the freedom of a guaranteed-income society would be those who have long experienced the situation of being claimants of benefits under our present Welfare State. The rules attached to social security in particular enforce a kind of passivity and a mental set which it is difficult to overcome. They insist that a man is only entitled to benefits if he is totally unfit to work, or unable to find full-time work, and that while he is claiming he should do no work; or at least if he does any, he should not profit by it. They thus make a rigid distinction between workers and claimants, which promotes an attitude of mind that sees work and claiming as inconsistent. From my own experience, I have found that many long-term claimants see any attempt to organise self-directing activities or group projects as endangering rights to provision, or encouraging inadequate provision by the state.[11] They often become, by virtue of the passivity prescribed for them, either convinced that their only security lies in complete inactivity, or even become content to be completely inactive. Some develop a dislike for work, or even for workers, who seem to despise them. Instead of using the limited freedom they have as claimants, they restrict their lives even more than restrictive rules constrain them to do. Segregated from workers, given an inferior status, and bound by their own peculiar regulations, they would be the last people to see the opportunity to work as a valuable freedom, and would be lost in a world which valued enterprise and co-operation between citizens, to build a better society. Their notion of benefits is based on a concept of claimants as totally dependent on the state, a notion which the authorities have allowed as the only alternative to independence through full-time work.

The type of Welfare State I have proposed, based on a guaranteed income for all citizens, would have to educate its citizens to a new attitude towards these benefits. Instead of seeing them as alternatives to earnings, they would need to be encouraged to see them as constituting a universal minimum standard of living, upon which everyone was expected to build in his own way, according to his choice, and through his individual contribution to society. Presumably everyone already agrees that every citizen in a prosperous industrialised nation should have the means of enjoying a decent standard of life, and presumably everyone also agrees that this standard can only be maintained if every citizen feels some obligation to work towards producing the necessary goods and services. Instead of relying on stigma and coercion to get the least skilled and least fit to work, or forcing them out of work, a true Welfare State would guarantee them a basic standard, and encourage them to make the contribution they could. In my view, this would create not only a freer, but also a fairer and happier society.

15

'A Decent and Secure Life'

In this book I have examined three traditions of thought about welfare and freedom. I have looked at the present-day manifestations of these traditions, and compared their approaches to current social problems. I have suggested ways in which the future development of welfare is related to key arguments about freedom and social obligation. It seems to me that each of these traditions has important insights to offer which are relevant to us in our present dilemmas. I shall now attempt to summarise the strengths and weaknesses of the analyses of freedom and welfare in each tradition.

In its heyday, nineteenth-century liberalism advanced a notion of citizenship which has still to be challenged by an adequate alternative. Its great appeal was that it suggested a line of development towards a state in which the injustices of inequality would be overcome without a fundamental change in economic or social institutions. It was possible then to believe that this notion was more powerful than the obstacles in its path. Full citizenship for all was an ideal towards which society was striving—a state in which all members would be equal with respect to rights and duties. This ideal was expressed quite separately by T. H. Green[1] and Alfred Marshall[2] in terms of a society in which all honest men would recognise themselves and be recognised as gentlemen. Such moral equality between all members of a state would not be achieved by equalisation of incomes, but by manual workers' learning to value education and leisure more than the 'mere increase of wages and material comforts', and their 'steadily developing independence and a manly respect for themselves and, therefore, a courteous respect for others'.[3] Marshall saw clear signs of progress towards this ideal as early as 1873: 'they are steadily accepting the private and public duties of a citizen; steadily increasing their grasp of the truth that they are men, and not producing machines. They are steadily becoming gentlemen.'[4]

The rights of citizenship were mainly civil, and to a lesser extent political rights. Civil rights rested on laws which defined both obligations and freedoms. The individual liberty of each citizen rested on his right to protect himself from undue or unfair influence or constraint by taking action through the courts. Because the law gave him not only freedom of speech and of assembly, but also freedom to earn and save, to acquire property, and thus to become eligible for a vote, nineteenth-century liberals saw no great contradiction in universal civil rights being associated with a limited franchise. Increasing prosperity, the strenuous use of liberty by working men and prudent electoral reform were all steadily increasing political rights, as progress to the ideal society advanced. In the meanwhile, equality before the law was, in principle if not in practice, the expression of citizenship. The courts should dispense an impartial justice, giving objective decisions about clashes of interests, treating each individual as a citizen, irrespective of his social status.

However, as T. H. Marshall has pointed out, nineteenth-century liberalism saw the state's assistance to and protection of unfortunate individuals not as additional rights of citizens but rather as alternatives to full citizenship. For instance, claims for public assistance[5]

> could be met only if the claimants ceased to be citizens in any true sense of the word. For paupers forfeited in practice the civil right of personal liberty, by internment in the workhouse, and they forfeited by law any political rights they might possess . . . The stigma which clung to poor relief expressed the deep feelings of a people who understood that those who accepted relief must cross the road that separated the community of citizens from the outcast company of the destitute.

By the same logic, the protection given to women and children as workers by the early Factory Acts was withheld from the adult male. The legislators did this 'out of respect for his status as a citizen, on the grounds that enforced protective measures curtailed the civil rights to conclude a free contract of employment.'[6] Similarly, compulsory state education was not an infringement of liberty, because the child was not a citizen: 'it should be regarded, not as the right of the child to go to school, but as the right of the adult citizen to have been educated.'[7]

At the same time when T. H. Marshall gave his famous lecture, *Citizenship and Social Class* (1949), it was possible for him to be optimistic that this nineteenth-century distinction between citizens' rights on the one hand, and the social rights of people who were less than citizens on the other, was being abolished. He argued that the direction of social change was towards 'incorporating social rights in the status of citizenship and thus creating a universal right to real income which is not proportionate to the market value of the claimant.'[8] The new social services of the Welfare State were contributing to[9] a general enrichment of the concrete substance of civilised life, a general reduction of risk and insecurity, an equalisation between the more and less fortunate at all levels—between the healthy and the sick, the employed and the unemployed, the old and the active, the bachelor and the father of a large family. Equalisation is not so much between classes as between individuals within a population which is now treated for this purpose as though it were one class. Equality of status is more important than equality of income.

Social rights were no longer confined to the poorest, outcast sector, but seen as means of ensuring a decent, civilised life for all. The new principles embodied in the social services were, he claimed, a counterbalance to the rights to individual economic liberty enshrined in nineteenth-century liberalism. The divorce of real incomes from money incomes achieved by social services would allow both the earnings differentials and status hierarchy of the industrial structure—as incentives to work and initiative—and the egalitarian provisions of the Welfare State, safeguarding the living standards of all. Within the tensions between these two conflicting principles lay the possibility of a new and fully democratic citizenship, guaranteeing all the 'essentials of a decent and secure life at every level, irrespective of the amount earned.'[10]

   That these optimistic predictions have not been fulfilled has resulted largely from the central weakness of the liberal view on which they are based. Its concern for the moral quality of the lives of full citizens forbade it to attempt to raise up the deprived by material means alone. Yet it never discovered how to give social benefits in other than the material terms it so deeply distrusted; thus it was constantly caught between assisting the poor and needy, and reminding them of the unworthiness of requiring assistance. It still felt it necessary to make the working class work and support their dependants. However much the state might be committed in theory to allowing workers the freedom and leisure to live civilised and cultured lives, in practice it could never trust them not to take advantage of its generosity. The regulations governing national insurance benefits, for instance, still enforced the obligation to do full-time work, if it was available, and the responsibility to provide for dependants out of earnings. Furthermore, selective assistance, which became an increasing feature of the social services, retained the old system of rationing benefits by deterrent and stigmatising features like the means test, the cohabitation rule and the wage stop, and the old awareness of the danger of 'abuse', while introducing a new form of rationing by complexity and multiplicity of provisions. The new conservatism more dramatically reflects these deep traditional doubts about the possibility of giving state assistance as an enhancement and enrichment of citizenship. It implicitly rejects the experience of nearly three-quarters of a century of old-age pensions, of the health service, of municipal housing and even of a century of state education. In Sir Keith Joseph's words,[11]

> Parents are being divested of their duty to provide for their family economically, of their responsibility for education, health, upbringing, morality, advice and guidance, of saving for old age, for housing. When you take responsibility away from people, you make them irresponsible. Hand in hand with this you break down traditional morals.

This very strong expression of traditional liberal doubts about welfare provision is largely in reaction against the recent trend towards a more paternalistic type of interventionism in the social services, as well as the expansion of welfare expenditure. Nineteenth-century liberal concepts of citizenship were developed largely as a rejection of the divisive and destructive practices of the old Poor Law. But some aspects of this critique are valid again today only because paternalism has to such a detailed and disastrous extent reproduced all the old weaknesses of protective provision for a pauper sector of the population. What the liberal tradition does is to identify the corruption and debasement of citizenship which is inevitable in some *forms* of provision with provision itself. It is still true that selective benefits and wage subsidisation create a poverty trap which turns work into a form of slavery for the poor; that the existence of a whole class of people who receive a concentration of provision on the grounds of their social problems gives rise to resentment and lowering of morale among others whose needs are not met; and that assistance given on grounds of irresponsibility cannot increase responsibility. It is not true, and there is much evidence to show that it is not, that *all* forms of provision have these effects. What the nineteenth-century liberal concept of citizenship should show us is that only a universal and all-embracing notion of social obligation allows people to think of each other as fellow citizens, and that only provision which is part of citizenship for all can strengthen people's sense of being citizens.

To contribute to a true Welfare State, the insights on freedom derived from nineteenth-century liberalism would have to be separated from its characteristic system of economics. There is by now massive and widespread evidence that giving people the freedom to exploit their economic advantages to the full produces a society which is intolerably unequal and unjust. The problem for a society like ours, therefore, is how to create a basis for a decent standard of living for all citizens, while simultaneously allowing them free choice of what work they do, and some control over what they earn. Instead of trying to meet the social needs that arise under conditions of exploitation and inequality, the state should try to provide an equal basis for a decent life, and the conditions for each citizen to make his individual contribution, and a meaningful existence for himself.

I have argued throughout this book that the most sensitive and problematical area of state provision is income maintenance. In a money economy, people value highly the freedom to choose how to spend their income; therefore the provision of a money income is seen as fundamental to all else. However, capitalist economics is unwilling to allow a source of money income for all citizens other than wages from work; it therefore insists on the strictest controls over benefits paid in cash. A true Welfare State would have to achieve the separation of income from earnings, so that freedom to earn was seen as secondary to a basic right to an adequate income for all.

It has already been recognised that the state covertly makes cash benefits available to citizens who are not in receipt of income maintenance provisions. Tax allowances are, in effect, a benefit paid to people in full-time work who earn sufficient to pay income tax. This recognition could form the basis of an income maintenance system giving an adequate income to all citizens. To do this it would be necessary to go well beyond the principles suggested in the proposed tax credit system.[12] The more radical proposal I have raised is the provision of a guaranteed income (or social dividend), payable at the same rate to every citizen, man or woman, married or single. It could be issued in the form of a book, like a Family Allowance Book, to all adults for life, with children's benefits attached to those of the adult who had custody of them. This would be the basic income of every individual and family, to which other forms of income could be added. It would replace tax allowances, family allowances, supplementary benefits, rent and rate rebates and family income supplements. In principle, it could also replace sickness and unemployment benefits. If the guaranteed income could be made adequate for a decent subsistence, then it would only be necessary to give extra income maintenance support to people who were quite unable to do any work in the long term—the very elderly and the physically and mentally handicapped. It would thus dismantle the bureaucratic structure of social security, with all its contributions, regulations and controls, and replace it with an absolutely simple system which gave the same free and equal status to every citizen.

Yet it is the nineteenth-century liberal tradition that insists that working people 'have nothing to stir them up to be serviceable but their wants, which it is prudence to relieve but folly to cure'.[13] It objects to the level of taxation on earnings and production required to finance such a scheme. Most of the extra taxation (which has raised tax revenue to 42 per cent of the gross national product) already falls on people with modest incomes. For instance, before the war only four million people paid income tax; now twenty million people do so.[14] The present system is so complex that some people both pay income tax and get income supplements, or other selective benefits. In raising the level of taxation much higher, the proposed scheme would require that people understood its principle, and saw themselves as equal beneficiaries with others from it, since their basic income would come from the state, and their earnings would merely supplement it. Everyone would have the incentive of their earning power to work, but no individual would be punished for not working. The new conservatism insists, in the manner of the 1834 Poor Law Report, that the idle must be made to suffer for their idleness; yet it also argues that long-term economic growth requires the toleration of higher rates of unemployment for longer, for 'the greatest good of the greatest number'.[15] It therefore demands that some members of the working class should suffer the stigma and deprivation of unemployment for the good of the rest to encourage them to work harder. It insists that coercion and the threat of hardship are the motivations for greater productive efforts by workers. Instead of sharing prosperity and leisure among all citizens, it argues that a vast paraphernalia of threats and punishments, as well as a steeply graded hierarchy of rewards, is necessary to ensure economic growth. What has become clear over the past hundred years is that increasing affluence does not create an equal citizenship under these terms, and that a new notion of social rights is required to bring about a tolerable measure of justice and equality. The opportunity for all to learn to live in freedom will never be provided under a philosophy that allows a civilised life for some at the expense of the enforced labour of many.

In spite of this central weakness, the nineteenth-century liberal tradition has given us several important concepts of citizenship which a true Welfare State would seek to embody. One is the individual's right to a definition of his freedoms and obligations in law, and access to the courts to settle disputes about them. Our recent experiences suggest that clear legal definitions, if necessary reinforced by penalties, have much to recommend them as compared with vague attempts by the state to promote welfare and provide programmes for the prevention of social problems. Civil rights are in the long run more fundamental than social services; and some forms of provision do undermine civil rights. A second is the real danger of destroying the quality of life by provision of the wrong kind, and particularly by provision which assumes moral inferiority or irresponsibility. In so far as a guaranteed income would really be an economic rather than a social intervention, it would embody these insights.

To turn now to the second tradition: the major contribution of the libertarian standpoint is its emphasis on personal freedom. It is most convincing and moving when it argues, as it frequently and passionately does, for the right of the individual to live in his own way, and above all to love in his own way. It insists that no regulations or responsibilities can rule the human heart, and it asserts the victory of spontaneous, primitive feeling over every attempt to constrain or channel it.

This leads it to be profoundly distrustful of formal definitions of social obligation. Other people's expectations, more particularly when they are formalised into the prescribed duties and responsibilities of a social role, are antagonistic to personal freedom. The libertarian notion of individual identity presupposes a degree of separation between the self and its social role (at least under the present social order), and that freedom resides in this separation. Personal freedom concerns the expression of what is unique to the self. Authentic experience is that which reflects the struggle of the self to win itself autonomy, and resist others' expectations. Social obligations thus become an infringement of personal liberty.

The libertarian tradition provides a sometimes withering, sometimes inspiring critique of the way we as individuals live our lives and conduct our relations with others. It forces us to look at the day-to-day dynamics of interpersonal influences, the subtle dishonesties and deceptions, and the crude manipulations and cruelties of some of our intimate as well as our formal relationships. It also makes us consider the connections between these small-scale patterns of influence and the norms and role definitions of wider society. It suggests that the framework for both societal and personal obligations stems from the organised exploitation of greed and insecurity. Because people have been socialised and conditioned to try to hold, to possess, to coerce others as a means to satisfying their personal needs, the materialistic ethos of capitalism can establish its control over them, and its bosses are able to bribe them to do its work and to consume its products. The obligations and responsibilities, the rewards and pleasures of everyday life in modern society are presented as monstrous fantasies which we are conditioned from birth to accept with unquestioning obedience.

From this analysis, the libertarian school goes on to make two further assertions about social obligations. First, it suggests that all external attempts to constrain and define the individual stem from characteristics of our particular social and economic system and institutions, and hence affect all individuals similarly. Second, it argues that since this system and its institutions are adventitious accretions upon the individual, we can conclude that human nature, left to its own devices, and without such distorting controls, would be good, kind, co-operative and benevolent. This point of view is not confined to libertarians of self-consciously extreme views; it is also expressed by a number of therapists and counsellors of individualistic and permissive persuasion. Thus, for instance, Carl Rogers[16] and Abraham Maslow[17] suggest that what disturbed people need to learn is to be true to their real, original, basic feelings, something which they can gain through genuine acceptance by another. Similarly, the influence of Zen Buddhist teaching is towards liberating 'all the energies properly and naturally stored in each of us, which are in ordinary circumstances cramped and distorted so that they can find no adequate channel for activity'. The freedom this provides is to give play 'to all our creative and benevolent impulses inherently lying in our hearts'.[18]

Whether or not this is good psychology, it is certainly very dubious sociology. Social influences comprise a vast and intricate network and, in so far as a society is a single structure, are necessarily interlinked. But how an individual actually experiences such influences, and which influences affect him most strongly, are determined by his position in society as a whole as well as by his personal situation. The deprived and underprivileged are held in their particular social roles by the prescriptions of more powerful members of society of how they should behave. The latter have at their disposal a vast array of institutional tools for shaping the lives of the poor—the industrial structure, the wage system, the social services (including education) and the penal system. The deprived are the constant objects of other people's definitions of their obligations, and have very little opportunity to exercise meaningful choice over their own lives. At the level of society as a whole, they are coercively, persuasively and cajolingly influenced; but their own influence on others' role definitions is small. Except by acting collectively, violently, unexpectedly and impulsively, they are unlikely to be able to affect their situation; and even then the outcomes of their actions are very unpredictable. Perceiving quite realistically that their life problems are inextricably connected with society's control over their roles as members of a large aggregate of people like themselves, they tend either to accept this role definition, or to engage in active, often collective, resistance against it. They are relatively uninterested in personal liberation, or the introspective search for individual identity, because they feel the weight of society's constraints so heavily upon them.

By contrast, middle-class people feel constraints on their personal freedom more strongly, since they are by no means to the same extent victims in the economic and political order. While they may experience a form of alienation, and may be the objects of some similar conditioning in materialistic values, they have freedoms the underprivileged do not enjoy, and in many ways they have these at the expense of those who lack them. Having the education and leisure to be aware of alternatives to their social and family roles, they can cultivate ways of developing individual identity and experience. But their struggle against what they experience as oppressive and distorting expectations of their behaviour in the personal sphere is of only limited relevance to the oppressions of the poor. Indeed, as I have tried to show in the last two chapters, their means of escape from their oppressive obligations often involve further additions of the same to members of the lower orders. There always has to be someone to do the dirty work, whether it is looking after children, preparing food or sweeping the factory floor.

Any quest for personal liberty which is no more than a search for the self has little social relevance. The notion of a society presupposes ends other than individuals and their personal identities. It presupposes some institutional expression of society's sense of order, of justice, of compassion, which indicates its priorities and its dislikes. A society would not be a society without an organised defence of its ideals; similarly, resistance and pressure for social change imply organised dissent, rather than simply personal, individual rebellion. I have argued in this book that libertarians are right in many of the criticisms they have advanced of our present institutions and systems of welfare—their bureaucratic structures, their attempts to regulate and control their clients. The weakness of their critique is that they imply that no organisational or institutional replacement of their structures is necessary or desirable.

The purpose of organisation should be to hold people to difficult tasks, or to ensure the means of their performance. Organisation and structure is necessary where tasks would not be done, or would not regularly be done well, without them. It is consistent with the other notions of freedom discussed in this book that people should want to achieve things, but should find them difficult to accomplish without the support of organisations. Even the creation of the necessary ethos for the accomplishment of goals may require a structure of interrelated roles, enabling the maintenance and revitalisation of a philosophy of action, and the assessment and evaluation of the work performed. What libertarians have shown, however, is that the difficult tasks which justify institutional structures are seldom, in fact, the real purposes of formal organisations. Whether in the family or in the factory, the church or the political party, the complexities or conflicts of the task are used as excuses for mystification, dishonesty and exploitation. The task is not the real purpose; it serves as a pretext for power relationships, for influence and control. For instance, in social work agencies, instead of helping to hold workers to the difficult job of relating to people in distress, managers usually obscure the real issues and conflicts, and create an ethos of defensiveness, evasion and protectiveness which transmits itself downwards, and is reflected in low morale among social workers, and in a similar kind of anxious and ineffective work with clients. The real purposes of social work agencies are thus often the creation of the powerful bureaucracies themselves, and the regulation and control of clients. But this insight into the workings of agencies does not indicate that a structure for social work is always damaging; it shows how easily such a structure can be diverted from a useful purpose. It seems very likely that, left to their own devices, social workers would be ineffective in other ways, and that they do need the organised help of others to do their best work.

The libertarian standpoint rests on a notion of the 'natural' virtue of man–that freed from the constraints of formal expectations, as our 'true' selves, we are capable of being sufficiently responsive to others' needs to make the whole concept of organised welfare superfluous. I do not believe that there is a natural human condition which is easy, conflict-free and happy. In a society that allows or encourages the development of individuality and the diversification of expressions of the self, people's needs become fairly complex and conflictual. The dichotomy of true, private self and false, social behaviour becomes an oversimplification. As Hermann Hesse argued,[19]

> It is a forcing of the truth to suit a plausible, but erroneous, explanation of that contradiction which this man discovers in himself and which appears to himself to be the source of his by no means negligible sufferings . . . [He] consists of a hundred or a thousand selves, not of two. His life oscillates, as everyone's does, not merely between two poles . . . but between thousands, between innumerable poles.

In all our relationships with others, we express a different, but always imperfect reflection of our many potentialities. Perhaps we may be fortunate enough to make one relationship in which we can, often painfully and with many mistakes, learn to live with all the contradictions contained in these aspects of ourselves. Such relationships do not simply develop in a natural and spontaneous way, out of being our real selves. Even if we are able to construct one out of the chaos of our lives, it will be vulnerable to many pressures from our other relationships, from demands upon us which are as 'real', and from the needs of people who have as much legitimate call upon our resources.

Similarly, meaning, value and significance in life are not natural properties of a spontaneous existence, but things which an individual either constructs for himself, or allows others to construct for him. In the latter case, if he accepts others' definitions of what are to be his satisfactions and his duties, then he lives by an external code–of honour, professional dedication, religious self-denial, or whatever. But in the former case, if an individual chooses his own meaning, and places his own interpretation on his experience, he does not escape into a realm beyond social significance, beyond the expectations of others. His own construction of reality has to be tested against the reactions of others to him, and ultimately is dependent on these reactions. Even the rebels and outsiders in Camus's novels need an audience to confirm that there is something to rebel against. Both kinds of construction of meaning can survive or thrive in the face of constraints, of persecution, of drastic curtailments of liberty. People can retain their values under the most adverse of conditions. But equally, both kinds of meaning can be lost; and libertarians are right to argue that once the significance has been drained out of a life or out of a relationship, it cannot be restored simply by the imposition of a formal framework of obligations. The subjective experience of choice, of will, is essential to any construction of a meaning in life, even if the values which give a life significance are entirely derived from some external code, political, religious or professional.

Libertarians sometimes make a distinction between true and false experience, which suggests that there is a qualitative difference between the two which is connected with their relation to conventional values. This seems to me to be misleading. Whether experience is true or false to the individual depends upon its entire context, his social situation as well as his personal qualities. One form of personal authenticity consists in the total integrity of some individuals within the narrow confines of a very deprived or constrained social role. Such authenticity and integrity is often the most inspiring and moving. An example is the life described in the book *Tonguetied*, written by a long-term patient in a subnormality hospital.[20] There can be no objectivity in judging what is true and what is false experience; such a judgment depends on empathy. It is perhaps harder to perceive whether people who ostensibly reject conventional attitudes and values are authentic in this unorthodoxy than to judge others who behave according to conventional expectations. This becomes particularly evident as, in a more affluent and permissive society, middle-class upbringings issue few moral imperatives and children can grow up without experiencing either material hardships or strict parental proscriptions. Even Marcuse notes that in such circumstances, without external constraints and difficulties 'the formation of the mature ego seems to skip the stage of individuation',[21] and the self which emerges lacks a strong sense of identity, an authentic sense of its own being. Thus not only is a rich and pleasure-orientated society able to control its citizens more effectively than a traditional society, but also these citizens are less likely to have learnt the moral intransigence and rebellious activism that only renunciation and sublimation can teach. On Marcuse's own evidence, therefore, personal authenticity requires the proscriptions of society for its production and maintenance. True experience is not the natural state of the unimpeded real self, but the definition of a self by the experience of opposition, of suffering, and of the expectations of others. A true Welfare State should not be overconcerned that the organised expression of its values would destroy the freedom of its citizens; for those who could not live authentically within its expectations could make use of them in defining their own individual alternatives. The mark of a true Welfare State would not be its total lack of structured attempts to fulfil social needs, but its respect for unorthodoxy, its recognition of the distinctive contribution of its less conventional citizens, and the value it placed on personal liberty and the right to a private life.

Finally, the third tradition, that of paternalistic state intervention, has its strengths as well as its weaknesses. Its importance is in reminding us that the power of the state can be used to protect people who need special care. There are individuals who are weak, handicapped and dependent, and who need lifelong attention and assistance. There are stages in everyone's life when we are helpless and depend on others—in infancy, sickness and old age. The state does need to make special provision for people who cannot fend for themselves. It may even have to take decisions on their behalf, or to protect them from exploitation.

The paternalistic tradition of the old (pre-1834) Poor Law contributed a good deal of practical wisdom on the care of these groups. In particular, in relation to the sick, the old Poor Law was able to develop a flexible, sympathetic and quite effective service. In respect of medical provision,[22]

> [the] expansion and diversification of poor relief represents one of the greatest achievements of the old Poor Law . . . the precepts of the 1601 Act could be exploited to discover new forms of need and new methods of relief and, by bringing the two together, create a vastly improved relief service.

The indoor and outdoor relief of the elderly was similarly more sensitively handled. In the same way we can see how today's social services departments of local authorities, which have disastrously mismanaged so many issues concerning the young and able-bodied, and families with children, have often been able to improve standards of care for more dependent groups. With their more systematic research methods, their awareness of the needs for non-institutionalised residential provision, for domiciliary support services and so on, the new unified social services departments have expanded and improved provision for groups like the mentally and physically handicapped, and for some of the elderly, who previously had a stark choice between total independence and total residential care. Furthermore, in relation to these groups, the preventive principle can be much more beneficially applied, particularly if interventions take the form of medical assessment and provision. While the elderly and handicapped have ambivalent views about assistance with social needs, they find preventive medical attention acceptable and helpful, and it may reduce the long-term need for social provision. In housing, also, the preventive principle could usefully be further developed in relation to these groups; more purpose-built or supervised accommodation could diminish needs for residential care.

However, the great weakness of paternalistic provision has been its failure to recognise the dangers of excessive interventions with other groups and how well-meaning assistance, especially in the name of the state, may crush or distort the lives of those who receive it. It tends to overestimate the value of supervision, and underestimate the frustrations of interference. It has little idea of the preciousness of freedom to marginal members of society, or the resentment that can be engendered by dispensing advice and assistance from a position of superiority. It has no clear concept of citizen's rights. It assumes that people value help more than equality, so it gives them help at the expense of equal status. It distrusts the decision-making powers of all but the benevolent, ruling elite, and is anxious to control and keep a watchful eye on all, and especially on the deprived. It has an inflated opinion of its ability to solve people's problems for them, and to avert potential dangers and catastrophes in their lives. In trying to overprotect, it infuriates many and ruins others.

The paternalistic tradition has had a great influence upon our present structure of welfare provision. As I have tried to show, our income maintenance services reproduce in detail the methods used in the early nineteenth century. Just as the old Poor Law moved from providing relief in weekly pensions towards the occasional provision of specific grants to cover particular needs,[23] so our social security system has moved from flat-rate benefits to a multiplicity of need-related assistance, with rent, rates, food, medical and other items. The social work services have adopted an approach based on preventive supervision, combined with conditional relief, which is in the paternalistic tradition, both in its method and its rationale. These interventions have undermined the freedom and the citizenship of recipients of welfare provisions. In their anxiety to protect and control, they have had no regard for human dignity, nor for the complexity of people's motivations.

Paternalism prescribes multiple interventions on grounds of generalised welfare investigation and assistance. It advocates the wholesale referral of people to social workers and other professionals and experts, on the sole ground of the apparent possibility of their getting in some kinds of difficulties. Such a policy is dangerous and destructive in many ways. The purpose of interventions should always be clearly defined, and clients' rights should be stipulated. Where supervision occurs, its nature and purpose should be identified. Social workers and others should be aware of the possible negative outcomes of supervision, the steps in a client career. Clients should have these dangers explained to them too; attempts should be made to define when the continuation of supervision leads to a new stage in a career where the possible outcomes change. Social workers should be self-critical and questioning about the value of intervention and supervision, and aware of the positive value of non-intervention and non-interference.

Paternalism tends to obscure the differences between liberty and loss of liberty in its dealings with deviant behaviour and social problems by providing a range of supervisions, treatments, controls, checks and intermediate facilities. Once they become clients, people pass imperceptibly from one to another, ending up in restrictively punitive conditions without knowing how they got there. Because decisions are often taken for them, on the basis of their unreadiness for responsibility for their own lives, they lose the sense of controlling their own destinies. They literally forget how to be free. Freedom only exists if we are free to lose it. Preventive welfare interventions can take away people's liberty to lose their liberty in any other way, except by the slow process of being welfare cases. Whether in crime, debt or any other form of deviance, people need to know what the consequences of their actions are, and to experience these as their own, rather than as the result of decisions made by experts about them. They need to know what they can do for themselves to keep their freedom, not to lose it by degrees in a process they cannot understand.

In the case of 'deserving' dependent categories of people, the paternalistic tradition shows that the power of the state can be used to defend the weak, and to improve the quality of their lives. In the other categories, it reminds us of the dangers of inappropriate interventions by so powerful a body. A true Welfare State would try to differentiate between situations in which the state can only really help by detailed, day-to-day involvement in the lives of handicapped citizens, and the much larger class of situations in which only the most general assistance (cash or a house) is appropriate, and where any other form of intervention will be destructive. The state has to learn to trust its citizens, to help them unconditionally. It has to learn that a few will always make a mess of their lives, and that it cannot hope to prevent this from occurring, however it makes provision. It could well be that state social work services are, as a general rule, best provided at the point where people have experienced failure, breakdown or crisis, and are at the stage of having to reconstruct their lives. Social work may perhaps be best as a compassionate rather than a preventive service, giving recognition to some tangible distress, and support to the client's efforts to overcome his problems and build afresh, rather than drawing anxious attention to the possibility of outcomes which may never occur.

In this critique of the three traditions of thought about welfare and freedom I have tried to suggest the outlines of an approach to the Welfare State which balances the concepts of citizenship, personal liberty and state intervention. A necessary element in the success of any future policy will be the ability of governments to translate their intentions into a clearly stated social philosophy, which will be comprehensible to all sectors of the population. I have suggested that no such philosophy has emerged (except during the brief period immediately after the last war) to replace that of nineteenth-century liberalism. It is not surprising, therefore, that modern conservatism has tried to resurrect that ethos at a time of economic crisis. However, short of using extreme measures of political repression, it is difficult to see how this philosophy could be put into practice in the immediate future. The paternalistic Welfare State is too extensive and established to be abolished at a single stroke, as happened to the paternalism of the old Poor Law in 1834. What is more likely is that a prolonged crisis in our welfare institutions, a new and invigorated debate about these, and increasingly violent social conflict, will eventually create a situation in which change can take place. I hope that by then we will have learnt the lessons of our past, and have come to recognise the conditions necessary for a true Welfare State.

Notes

Chapter 2 Liberty and Liberation

1 Sir Isaiah Berlin, 'Two Concepts of Liberty', in *Four Essays on Liberty*, Oxford University Press, 1969.
2 Ibid.
3 J. S. Mill, *Essay on Liberty* (1859), Blackwell, 1946, p.9.
4 Ibid., p.11.
5 Ibid., p.54.
6 Ibid., p.104.
7 Ibid., p.85.
8 Ibid., pp.78-9.
9 Ibid., p.79.
10 H. Marcuse, *Essay on Liberation*, Penguin, 1969, p.vii.
11 Ibid., p.11.
12 Ibid., p.69.
13 Ibid., pp.69-70.
14 Ibid., p.21.
15 Mill, op. cit., p.4.
16 Ibid., p.67.
17 Ibid., p.70.
18 See, for example, A. I. Melden, *Rights and Right Action*, Blackwell, 1959.
19 Mill, op. cit., p.18.
20 E. Aronson, *The Social Animal*, Freeman, 1972.
21 B. F. Skinner, *Beyond Freedom and Dignity*, Knopf, 1973, p.97.
22 Stanley I. Benn, 'Freedom and Persuasion', *Australian Journal of Philosophy*, vol. 45, 1967, pp.259-75.
23 J. P. Plamenatz, *Consent, Freedom and Political Obligation*, Oxford University Press, 1938, pp.105-30.
24 Marcuse, op. cit., pp.45-6.
25 Plamenatz, op. cit., p.139.
26 Mill, op. cit., p.52.

Chapter 3 The True Nature of 'the Social Being'

1 William Godwin, *An Enquiry Concerning Political Justice*, London, 1793, vol. 1, p.11.
2 Ibid., p.31.
3 J. P. Proudhon, *Système des contradictions économiques*, Paris, 1923, vol. 2, p.361.
4 K. Marx, *Wage Labour and Capital* (1849). Quoted in T. B. Bottomore and M. Rubel, *Karl Marx. Selected Writings in Sociology and Social Philosophy*, Watts, 1956, p.147.
5 K. Marx, *Economic and Philosophical Manuscripts* (1844). Quoted in Bottomore and Rubel, op. cit., pp.169-70.
6 K. Marx, *Economic and Philosophical Manuscripts* (1844). Quoted in Bottomore and Rubel, op. cit., p.170.
7 K. Marx, *Economic and Philosophical Manuscripts* (1844). Quoted in E. Fromm, *Marx's Concept of Man*, Ungar, 1963, p.130.
8 R. D. Laing, *The Politics of the Family and other Essays*, Tavistock, 1971, p.101.
9 D. Cooper, *The Death of the Family*, Penguin, 1971, p.25.

10 Ibid., p.47.
11 Ibid., p.65, p.106.
12 D. Martin, *Adventure in Psychiatry*, Casner, 1962.
13 R. Rapoport, *Community as Doctor*, Tavistock, 1960.
14 E. Goffman, *Asylums* (1961), Penguin, 1968.
15 Diane Hart, 'The Therapeutic Community as a Total Institution', unpublished dissertation for a B.Phil. in Social Work, Exeter University, 1975.
16 L. Yablonsky, *The Tunnel Back*, Penguin, 1967, p.9, p.203.
17 E. Aronson, *The Social Animal*, Freeman, 1972, pp.17–19.
18 Rapoport, op. cit., pp.92–3.
19 E. J. Lifton, *Thought Reform and the Psychology of Totalism*, Norton, 1971.
20 T. Mahon, 'The Therapy of Brainwashing', in *Drugs and Society*, vol. 2, pp.7–10.
21 S. M. Lipset, *Political Man*, Heinemann, 1960.
22 Ibid., p.197.
23 D. Riesman, *The Lonely Crowd*, Yale University Press, 1950.
24 C. Wright Mills, *The Power Elite*, Oxford University Press, 1956, p.324.

Chapter 4 'Alternative Realities'

1 J. S. Mill, *Essay on Liberty* (1859), Blackwell, 1946, p.85.
2 D. Matza and G. Sykes, 'Juvenile Delinquency and Subterranean Values', *American Sociological Review*, no. 26, 1961, p.716.
3 J. Young, *The Drugtakers: The Social Meaning of Drug Use*, Paladin, 1971, p.128.
4 Ibid., pp.83–4.
5 Ibid., p.127.
6 Ibid., p.42, p.147.
7 Ibid., pp.136–7.
8 J. Young, 'Mass Media, Drugs, and Deviance', in *Deviance and Social Control*, ed. P. Rock and M. McIntosh, Tavistock, 1974, p.237.
9 A. Malleson, *Need Your Doctor Be So Useless?*, Allen & Unwin, 1973.

10 J. Young, in Rock and McIntosh, op. cit., p.252.
11 J. Young, *The Drugtakers*, p.137.

Chapter 5 Freedom and Social Control

1 M. Phillipson and M. Roche, 'Phenomenology, Sociology and the Study of Deviance', in *Deviance and Social Control*, ed. P. Rock and M. McIntosh, Tavistock, 1974, p.146.
2 Ibid., pp.146–7.
3 H. S. Becker, 'Labelling Theory Reconsidered', in *Outsiders*, Free Press, revised edn., 1973.
4 Jock Young, *The Drugtakers*, Paladin, 1971, p.33.
5 Becker, *Outsiders*.
6 G. Bateson, D. D. Jackson, J. Weakland and J. Haley, 'Towards a Theory of Schizophrenia', *Behavioural Science*, 1956, vol. 1, pp.251–64.
7 A. I. Schuham, 'The Double Bind Hypothesis a Decade Later', *Psychological Bulletin*, 1967, vol. 68(6), pp.409–16.
8 E. Bott, *Family and Social Network*, Tavistock, 1957.
9 J. Boissevain, *Friends of Friends*, Blackwell, 1974.
10 R. Robertson and G. Taylor, 'Problems in the Comparative Analysis of Deviance', in *Deviance and Social Control*, ed. P. Rock and M. McIntosh, Tavistock, 1974, p.114.

Chapter 6 'Perfect Respectfulness' and 'Painful Nearness'

1 L. Trilling, *Sincerity and Authenticity*, Oxford University Press, 1972, ch. 4.
2 Ibid., p.111.
3 Ibid.
4 Ibid., p.82.
5 A. E. Dyson, *Bleak House: A Selection of Critical Essays*, Macmillan, 1969, p.263.

6 Una Cormack, 'Developments in Casework', in *Voluntary Social Services*, ed. A. Bourdillon, Methuen, 1945, p.97.
7 Charles Dickens, *Bleak House* (1852), Chapman & Hall, 1911, p.127.
8 John Berger, *A Fortunate Man*, Penguin, 1967, p.76.
9 Ibid., p.144.
10 Ibid., p.147.
11 Dickens, op. cit., p.483.
12 Thomas Hardy, *Jude The Obscure*, Macmillan edn., 1894, p.153.
13 Ibid., p.416.
14 Ibid., p.427.
15 Ibid., p.394.
16 Ibid. (second preface).
17 Ibid., p.444.
18 Ibid., p.427.
19 Ibid., p.416.
20 D. H. Lawrence, *Sons and Lovers* (1913), Penguin edn., 1974, p.340.
21 Ibid., pp.353-4.
22 Ibid., p.341.
23 Sigmund Freud, 'Civilization and its Discontents' (1929), in *Civilization, War & Death. Psycho Analytical Epitomes*, No. 4, Hogarth Press, 1939, p.35.
24 Ibid., pp.45-6.
25 Ibid., p.46.
26 Ibid., p.43, pp.47-8.
27 Ibid., p.61, p.57.
28 Ibid., p.61, p.68.
29 Trilling, op. cit., p.41.
30 Lawrence, op. cit., p.461.
31 Philip Rieff, *Freud: The Mind of the Moralist* (1959), Methuen, 1965, pp.11-12.
32 John Fowles, *The French Lieutenant's Woman* (1967), Panther, 1970, pp.123-4.
33 Ibid., p.159.
34 Ibid., p.164

Chapter 7 The Ethics of Intervention

1 F. P. Biestek, *The Casework Relationship* (Loyola University Press, 1957), Allen & Unwin, 1961, p.101.
2 Ibid., p.111.
3 Ibid., p.113.
4 Ibid., p.115.
5 Una Cormack, 'Oxford and Early Social Work', unpublished.
6 R. L. Nettleship (ed.), *The Works of T. H. Green*, Longmans, 1899, vol. 3, p.81.
7 Cormack, op. cit.
8 Ibid.
9 Quoted by Madeleine Rooff, *A Hundred Years of Family Welfare*, Joseph, 1972, p.256.
10 T. H. Green, lecture addressed to Wesley Literary Society, 19 December 1881. Quoted in Cormack, op. cit.
11 See, for instance, H. H. Perlman, 'Self-determination: Reality or Illusion?', in *Self-determination in Social Work*, ed. F. E. McDermott, Routledge & Kegan Paul, 1975.
12 R. W. Witkin, *The Intelligence of Feeling*, Heinemann, 1974, pp.33-4.
13 Perry London, *The Modes and Morals of Psychotherapy*, Holt, Rinehart & Winston, 1964, p.34.
14 Ibid., pp.63-4.
15 Alan Keith-Lucas, 'A Critique of the Principle of Client Self-Determination', in McDermott, op. cit., pp.49-50.
16 David Soyer, 'The Right to Fail', in McDermott, op. cit., p.57.
17 Janet Mattinson, *The Reflection Process in Casework Supervision*, Institute of Marital Studies, 1975, pp.23-4.
18 Ibid., p.36.
19 Ibid., p.40.
20 Ibid., p.41.
21 Philip Rieff, *Freud: The Mind of the Moralist* (1966), Methuen, 1965, p.12.
22 London, op. cit., p.62.
23 J. Frank, 'The Dynamics of the Psychotherapeutic Relationship', in *Mental Illness and Social Processes*, ed. J. Scheff, Harper & Row, 1967, pp.168-206.
24 A. A. Lazarus, *Behaviour Therapy and Beyond*, McGraw-Hill, 1971.
25 W. J. Reid and A. W. Shyne, *Brief and Extended Casework*, Columbia University Press, 1969.
26 London, op. cit., p.80.

27 Ibid., p.120.
28 D. Jehu, *Learning Theory and Social Work*, Routledge & Kegan Paul, 1967, p.62.
29 W. Glasser, *The Identity Society*, Harper & Row, 1972, p.102.

Chapter 8 Flattery and Dumb Service

1 J. S. Mill, *Essay on Liberty* (1859), Blackwell, 1946, p.54.
2 Ibid., p.8.
3 S. Milgram, *Human Relations*, vol. 18, 1965, no. 1.
4 G. W. F. Hegel, *The Phenomenology of Mind* (1807), pp.509–48.
5 Mill, op. cit., pp.69–70.
6 J. Magruder, *An American Life: One Man's Road to Watergate*, Hodder & Stoughton, 1974.
7 Jock Young, *The Drugtakers*, Paladin, 1971, p.153.
8 Ibid., p.160.
9 Ibid., p.148.
10 H. Marcuse, *Essay on Liberation*, Penguin, 1969, p.58.
11 B. Bernstein, 'Language and Social Class', *British Journal of Psychology*, 1963.
12 R. Witkin, *The Intelligence of Feeling*, Heinemann, 1974.
13 Charles Dickens, *Bleak House* (1852), Chapman & Hall, 1911, pp.203–4.
14 Thomas Hardy, *Jude the Obscure*, Macmillan edn, 1894, p.30.
15 Ibid., p.38.
16 D. H. Lawrence, *Sons and Lovers* (1913), Penguin edn, 1974, pp.68–9.
17 Ibid., p.93.
18 *Supplementary Benefits Handbook*, HMSO, 1971, p.44.
19 Evidence of Supplementary Benefits Commission to Fisher Committee, Report of the Committee on Social Security Benefits, HMSO, 1973, p.109.
20 *Supplementary Benefits Handbook*, p.10.
21 J. Handler, *The Coercive Social Worker: British Lessons for American Social Services*, Markham, 1973, p.65.

22 Ibid., p.66.
23 Witkin, op. cit.

Chapter 9 The Origins of Social Engineering

1 *The Times*, 16 October 1868.
2 S. E. Finer, *The Life and Times of Sir Edwin Chadwick*, Methuen, 1952, p.514.
3 Quoted in B. L. Hutchins and A. A. Harrison, *A History of Factory Legislation*, Cass edn, 1966, p.55.
4 *The Charter*, 28 April 1839.
5 Ibid., 16 May 1839.
6 Herald, 4 May 1839.
7 Finer, op. cit., p.180.
8 E. Chadwick, 'On the Means of Insurance etc.', *Westminster Review*, April 1828.
9 *The Poor Law Report of 1834*, ed. S. G. and E. O. A. Checkland, Penguin, 1974, p.349.
10 Finer, op. cit., p.26.
11 Ibid., p.15.
12 E. Halevy, *The Growth of Philosophical Radicalism*, Faber, 1928. p.36.
13 Finer, op. cit., p.16.
14 Ibid., p.428.
15 Ibid., p.70.
16 Ibid., p.166.
17 *Fraser's Magazine*, June 1833.
18 *The Times*, 3 May 1833.
19 *The Poor Law Report of 1834*, p.152.
20 Finer, op. cit., p.157.
21 Ibid., p.478. (Letter from E. Chadwick to the Prince Consort, 1955.)
22 Ibid., p.475.
23 Ibid., p.476.
24 Ibid. (E. Chadwick, 'On Different Principles of Legislation and Administration in Europe', 1859.)
25 Ibid., p.477. (Letter to the Prince Consort, 1855.)
26 Philip Magnus, *Gladstone*, John Murray, 1954, p.395.
27 J. R. Hay, *The Origins of the Liberal Welfare Reforms, 1906–1914*, Macmillan, 1975, p.52.
28 Ibid.
29 S. Reynolds, B. and T. Woolley, *Seems So*, 1911, pp.315–16.

30 H. Belloc, *The Servile State*, 1912.
31 G. Dangerfield, *The Strange Death of Liberal England* (1935), MacGibbon & Kee, 1966, p.32.
32 Ibid.
33 C. Cockburn, *The Devil's Decade*, Sidgwick & Jackson, 1973, p.80.
34 *Social Insurance* Part 1, Cmd 6550, 1944, p.6.
35 Ibid., p.6.
36 *The Poor Law Report of 1834*, p.139.
37 C. A. R. Crosland, *The Future of Socialism*, Cape, 1956, p.27.
38 Ibid.
39 Ibid., p.70.
40 Quoted in Sir H. Bunbury and R. M. Titmuss, *Lloyd George's Ambulance Wagon*, Methuen, 1957, p.24.

Chapter 10 Two Concepts of Welfare

1 *The Poor Law Report of 1834*, ed. S. G. and E. O. A. Checkland, Penguin, 1974, p.335.
2 Ibid., p.375.
3 Ibid., p.376, p.378.
4 Ibid., pp.376-7.
5 Quoted in M. Bruce, *The Coming of the Welfare State*, Batsford, 1961, p.42.
6 36 Geo. III c.23 (1796).
7 *The Poor Law Report*, p.102.
8 Ibid., p.103.
9 Ibid., p.136.
10 Ibid., p.137.
11 Ibid., p.155.
12 Ibid., p.241.
13 Ibid., p.83.
14 Ibid., p.84
15 Ibid., pp.101 and 161.
16 Ibid., p.141.
17 Ibid., p.216.
18 Ibid., p.349.
19 W. Beveridge, *Full Employment in a Free Society*, Allen & Unwin, 1944, p.42.
20 Ibid., pp.18-19.
21 P. Townsend and B. Abel-Smith, *The Poor and The Poorest*, Bell, 1965.
22 Sir Keith Joseph, Speech in House of Commons on the second reading of the Family Income Supplements Bill, *The Times*, 11 November 1970.
23 *The Poor Law Report*, p.216.
24 M. P. Jackson and M. Valencia, 'Financial Aid Through Social Work: A Review of Recent Developments', unpublished.
25 *The Poor Law Report*, p.86.
26 Jackson and Valencia, op. cit.
27 A. Malleson, *Need Your Doctor Be So Useless?* Allen & Unwin, 1973.
28 Sir Keith Joseph, Speech on Unemployment, 7 September 1974.
29 Sir Keith Joseph, Speech on Morals, *Guardian*, 21 October 1974.
30 Ibid.
31 *The Poor Law Report*, p.135.
32 Sir Keith Joseph, Speech on Morals.
33 Sir Keith Joseph, *The Family Way*, interview in *Guardian*, 4 June 1973.
34 Sir Keith Joseph, Speech to Pre-School Playgroups Association, 29 June 1972, DHSS official version, p.4.
35 Ibid.
36 Sir Keith Joseph, 'The Next Ten Years', *New Society*. 5 October 1972.
37 Sir Keith Joseph, Speech to Pre-School Playgroups Association, p.5.
38 P. Sainsbury, *Suicide in London*, Chapman & Hall, 1935.
39 Jean Packman, *Child Care: Needs and Numbers*, Allen & Unwin, 1969.
40 *The Poor Law Report*, p.333.

Chapter 11 Punishment, Treatment and Control

1 For instance, Hobbes, Locke and Rousseau.
2 J. Bentham, 'Principles of Penal Law', in *Collected Works*, ed. J. Bowring, William Tait, 1843, vol. 1, p.396.
3 J. Bentham, 'Panopticon', *Collected Works*, vol. IV, pp.122-3.
4 E. Chadwick, 'Letter to Spencer', 28 April 1838. Quoted in S. E. Finer, *The Life and Times of Sir Edwin Chadwick*, Methuen, 1952, pp.74-5. See also *The Poor Law Report of 1834*, ed. S. G. and E. O.

A. Checkland, Penguin, 1974,
p.335.
5 Ibid., p.376.
6 Ibid.
7 T. Hobbes, *Leviathan* (1651),
Collins, Fontana Library, 1961,
p.282.
8 *The Poor Law Report of 1834*,
p.135.
9 Ibid.
10 Ibid., p.156.
11 Charity Organisation Society, *Fifth
Annual Report*, 1875, pp.5–6,
12 Charity Organisation Society,
Second Annual Report, 1870, p.5.
13 H. B. Acton (ed.),*The Philosophy
of Punishment*, Macmillan, 1967,
p.24.
14 J. E. Thomas, *The English Prison
Officer since 1850: A Study in
Conflict*, Routledge & Kegan Paul,
1972, p.16.
15 Ibid., p.117.
16 *Report from the Departmental
Committee on Prisons* (Gladstone
Report), c.7702, HMSO, 1895.
17 Thomas, op. cit., p.132.
18 Ibid., p.133.
19 Prison Commissioners, *Annual
Report*, 1913–14, Part II, p.127.
Quoted in Thomas, op. cit., p.133.
20 Thomas, op. cit., p.134.
21 Ibid., p.159.
22 B. Glueck, 'Changing Concepts in
Forensic Psychiatry', *Journal of
Criminal Law, Criminology and
Police Science*, July–August, 1954,
p.130.
23 B. Wootton, *Social Science and
Social Pathology*, Allen & Unwin,
1959, p.27.
24 B. Wootton, 'Sickness or Sin?',
Twentieth Century, May 1956,
p.442.
25 B. Wootton, *Social Science and
Social Pathology*, p.289.
26 *Crime–A Challenge to Us All*,
Report of the Labour Party's Study
Group (Longford Report), 1964,
p.1.
27 Research projects as yet
unpublished. Quoted by Jean
Packman, *The Child's Generation:
Child Care Policy from Curtis to
Houghton*, Blackwell, 1975, p.123.

28 M. Berlins and G. Wansell, *Caught
in the Act*, Penguin, 1974, p.28.
29 Packman, op. cit., p.113.
30 Dr A. Schapiro, in *The Mentally
Abnormal Offender*, ed. A. V. S. De
Reuck and R. Porter, Little, Brown,
1968, p.183. Quoted in A. Flew,
Crime or Disease? Macmillan, 1973,
p.57.
31 Flew, op. cit.
32 T. Szasz, *The Myth of Mental
Illness*, Harper & Row, 1961.
33 R. D. Laing, *The Divided Self*,
Tavistock, 1960.
34 D. Cooper, *Psychiatry and
Anti-Psychiatry*, Tavistock, 1967.
35 Mary Barnes and Joseph Berke,
*Mary Barnes: Two Accounts of a
Journey Through Madness*,
Penguin, 1973.
36 A. Malleson, *Need Your Doctor Be
So Useless?* Allen & Unwin, 1973.
37 T. Szasz, *Ideology and Insanity:
Essays in the Psychological
Dehumanization of Man* (1970),
Penguin, 1974, p.144.

Chapter 12 Citizenship and Social
Work

1 Quoted in Una Cormack,
'Developments in Casework', in
Voluntary Social Services, ed. A.
Bourdillon, Methuen, 1945.
2 *Report of the Committee on the
Care of Children* (Curtis
Committee), HMSO, 1946, para.
441.
3 Ibid., para. 461.
4 Jean Packman, *The Child's
Generation*, Blackwell, 1975, p.16.
5 Ibid., pp.55–62.
6 Ibid., p.62.
7 Bill Jordan, *Poor Parents: Social
Policy and the Cycle of
Deprivation*, Routledge & Kegan
Paul, 1974, ch. 6.
8 M. P. Jackson and M. Valencia,
'Financial Aid Through Social
Work: A Review of Recent
Developments', unpublished.
9 F. Lafitte, 'The Relief Function', in
*Social Issues and the Social
Services*, ed. Malcolm Brown,
Charles Knight, 1974, pp.231–2.

10 Packman, op. cit., p.124.
11 A. Skinner and R. Castle, *78 Battered Children: A Retrospective Study*, NSPCC, 1969.
12 C. Cannan, 'The Ideology of Casework and Professionalism', *Case Con.* no. 3, 1972, p.4.
13 W. Jordan, *Client–Worker Transactions*, Routledge & Kegan Paul, 1970.
14 C. D. Tait and E. F. Hodges, *Delinquents, their Families and the Community*, Thomas, 1962. See also W. and J. McCord and I. K. Zola, *Origins of Crime*, Columbia University Press, 1959.

Chapter 13 Family—Support or Suppression?

1 C. Cockburn, *The Devil's Decade*, Sidgwick & Jackson, 1973, p.80.
2 *Report on the Committee on One-Parent Families* (Finer Report), Consid. 5629, HMSO, 1974, para. 2.54, p.20.
3 Ibid., para. 2.31, p.14.
4 T. Parsons and R. Bales, *Family: Socialisation and Interaction Process*, Routledge & Kegan Paul, 1956, p.16.
5 Finer Report, para. 9.10, p.492.
6 J. Handler, *The Coercive Social Worker*, Markham, 1973, p.66.
7 M. P. Jackson and M. Valencia, 'Financial Aid Through Social Work: A Review of Recent Developments', unpublished, p.3 (quoting Home Office Statistics).
8 Finer Report, para. 5.163, pp.306–7.
9 Ibid., para. 5.164, p.307.
10 Quoted in Finer Report, para. 4.183, p.135, from 'Cohabitation' and *Report by Supplementary Benefits Commission*, HMSO, 1971, para. 7 and 30.
11 *Annual Abstracts of Statistics.*
12 According to evidence given to Robbins Committee.
13 A. Oakley, *The Sociology of Housework*, Martin Robertson, 1974, p.139.
14 Ibid.
15 Ibid., p.145.

16 J. M. Shaw, 'Some Implications of Sex Segregated Education', in *Sexual Divisions in Society*, ed. D. L. Barner and S. Allen, Tavistock, 1976.
17 Evidence to Robbins Committee.
18 Oakley, op. cit., p.126.
19 Ibid., p.77.
20 Ibid., p.145.
21 F. Nietzsche, 'Thus Spoke Zarathustra', in *Complete Works*, ed. O. Levy, Foulis, 1911, vol. 11, p.232.
22 G. Greer, *The Female Eunuch* (1970), Paladin edn, 1971, p.67.
23 Ibid., p.329.
24 Ibid., p.235.
25 Ibid., p.236.
26 Ibid., p.323.
27 Ibid., p.243.

Chapter 14 Work: an Essential Characteristic of Man?

1 Barry Hines, *A Kestrel for a Knave*, Penguin, 1969.
2 Ivan Illich, *Tools for Conviviality*, Calder & Boyars, 1973, p.41.
3 C. M. Cippolla, *Literacy and Development in the West*, Penguin, 1969.
4 Illich, op. cit., p.63.
5 See for instance, J. W. B. Douglas, *The Home and the School: a Study of Ability and Attainment in the Primary School*, MacGibbon & Kee, 1964.
6 Illich, op. cit., p.46.
7 Ibid., p.12.
8 Ibid., pp.20–1.
9 Ibid., p.25.
10 *Report of the Committee on Abuse of Social Security Benefits*, HMSO, 1973, p.109.
11 See Bill Jordan, *Paupers: The Making of the New Claiming Class*, Routledge & Kegan Paul, 1973.

Chapter 15 'A Decent and Secure Life'

1 T. H. Green, lecture addressed to Wesley Literary Society, 19 December 1881.

2 Alfred Marshall, *The Future of the Working Classes* (1873). Quoted in T. H. Marshall, *Citizenship and Social Class,* Cambridge University Press, 1950, p.4.
3 Ibid., p.5.
4 Ibid.
5 Marshall, op. cit., p.24.
6 Ibid.
7 Ibid., p.25.
8 Ibid., p.47.
9 Ibid., p.56.
10 Ibid., p.82.
11 Sir Keith Joseph, Speech on the Population, 19 October 1974.
12 Green Paper on Proposed Tax Credit System, Cmnd 5116.
13 Sir John Mandeville, *The Fable of the Bees* (1732), 6th edn, p.213.
14 M. Cooper, 'Tax Credits: Problems and Proposals', *Social and Economic Administration*, May 1973, vol. 7, no. 2.
15 Sir Keith Joseph, Speech on Unemployment, 6 September 1974.
16 C. Rogers, *On Becoming a Person: A Therapist's View of Psychotherapy*, Constable, 1961.
17 A. Maslow, *The Further Reaches of Human Nature*, Penguin, 1973.
18 D. Suzuki, *Introduction to Zen Buddhism*, Rider, 1944.
19 H. Hesse, *Steppenwolf* (1927), Penguin edn, 1965, pp.69–70.
20 J. J. Deacon, *Tonguetied*, Society For Mentally Handicapped Children, 1975.
21 H. Marcuse, *Eros and Civilisation*, Routledge & Kegan Paul, 1956, pp.96–7.
22 G. W. Oxley, *Poor Relief in England and Wales 1601–1834*, David & Charles, 1974, p.73.
23 Ibid., p.64.